D1740621

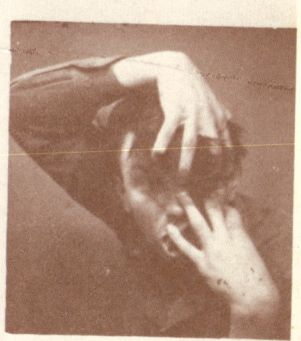

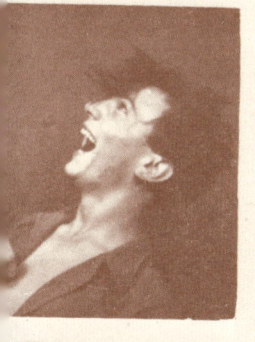

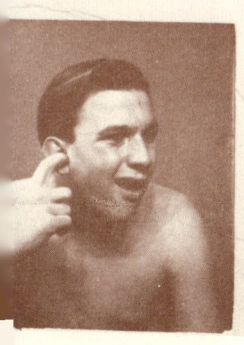
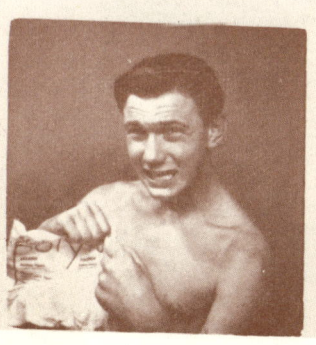

The Prince
LAURENCE HARVEY

Melvyn, you are a
wonderful man — I
miss you so much
I don't wish to carry
on.
Love c X

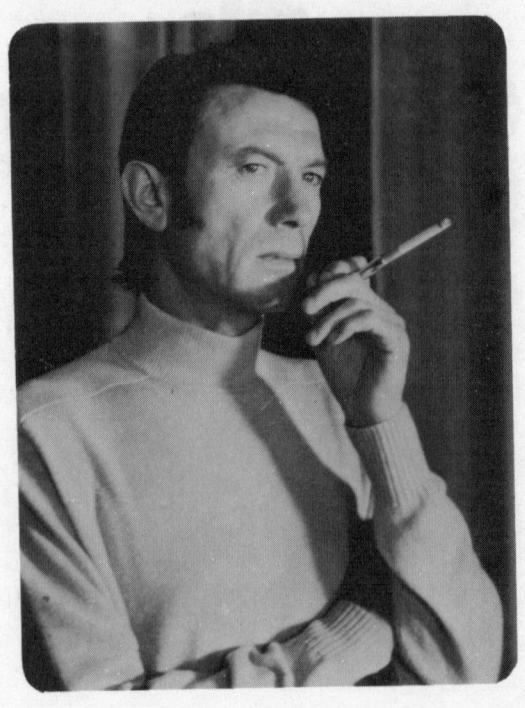

Des Hickey and Gus Smith

The Prince

Being the Public and Private life
of Larushka Mischa Skikne, a Jewish
Lithuanian Vagabond Player,
otherwise known as

LAURENCE HARVEY

Leslie Frewin of London

Also by Des Hickey and Gus Smith

A Paler Shade of Green
My Life With Brendan (in collaboration with Beatrice Behan)

World Rights Reserved

No part of this book may be reproduced, stored in a retrieval system or transmitted in any other form whatsoever, or by any means, mechanical, electronic, recording, photocopying, or otherwise, without the prior written permission of the Publisher and the copyright owners.

© Des Hickey, Gus Smith and Leslie Frewin Publishers Limited, 1975

First published in 1975 by

Leslie Frewin Publishers Limited,
Five Goodwin's Court,
Saint Martin's Lane,
London WC2N 4LL, England.

This book is set in Garamond Bold
Photoset, printed and bound in Great Britain by
Weatherby Woolnough,
Sanders Road, Wellingborough, Northants.

ISBN 0 85632 121 4

Illustrations

Contents

Co-Starring
(in Alphabetical Order)

Hermione Baddeley
Harry Barr
George Barrie
Claire Bloom
John Braine
David Butler

Sammy Cahn
Michael Caine
Constance Chapman
Edward Chapman
Jack Clayton
Joan Cohn Harvey
Richard Condon
Jack Cushingham

Basil Dean
Vincent Donohoe
Patricia Duschak

'Jock' Falkson
Bryan Forbes

Brian Gibbs
Lewis Gilbert
Sydney Guilaroff

Gordon Harbord
Joseph Hardy
Don Hensman
John Huston
Ken Hughes
Brian Desmond Hurst

John Ireland

Harold Karpman

Sid James
Jean Louis and Maggie

Sylvia Kotcheff
Stan Krell

Elizabeth Larner
Margaret Leighton
Robert Lennard
Olga Lowe

Cyril Count McCormack
Siobhan McKenna
George McLean
Wolf Mankowitz
Robert Marasco
Charles Moses

Alun Owen

Peter and Kathy Powrie
Jim Potter

John Quested

Hymie Siegel
Joshua Sinai

Robert Sinai
Nahum and Henya Sneh

Eric Uttley

Cody Wietzel
Billie Whitelaw
Michael Wilding
John Woolf

whose co-operation helped make this book possible.

Off-Screen credits to:

Margery Barzey
Tom Curran
Helen Fishman
Christopher Green
Marie Howlett
John Maroni
Peter Skelton
Lurena Deutsch
Jack Gallagher
Knox Laing

Noel Purcell
Patrick Magee
Sandie Stubbs
Roy Everson
Peter Holdsworth
Cyril Cusack
Gloria MacGowran
David Scase
Raymond Vignale
Peter Woor

and to:

the Editor of the *Bradford Telegraph and Argus* and the members of the Bingley Little Theatre for their assistance; the staffs of the British Film Institute, London; the American Academy of Motion Picture Arts and Sciences, Los Angeles; the *Daily Express* library, London; Romulus Films, and the libraries and art departments of the *Sunday Independent* and *The Irish Press* for their patience and co-operation; to *Time* Magazine, *Variety* and *The Observer* for permission to reproduce material; and especially to George Barrie, 'Jock' Falkson, Gordon Harbord, Don Hensman (Buff and Hensman, Architects and Associates, Los Angeles), Joan Cohn Harvey, Margaret Leighton, Robert Lennard and Nahum and Henya Sneh for their generous permission to reproduce letters, telegrams and photographs. The *Elegy* is reproduced by permission of Wolf Mankowitz.

Cover photograph by courtesy of Avco Embassy Pictures.

1 | 'Why did it have to happen to me, John?'

HOLLYWOOD, MAY 6, 1974. FOUR O'CLOCK IN THE AFTERNOON. Producer George Barrie was screening a film for a group of friends in the private theatre downstairs in the rambling, pink-stuccoed Beverly Hills Hotel. A blonde girl in a tan dress moved easily among the dozen guests dispensing glasses of white wine. Vidal Sassoon was there, photographer Yousef Karsh, film executive James Aubrey, wives and girl friends. Barrie's wife Gloria, a small, well-shaped, pretty woman, her orange print dress complementing her tanned skin, her fair hair drawn back in a bun, announced, 'George is busy right now. He'll be along later.'

The lights dimmed. The guests seated themselves in armchairs and in the extra chairs that had been hastily arranged. Aubrey, in white shirt and dark slacks, couldn't find an armchair before the theatre went dark, so he perched himself on the beige-carpeted steps near the door. A guest with foresight grabbed a bottle of white wine as the curtains parted, hoping to make it last for ninety-nine minutes.

The titles on an Eastmancolor background of Santa Barbara coastline announced:

Laurence Harvey in Welcome to Arrow Beach.

At the end of the list of credits the name appeared again:

Directed by Laurence Harvey. Undisguised curiosity had brought most of the guests to the screening that afternoon to witness the epitaph of a star and director who had died six months previously.

Before the end of the first reel Harvey had made his appearance on the screen, his tall figure in a dark blazer and polo sweater looming above a hippy girl on the beach below his Santa Barbara mansion. The star, unusually gaunt, was portraying a Korean war veteran with a taste for human flesh. Despite the protests of his incestuous sister, he invites the hippy home to a dubious meat dinner from the deep freeze and before the night is out chases her around the mansion with a meat cleaver. She escapes and is hospitalised as a junkie, unable to convince the police she's telling the truth. When she makes friends with a clean-cut hospital technician the pair return to the mansion to reveal the truth about Harvey.

As the audience probably anticipated, Harvey becomes the victim of his own meat cleaver. In jump cuts there were glimpses of his bloodied corpse, and the film ended with a zoom into the corpse's staring eye.

Over the end titles a man's voice sang, *Who can tell us why we do the things we do?* The credits listed, *Music by Bert Keyes and George Barrie, lyrics by Sammy Cahn.* The guests applauded generously, if politely, as the lights went up. When they looked around they saw a stocky, middle-aged man in a cream waist-length jacket over a blue open-necked shirt standing at the back of the theatre: George Barrie, whose Brut Productions had backed the film. The guests gathered around him.

'George, it's incredible.'

'It's commercial, George'.

'Thanks a lot, George.'

'Guess it'll turn them vegetarian, George.'

Barrie accepted their comments placidly. He seemed happy enough that his friends had come along. 'It's no *Gatsby'*, he remarked with a craggy smile. 'But it'll take money.'

Nobody asked him why he had given Laurence Harvey the money to make the film.

Outside in the sunlight traffic was heavy along Sunset

Boulevard. The car radio reported a back-up for a mile on Sunset and Santa Monica Boulevards. The Sam Goldwyn Studios, a Hollywood landmark on Santa Monica and Formosa for more than half a century, said the newscaster, had been partially destroyed by fire. Actress Ali McGraw was watching while her husband Steve McQueen helped the firemen. The fire had started at 4.22 p.m.

Hollywood would transcend the ten million dollar blaze, as it would transcend the possible miscalculation of *Welcome to Arrow Beach,* and as it had transcended the death of one of its stars, Laurence Harvey.

THE STORIES PUBLICISTS weave around film-making seldom bear much resemblance to reality. There had been no publicist to report on the frustrating months Harvey had spent in search of a backer for *Arrow Beach.* It was not until an evening late in 1972 that the making of the film became a probability. Harvey's dinner guest in his white, hilltop house on Cabrillo Drive in Beverly Hills was George Barrie. Harvey poured a glass of white wine for both of them, a Pinot Chardonnay labelled 'Specially bottled for Laurence Harvey'.

Wearing a bright blue jumpsuit that hung loosely on his thin body and nervously fingering a long black and gold cigarette holder, he paced the off-white carpet of the lounge that looked out across the valley to Los Angeles and the ocean beyond. Barrie, sitting on one of the off-white sofas, listened in silence as Harvey enthused about yet another project.

'What are you talking about, Larry?'

The actor stopped pacing and looked directly at Barrie.

'George, I want to direct a perfectly marvellous script about cannibalism . . . I mean cannibalism *today.*'

'Can I read it?'

Harvey picked up a folder from a low table. Between the covers were sixty pages of typescript. He handed it to Barrie as though it were the hottest film property since *Gone with the Wind.* Barrie flipped through the pages quickly. He was a former musician, still paying his dues to the union, who had in a few years built up the international toiletries firm of Brut Fabergé. Selling cosmetics had proved more profitable than writing songs, and from toiletries his company had diversified into films. Brut Productions had helped back a successful comedy, *A Touch of Class,* combining the talents of Glenda Jackson and George Segal, and a thriller, *Night Watch,* in which Harvey had co-starred that summer in London with Elizabeth Taylor and Billie Whitelaw.

During the making of *Night Watch* Barrie had first met Harvey and listened to his engaging talk of future projects, not just plays and films, but dream houses and antique shops. They travelled together, Harvey's image helping the Fabergé business, and eventually agreed to produce a series of television *Movies of the Week* together. Harvey would narrate the movies, star in some of them, and occasionally direct. But his immediate aim was the realisation of this new script. Barrie, accustomed to reading scripts which piled up on his desk at the Brut office in the Warner studios at Burbank, saw the possibilities of *Welcome to Arrow Beach.* As he neared the gory end of the treatment he accepted another glass of Pinot Chardonnay and looked at Harvey.

'It's a great idea, Larry. Tell me, what's your problem?'

Harvey's eyes narrowed anxiously. 'It's this, dear heart. Some people promised to finance the picture. Now they tell me it's off. That's my problem.'

He lay back among the coloured cushions on the sofa that backed against a shelf of T'ang dynasty carvings ('the best collection outside the British Museum', he liked to boast) and listed friends who would appear with him in the film, of which he would be the director and star: John Ireland, Stuart Whitman, Joanna Pettet. Jack Cushingham, who had made a successful sleeper, *Quackser Fortune Has A Cousin In The Bronx,* would produce it. Peter Murton, the art director on *Night Watch,* would come over from London. And Wolf Mankowitz, his friend in Dublin who had scripted *Expresso Bongo* fourteen years previously, would work on the screenplay.

Barrie was impressed. Imposing names. 'And I can make it for 400,000 dollars,' Harvey continued, the baritone returning to his voice that rose to a tenor when nervous.

'Absurd. It just can't be done.'

'I'll even put up the completion bond for them. I'll guarantee completion, George, with my own money. I can sell property, securities. It *can* be done.'

They were still talking about *Arrow Beach* when George Barrie got up to go. 'Cannibalism does exist, you know,' Harvey assured him. 'I thought I might call it *The Vegetarian*. But that's rather sick, don't you think?' At the door his gaunt face was lit by a smile. 'They do say, George, that once you acquire a taste for human flesh it can become quite habit-forming.'

Barrie looked incredulous. 'That so?'

As he drove his car down the winding Cabrillo Drive he knew that within a couple of months *Arrow Beach* would be shooting.

Screw the insurance companies, Harvey swore, returning to the lounge and helping himself to another glass of wine. In spite of major surgery that summer in London, which he had been assured was a success, the pain in his gut was just awful. If he were to become a bad insurance risk for films, then he had other plans. George Barrie was entrusting Fabergé promotion to him; there might even be a seat on the board of directors, as there had been for Cary Grant.

He hadn't told Barrie that he and Jack Cushingham, with whom he had formed a company, had been humping the script around for months. Cushingham had sent *Arrow Beach* to Berlin when he was filming *Escape to the Sun,* a story loosely based on the Leningrad Jews' attempts to hijack a plane to Israel, in which he played a KGB man. The script caught up with him on location in Norway where he and John Ireland, also in the film, were holed up in their Oslo hotel. Outside the hotel they could find no restaurants to their taste. 'We can't even get a Norwegian sardine,' Ireland complained. Cushingham thought that Harvey had only himself to blame. For eight years he had been appearing in nondescript films made on foreign locations, films which

Cushingham maintained were doing him no good. But Harvey insisted they kept him working and brought in money. When he got back to the States he and Cushingham went to Texas and Canada in search of backing for *Arrow Beach,* and failed. The trouble was that for too long Laurence Harvey had been missing from American screens and American distributors didn't want to know about the dubbed films he had made in Yugoslavia or Italy or the Lebanon. While he was racketing around the European continent a new generation of filmgoers was queueing to see a new breed of star in a new style of film. Robert Redford, Dustin Hoffman, Al Pacino, Jon Voight and Ryan O'Neal were the young men forcing the older stars of Harvey's age into character parts.

IN THE TRADE papers a few weeks later a short item announced that Laurence Harvey was to produce a film, *Welcome to Arrow Beach,* with Jack Cushingham in association with George Barrie. Harvey was reported to be working with Jack Gross, Jr., in adapting an original treatment by Wallace C. Bennett, the story of a pilot who had been shot down in Korea and returned home a cannibal.

JOHN IRELAND, WHO found the location for the film in the Santa Barbara area, lived in a large beach house near the rambling mansion which became the setting for the story. The mansion, built in the 'thirties by a castor oil millionaire, had thirty rooms and had once been a girl's school. Tricia Nixon had been a student and Olivia de Havilland had made a film in the mansion. A knock-out place, Harvey reckoned, plunging into *Arrow Beach* as eagerly as when he directed his first film in Spain ten years earlier. But when filming began at Montecito in early February he realised that the daily problems he had coped with successfully in Spain were magnified. He was fighting the agonising pain in his gut, he had six weeks to turn the film in on schedule and within the budget, and long hours on the set gave him little time to be with his wife of just a month, the London model Paulene Stone, who had married him after his divorce from Joan Cohn.

Paulene and their love child Domino had arrived in California and moved into his bungalow at the Miramar motel. Harvey's temper didn't improve when some of the crew got themselves moved to better quarters because they said their rooms weren't as comfortable as his bungalow. Christ, he thought, they're going to add another 30,000 dollars to the budget. Angry, he didn't care if he kept them waiting on the set in the morning. They worked ten or eleven hours a day six days a week, usually starting at nine, and a few times he was half an hour late because he would sit down with the script over his final cup of coffee to refresh his memory or make last-minute changes. One can't always go by the book when making a film, he reasoned.

He had wanted Wolf Mankowitz to work on the script with him; out of friendship Mankowitz had already supplied ideas, but there was no money to pay his fare from Ireland to California. Just the same, in spite of the pressures and the tight budget, Harvey didn't alter his lifestyle. For twenty-five years he had gone out to dinner most nights and *Arrow Beach* wasn't going to make any difference. He and Paulene might have dinner at the motel occasionally; once or twice a week they would go to John Ireland's house; but usually they dined in the best local restaurants. And on Saturday nights caterers brought *hors d'oeuvres* and drinks to the mansion and a small party was held on the set. Harvey picked at his food or took a little from other people's plates, just to sample it, though he still managed to get through a couple of bottles of Pinot Chardonnay.

Most evenings they screened the 'rushes' of the previous day's filming. Jack Cushingham would be there with the cameraman Gerry Finnerman and the editor Jim Potter. Potter and his assistant had moved to Montecito to edit the film during production and Harvey suspected they were editing faster than he was filming. When a long scene between Joanna Pettet and himself was screened in the 'rushes' one evening the actress seemed displeased. A small mole had been removed from her face by surgery leaving a pinhole of a scar. She was self-conscious about it, claiming that if she was photographed from a certain angle the scar could be seen. She phoned Harvey the next morning at the Miramar.

'Larry, you photographed my scar deliberately. Are you trying to ruin my career?'

Unless he re-shot the scene she would not continue with the film. Joanna was a cool, blonde leading lady who had co-starred in films with Peter O'Toole and Stanley Baker, and Harvey admitted to Jack Cushingham that he couldn't afford to lose her. He held back his anger, reassuring her, 'Joanna, darling, you're beautiful. But this is a long scene and I can't possibly shoot it all from the same angle.'

'My God', he complained to Cushingham, 'we've lost an entire day's shooting. If she knows her face so well, all she had to say that day was, "Please can we do it again?" The furniture has been returned and we'll have to get it back and re-dress the set. That girl's just jerking me around, Jack.'

It was uncharacteristic of him to plead with women; his relationships with them had always been on his own terms. But that night he pleaded with Joanna Pettet to come back. 'You're the actress I want. You, Joanna, and nobody else.'

She agreed to return to Santa Barbara next day if he filmed the scene again.

WHEN THE FILMING of *Arrow Beach* was completed he ordered cases of Pinot Chardonnay to be delivered to Jim Potter's cutting rooms on Seward Street in Hollywood and moved in to supervise the editing. He and Potter examined the 'takes' together, deciding what to use and what to discard. When scenes were not shaping as they should it was sometimes too much effort for him to disagree because the pain in his gut was doubling him up. It hurt him to sit in the cutting room chairs and he found the only restful position was squatting on the carpet on his elbows and knees. His colleagues, aware of his pain, considered his attitude absurd, but they admired his courage. After fifty films he was working with the energy of an ambitious young actor.

The pain, like his moods, fluctuated. There were good days and bad. After five weeks in the cutting rooms they had assembled *Arrow Beach* in nineteen reels, and he flew to London in the Fabergé jet to join Paulene and Domino and Paulene's older daughter Sophie who was home from her first term in boarding school. He didn't stay long in the big white house on the hilly road in Hampstead, but decided to make up for his neglect of his young wife during those weeks in Hollywood and Santa Barbara by calling on the Fabergé jet to take them to Paris where they dined and danced. He seemed relaxed and in good spirits. Paulene, younger than his former wives, Margaret Leighton and Joan Cohn, had been described by the columnists as the perfect love partner for him. She would provide, they said, the affection and encouragement for which he craved.

But within days he was restless to discuss new projects with George Barrie. On the flight from Paris to New York he felt so ill that Paulene didn't leave the 'plane, as she had planned to do, in London; instead she went on to New York with him and stayed at Barrie's house in Connecticut. Harvey didn't complain about his illness, but to George he admitted, 'I just don't feel right.'

Barrie read the concern in his eyes.

'What's wrong, Larry?'

'I wish I knew. Something – something here.' He touched his stomach gently.

When Paulene returned to London, Harvey and Barrie took the jet to California and called on his doctor, Harold Karpman, in the tall, black medical building on North Camden Drive. He and Karpman often went out to dinner, but he called on his professional services only when he was really ill – and he felt really ill now. Within hours he was lying in an air-conditioned room at the UCLA hospital on Sunset Boulevard. By the weekend he had been operated on and Paulene had flown from London to be with him.

He knew, and she knew, it was cancer.

When the surgeon discovered how widespread the malignancy had become he stitched his patient up. It was decided to switch to chemotherapy treatment to kill or impede the growth of the tumour. This was a treatment that occasionally worked, and Harvey decided it would work for him. He would lick what he called the tiger in his gut.

As soon as they had removed the tubes and intravenous drip and he was able to sit up in bed he called Jim Potter. While he had been in hospital George Barrie offered suggestions to Potter about the editing of the film. Potter had made notes and then said, 'I'm sorry, I can't do it, George. I'm working for Larry Harvey.'

When the call from UCLA came through, Potter took the cans of film and the sound tracks to the electronics firm down the street and had them transferred to tape. Equipped with two Sony cassettes of videotape and a recorder he drove to the hospital and ran the film on a television screen in Harvey's room. He had read the newspaper reports that Harvey had cancer and the counter-reports that his condition was good, but when he saw him he knew the truth.

Harvey poured him a glass of white wine. 'The doctors say I can have red wine, but I prefer white, dear heart.'

His housekeeper was smuggling the wine to him in super-market bags, four bottles to each bag. A German nurse who was logging his intake of fluids protested at this wine drinking.

'Scheiss!' Harvey swore at her.

'I would prefer it if you didn't speak to me like that, Mr. Harvey.'

FOUR DAYS after George Barrie's screening of *Arrow Beach* for his friends at the Beverly Hills Hotel the critics from the trade papers had seen the film. On the Friday before he left for New York Barrie scanned *Variety*, which had arrived on his desk at the Brut office at Burbank. The paper had a review on Page Three:

Welcome to Arrow Beach is the kind of inept and distasteful horror film usually handled by one-office distribs with States–rights outlets, not a major like Warner Bros. In fact the Jack Cushingham-Steven North production, a sorry finale to the late Laurence Harvey's career, was an indie Brut venture that landed in WB's lap via the recent tie-in between the two outfits.

Variety considered the film's box-office prospects frailer than its artistic quality.

George Barrie didn't agree.

IN MAY HARVEY left UCLA hospital and joined Barrie and a few friends on a promotional flight to Australia aboard the Fabergé jet. Harold Karpman said it would be okay for him to make the trip. On the luxurious jet he would be among friends, so the flight need not be physically taxing. Anyway, it was better for him to travel than to lie in bed. Nobody said as much, but they thought the end result would be the same.

Barrie filled the aircraft's icebox with gallons of ice cream, the only solid food Harvey could eat. Dr. Karpman accompanied the group as far as Sydney, not because Harvey needed his attention, he said, but simply as a friend.

The 'plane touched down on a couple of South Sea Islands. Barrie set up newspaper interviews for Harvey in Sydney and Brisbane. They visited Singapore, Colombo, Ceylon and Teheran. In Rome Elizabeth Taylor was waiting to greet them. Her friend Larry, she decided, was going to live to be a hundred. Together they went to his tailor, from whom he ordered a dozen suits.

John Ireland telephoned him from California to ask if he should join them in Rome. 'Hold on, John,' Harvey replied, 'I'm on my way home.'

When he returned to California the house on Cabrillo Drive was lonely. He drove up to Montecito to see Ireland. Staring out of the picture window at the tanned surfers riding the breakers on their decorated plastic boards, he clenched his hands. Without turning, he asked his friend, 'Why me, John? Why? Why did it have to happen to me?' He felt he should go to London to spend some time with Paulene. 'But I'll be right back. If I don't go she'll come over here and bring Domino, and I don't want that. I don't want anybody here. I've got to be by myself to work this thing out.'

Ireland, his friend since they had first acted together in the film *The Good Die Young* twenty years earlier, knew the pain Harvey felt in sitting upright. He thought if he could get him to Los Angeles International Airport in a station wagon, at least he could stretch out in the back.

The garage where he bought his cars was keen to sell him a new Cadillac station wagon. 'Listen,' he told them. 'I'm taking a friend to the airport. Let me use the wagon for a day and I'll see how it drives.'

They agreed, and he and his wife Daphne drove down to Los Angeles from Santa Barbara that evening and up to the house on Cabrillo Drive where Harvey was waiting for them. They packed his monogrammed bags in the wagon.

'What a beautiful Cadillac, John,' he said. 'Do you mind if I drive?'

The Irelands exchanged anxious glances. Daphne gave her husband a look that said, 'If he wants to, better let him.' Harvey eased himself into the driving seat and sat stiffly behind the wheel. He drove slowly down Cabrillo and Beverly Drive and along Santa Monica Boulevard to join the traffic on the San Diego Freeway. It took them an hour to reach the off-ramp for the airport. Ireland looked at his friend. Harvey was tense and white-faced.

'You'll be okay on the 'plane,' Ireland said. 'They'll block off seats in economy for you so you can lie down. And if they can't, they'll move you into first-class.'

At the check-in desk the clerk told them the aircraft was fully booked. 'One seat in economy for Mr Harvey'. That was all. Ireland was about to argue when he realised that Harvey had turned on his heel and was walking out of the terminal. He cancelled the booking and called a porter to wheel the luggage back to the car.

Angrily, Harvey took the wheel of the Cadillac again and drove back along the freeway to Scandia, a favourite restaurant on Sunset Boulevard. They ordered sole, but started with the restaurant's varieties of herring which were brought to the table on a lazy susan. The Irelands ordered wine, Harvey settled for beer. He tried to be charming and witty, but before the main course arrived he was bent over with pain, his hands gripping his stomach.

'We'll get you home, Larry', Ireland said.

Next day Ireland called a friend in TWA who told him there were three seats available in economy on a Boeing 747 to London that night. Ireland agreed to take all three.

'But they're not together.'

'It's for Larry Harvey,' Ireland pleaded. 'He's too sick to sit up. He's got to lie down.'

'Okay,' said his friend. 'I'll get you three seats together.'

On board the aircraft Harvey eased himself across the seats. Dinner was served, a movie screened, people joked and drank in the bar. Then breakfast. Scrambled eggs, French toast, coffee. 'Why isn't everybody smiling this morning?' a cabin steward asked cheerily. Harvey saw nothing, ate nothing, heard little. He slept fitfully during the long flight.

Los Angeles was far behind. Laurence Harvey, the fading star, was a dying man. He wouldn't ever again dine with John Ireland in Montecito or lunch at New York's '21'. He had left Cabrillo Drive forever. He had also left behind in America a man whose name was unknown in Hollywood.

That man was his brother, Robert Sinai.

2   'What is there to be proud of in being a Lithuanian?'

ROBERT SINAI'S SON JOSHUA RAN FROM THE CAR IN THE POURING rain into the spartan waiting room at the airstrip at Massena not far from the Canadian border in upstate New York. He had come to provide a welcome on an unwelcome summer's day in 1974. He was over six feet tall, wide-shouldered, with straight dark brown hair. His face had broad cheek-bones and a wide mouth that conveyed a hint of a smile. He looked astonishingly like the early photographs of the young Laurence Harvey.

Massena is a couple of hours' flight from New York, a jet flight to Syracuse, then a bumpy commuter flight north to the small airstrip. Joshua Sinai lived with his parents half an hour's drive away in the small town of Potsdam. He had just got his driver's licence, so he handled the family's black secondhand Pontiac carefully.

In 1970, during a summer course at Oxford University, Professor Francis Warner had arranged for him to meet Laurence Harvey at the Chichester Theatre Festival. He had gone down to Chichester by train, been met by a secretary and introduced to Harvey after the performance.

It was their first meeting.

'He was nervous; so was I,' recalled the young man as he drove slowly through the rainswept countryside. 'Funny, I never thought of Uncle Larry as a real uncle. I had seen him only in the movies. But I knew he was a dynamic person, just like my father.'

The Sinai family were living in a two-storey house on a treelined road off Potsdam's main street. As Joshua entered by the kitchen, Robert Sinai came in from the living room.

A sturdily-built man of medium height with thinning dark hair, he could have passed for a football coach, but in fact he taught college at Potsdam and wrote books of original political thought, *The Challenge of Modernisation* and *In Quest of the Modern World*. Whatever resemblance there was between Robert Sinai and the actor who called himself Laurence Harvey was in the grey eyes and the soft intonation of the voice.

Sinai showed the way into a small living room. He began to speak about his brother with a caution mixed with some surprise that his visitors had come such a distance to explore the background of the man whose lifestyle had nothing of the simplicity of his Lithuanian upbringing.

'I never met my brother again after 1951, when we had a great quarrel in London,' he said. 'I went to live in Israel and six or seven years later we made it up. But even when I was living in New York and Larry had a film company there he never came to see me. I think he had become obsessed with material achievement. It was an obsession born of a deep psychological insecurity, an insecurity false to his nature.

'The image he tried to project was the image of an English aristocrat, and he couldn't carry it off. If Larry was an aristocrat then the word has no meaning at all. Once he lost his market value, then what was there to sustain him? There was no inner life. I'm sure Larry couldn't love anybody; he didn't even love himself.

'He had an exhibitionist quality in him, which is not the same as having a deep self-confidence. He was completely absorbed in the artificial world of outward show. He had even developed an accent which in a way was absurd; it was the accent of an outsider, something contrived.

'When he first went to London he showed talent. He thought of himself as a stage actor, yet he never had a conception of himself reaching the heights of his profession. I don't think he had the drive of an Olivier or a Gielgud. Later he sold out. That's what really destroyed him. On the one hand he was ambitious, on the other hand he never had the courage to sacrifice material rewards for artistic achievement. He didn't have that kind of courage. He stooped and he conquered'.

Outside it was still raining. Joshua came into the living room. He had probably not heard his father talk so frankly about his uncle. The elder Sinai, his voice conveying more detachment than bitterness, possibly wished to expound his own views about man's materialistic nature; he was examining Laurence Harvey as a character in a dramatic tragedy, a victim of his own ego.

He continued, as though wanting his son to hear more of this cautionary tale. Harvey's films he knew about. 'I thought *The Ceremony* wasn't bad, you know. The critics tore him to pieces, which was unfair, because the film had something. His best role was Joe Lampton in *Room at the Top*. Because he *was* Joe Lampton.'

Harvey's family name was Skikne. They were a very traditional family in the Jewish sense, and Robert Sinai had remained traditional and very consciously Jewish. 'I have certain intellectual difficulties with my Jewishness, but not emotional difficulties. Larry had many ambivalences, because on the one hand he was a great mimic and loved to tell Jewish jokes. He didn't try to conceal his Jewishness, yet he tried to create the image of being a Lithuanian.

'What is there to be proud of in being a Lithuanian?

'Lithuania was a little kingdom in the fourteenth century. When I went back there in 1970 I found it a miserable, gloomy, poverty-stricken place. The Lithuanians are nothing. They have produced nothing. And Larry tried to masquerade as a Lithuanian! That shows you his knowledge and sense of history.'

Despite such criticism of his birthplace, he talked fondly of his childhood.

'I can remember the village where Larry and I and my older brother Nahum were born. It was called Joniskis. There was a main street and houses of brick and wood. We played football in the orchards and, of course, went to synagogue; Joniskis was mainly Jewish.

'The Jewish community was being pushed out of Lithuania because of economic, social and political conditions. There was a continuous movement of migration. In the twenties the gates of America were closed because of the quota system, but South Africa lay open.

'My grandfather had gone to South Africa with his two sons before the Boer War and stayed for a few years before returning to Lithuania and then crossing to America. After the Boer War he decided to go back to South Africa, but he returned to Lithuania where he lived to the age of ninety. My father emigrated to South Africa in 1929 and we followed him in 1934. We had relatives in England, but there was no talk of us settling there. South Africa was the land of opportunity, a golden land.

'After my father left us we weren't too badly off. He sent South African rand home. We had quite a large house and there was my mother and my two brothers and me and my mother's sister, Chava Zotnik, an extraordinary woman, a hunchback. During the Russian Revolution Aunt Chava used to harangue the Russian soldiers.

'My family's connection with Lithuania must have gone very far back. But during the First World War the Jews of Lithuania were expelled, and many of those who were in the path of the German armies went to Russia. My parents spent the war years and the first years of the Revolution in Russia. They could speak Lithuanian and also some Russian and German, but I didn't know a word of Lithuanian. I spoke Yiddish, the language spoken by the Jews of Lithuania, and at school the language of instruction was Hebrew.

'Except for Larry, who was too young, we were all politically conscious. My aunt was very eloquent and right from the beginning we were caught up in socialism and Zionism. Nahum was a member of the Zionist movement; I wasn't, because I was too young, but I was conscious of all that was going on.

'My father had been in South Africa five years before we joined him. Larry had been born less than a year before my father left

Lithuania. During his time in Joniskis my father had done some house painting. He had no particular trade; he tried all kinds of jobs, even exporting eggs to England. If he had any trade, it was building. In South Africa he began to buy houses, renovating and selling them.

'The time of our going was the summer of 1934.

'There were just four of us: my mother, Nahum, Larry and me. Larry was six, I was ten and my elder brother fourteen. I can remember the journey. We travelled by train through Germany and when the train stopped in Berlin the platform was full of Nazi stormtroopers. Although there was nothing dangerous about our journey through Germany – we were citizens of Lithuania – the menace of Hitler was known to us and it was frightening.

'We took ship from Ostend to Dover and spent a few nights in the East End of London at a transit centre which had been set up for Jewish immigrants.

'That, you see, was Larry's first visit to London, though he may never have spoken of it again.

'I remember relatives from Sheffield coming down to see us. And I remember being taken on a sightseeing tour on a London bus. People were coming and going at the centre, which was probably administered by the Jewish community, and each family had a number of beds assigned to it.

'I don't know whether we could have stayed in England; anyway, England in 1934 was going through a depression and South Africa was not. The sea voyage took about three weeks. We travelled third-class aboard a Union Castle liner. When we reached Madeira Larry and I went ashore and bought bananas, oranges and peaches and ate them in our cabin. Mother gave us a terrific spanking.'

For the first time as we talked Robert Sinai began to laugh. If he was pained at the memory of his brother's life as an actor, the pain was forgotten in recollections of childhood.

'A family friend met us at Capetown and we made the long train journey to Johannesburg. My mother spoke no English, but my father had picked up some English in South Africa; it wasn't good English, but he got by. At first we stayed with relatives, then we moved into a house in a Jewish suburb. Most of the neighbours would have come from Lithuania.

'Larry was about ten when he began misbehaving at school. He was sent away to a private boarding school about thirty miles from Johannesburg so that he could be disciplined. At the age of fourteen he ran away to join the Navy and my mother went down to Capetown to get him back.

'He developed an aimless kind of rebelliousness, bordering on delinquency. When he came back to Johannesburg he went around in his naval uniform getting into scrapes and having a tooth knocked out. It wasn't just a problem of social adjustment. There were psychological difficulties, which we all had, stemming from our particular family situation. We had a mother who was an elemental force of nature. She was strong-willed with tremendous energy, volcanic energy, you might say.

'She was a good woman, but uneducated, and she couldn't channel her energy in any direction except her family's.

'She was extremely possessive. She tried to strangle all of us with her possessiveness and we all sought to escape from that stifling atmosphere. She dominated my father who was a gentleman, a wonderful man, liked by everybody. He was intelligent, but he was weak.

'My mother kept our house absolutely spotless. She was a great cook, an artist in cooking. She would get up at four on a Friday morning to prepare the dishes for the sabbath, but the food she cooked was more suitable to Siberia than South Africa. We'd come downstairs on a Friday morning and before we went to school there would be cheesecake and applecake for us on the table.

'Larry used to go around the house cleaning up. He inherited my mother's obsession with cleanliness. He also inherited her taste for cooking, except that he couldn't eat.

'The private school may have been a mistake, for a few years later he took off again. He wasn't very much interested in schoolwork, not was I for a time because I was so involved in sports. But we had a scheme whereby each of us had to select a

certain book during term. When my turn came I didn't know
what book to choose. I went to Nahum and he told me to ask for
Upton Sinclair's *The Jungle*. That novel changed the direction of
my life. I became obsessed with books and reading. But this never
happened to Larry.

'Yet there was a tremendous psychological ferment within him.
He went to a private college to finish his secondary schooling,
though I don't think he ever matriculated. At the age of fifteen he
was associating with some unsavoury characters. He tried his hand
as an architect's assistant for a few months and then began to move
among the theatrical groups in Johannesburg. When he was
seventeen he ran away a second time to join the Army. Of course
it wasn't really running away then because our parents consented.
In any case they couldn't do anything about it.

'By now I was involved in politics. Larry had a slight interest
in politics for a brief period. He joined one of those Zionist youth
movements when he was thirteen, but there was never any real
involvement. He didn't tell me what he wanted to do until he
came back from the Army. And then he went to London'.

As evening came on the rain continued to pour down outside
the house. Joshua listened to his father in silence.

'We are Jews. We have all the burdens of an oppressed
minority and at the same time certain creative capacities. We also
have the problem of passing from one culture to another, and this
can release compelling forces of creativity. Larry must have felt
that. I felt it – it was a traumatic shock, yet I was able to confront
it.'

A simple dinner prepared by Joshua of minced steak and
vegetables washed down with a glass of beer was served. The
setting might as easily have been the Middle European Potsdam as
Potsdam in upstate New York.

'I was a revolutionary at one time,' said Laurence Harvey's
brother. 'I changed my name from Isaac Skikne to Robert Sinai.
Did you know that Larry's real name was Hirsch, which is
Yiddish for Harry? In South Africa it was always Harry. But when
he began to move among theatrical people he changed it to Larry.'

3 | 'Hirschki,' said his mother, 'we're going to see Father.'

THE BARMITZVAH BOY WAS BITTERLY DISAPPOINTED. LIKE OTHER Jewish boys he wanted his day to be memorable, with his family and friends sharing the joy of his Confirmation, the Confirmation of thirteen-year-old Ztvi Moishe Skikne, the name by which rabbi had addressed him during the synagogue service that morning in October, 1941, Ztvi Moishe being the Hebrew for Hirsch Moses. But when he looked around the eager faces at the luncheon tables he faltered for a moment in his speech. Nowhere among those hundred relatives and friends in the Hebrew Order of David Hall in Johannesburg could he see his brother Nahum or Nahum's fiancée Henya.

Hirsch Skikne, the boy who was to become Laurence Harvey, gave the customary thanks to his parents, his family and teachers, promising to remain faithful to his Jewish heritage. He delivered his speech more successfully than most boys because he had rehearsed it carefully with Nahum and Henya. People wondered where his eldest brother was, but when he thanked Nahum in his speech he didn't refer to his absence; he dared not risk upsetting his mother further.

She disapproved of the courtship of her son Nahum and Henya Blacher, another Lithuanian refugee who had come with her family to South Africa a year before the Skiknes. She refused to invite Henya to the barmitzvah.

'If there's no Henya,' Nahum warned his mother, 'you won't see
me there'.

To Mrs. Skikne his words were an empty threat. She wouldn't
budge. Only Hirsch, whose friendship with Nahum and Henya
was close, hoped to change his mother's mind, and then tried to
persuade Henya to come to the barmitzvah in spite of her.

'No,' Henya told him, 'I can't go. It would be too unpleasant
– for you, for your parents and for Nahum.'

Ber Skikne explained to the girl that he could not invite her
against the wishes of his wife. Nonetheless, Henya had her hair
styled, slipped on a new dress and waited for the telephone call
that would announce Mrs. Skikne's change of heart. The call never
came.

A month later Nahum and Henya were married and at the end
of the year they left to begin a new life in Palestine. With a group
of family and friends Hirsch went to the station to see them off.
Ber Skikne said philosophically to Nahum, 'You could have
waited, son. But I suppose everybody has to get married sooner or
later.'

Nahum was twenty years old. His youngest brother cried at the
leave-taking, promising to follow the young couple one day. He
had always been close to Nahum, and in Henya he had found a
sister.

NAHUM, THE ELDEST of the three brothers, considered Hirsch
the emotional one and Isaac, who later called himself Robert, the
intelligent one. Hirsch was deeply attached to his mother, even
though the relationship was difficult. Isaac loved his father best. In
the days when they lived in Lithuania Ber Skikne kept a horse on
which he would ride into the countryside to work as a
housepainter on the estates of wealthy farmers. Once as he set off
on such a mission Isaac, not yet five, ran after him, shouting for
his father to come back. He ran for almost a mile until Nahum
brought him home.

Ber Skikne also covered roofs with sheet metal (housepainting and sheet metalwork went together in Eastern European countries) and made pots and pans for farmers and townspeople. These were the trades and handcrafts he had returned to in the second half of the 'twenties when the Lithuanian authorities restricted the activities of Jews in commerce and he could no longer work at exporting geese and eggs.

After Ber Skikne left for South Africa in search of a better life little Hirsch was to spend almost six years without a father.

His mother and aunt decided to let part of the house at 14 Vilnius Street to a Gentile family. The house was divided by a long corridor, with a yard and barn at the back where the father had kept his geese and eggs. The Skiknes lived on one side of the house, sharing it with Mrs. Skikne's sister Chava and her father, who was in his eighties.

The mother had her hands full looking after her three boys, especially Hirsch, but Chava was able to work as a seamstress, sewing underwear in her own workroom in the days when readymade underwear was still unknown in Lithuania.

When Nahum and Isaac went to a youth club in the evenings Hirsch was left on his own. He had no fear of solitude, and even as an infant he was sometimes entirely alone. Eager from the start to find out about the world, he came down the steep stairs to the living room one night on his backside when he was too tiny to walk.

At the age of four his mother took him to the Jewish kindergarten at Joniskis. Other children were crying and clinging to their parents in the strange new surroundings. Hirsch simply said goodbye to his mother and was inmediately at home.

The language of the kindergarten was Hebrew, in which he was taught songs, games and handcrafts. He excelled himself during the Jewish celebrations. When they staged playlets, including a Hebrew version of *Puss in Boots,* he was always the star. There was something special about him. In a photograph of his kindergarten class he didn't simply stare at the camera like the other children; he put a toy spade in his mouth.

When the time came for the family to leave for South Africa his mother told him, 'Hirschki, we're going to see Father.'

He took the news for granted, even though he had no idea who Father was. The long journey held no fears for him, nor the week spent with relatives in Kaunas, the capital, making last-minute preparations and waiting for papers from the British Consulate. Even in later years he did not remember the date, Saturday July 12, 1934, nor the moment when he and his mother and brothers boarded the train for Germany and were carried in the dark of night through the Polish Corridor. Stettiner Bahnhof, Berlin, was just another station to him, the men standing on the platform in stormtrooper uniforms just another soldiery.

Nahum went to the post office during their three-hour wait at Berlin to send postcards to his Aunt Chava and grandfather and friends in Joniskis. He was blond and Slav in appearance and could pass as a German boy, but when he talked to civilians in the street he admitted he was a member of a Jewish family emigrating to South Africa.

It was the ship, the *Dunluce Castle,* that excited Hirsch. He wandered freely from the third-class area into first-class until his worried mother sent his brothers to fetch him. At Capetown a kinsman of the family met the little group, put them up at his house for a few days and then saw them off on the train for Johannesburg. At Germiston, a station half an hour's ride from Johannesburg, Ber Skikne boarded the train. Nahum and Isaac recognised him at once. Their mother flung her arms around her husband and kissed and hugged him. Hirsch hung back diffidently. In Yiddish he asked of Nahum, *'Wer is dos mensch, Nahum?* Who is this man?'.

His mother, startled, drew the boy to her, explaining, *'Er is dein Fotter.* He's your father.'

Ber Skikne hugged his six year old son. But it was many weeks before Hirsch came to accept the fact that he had a father. To him the dark-haired man was a stranger.

'HE HAD DREAMS,' said Henya. Her husband nodded in agreement. In 1970 the couple had been able to buy their own house in Beersheba, where Nahum, silver-haired, with a short, neat beard and a preference for open-necked shirts, was a deputy Mayor, and Henya, raven-haired as in her youth, a busy housewife and teacher.

Henya and Nahum treasured the memory of the boy who was Hirsch Skikne. In those early days in Johannesburg his mother gave him sixpence to go to the films once a week, but he wanted to go three and four times. He would say to Henya, 'Will you come to the cinema with me?'

'You know I'm busy, Harry.'

'I can't go by myself, Henya.' And then he would admit, 'You know I don't have any money.'

His favourite stars were Clark Gable, Mickey Rooney, Shirley Temple and the boy singer of his own age, Bobby Breen. He saw Breen's films over and over again: *Rainbow on the River, Make a Wish, Way Down South.* He told his mother, 'I'll be a film star one day. I'll have my own aeroplane and I'll come and fetch you in it and take you to see my studios. I will, Ma. You'll see.'

His mother, who demanded the total compliance of her sons, never believed his promises.

'*Oi, dos Hirsch!* Nothing will come of him,' she complained to her husband.

Hirsch could not accept the discipline of his family. He became difficult to control, neglected his school work, arrived home whenever he felt like it. His worried parents decided to send him for a year to Meyerton College, a private school for recalcitrant Jewish boys. The day he was leaving he kissed Henya goodbye and whispered in her ear, 'I won't stay there. Don't worry.'

Nor did he stay. The school was an hour and a half away by train from Johannesburg and his mother soon began to wish he was home again. In his letters he convinced his parents that they should bring him back, and when they finally did his mother subconsciously rationalised the situation by persuading herself, 'Hirschki has taken his punishment. He'll be a good boy now.'

He joined the Zionist youth movement, Hashomer Hatzair, of which Nahum and Henya were active members. It was a Young Guard dedicated to the conversion of young Jews to the cause of Zionism. Hirsch couldn't grasp its ideological aspects, but for junior members like himself there was camping and scouting and woodcraft.

He became the camp bugler and each morning took it on himself to stand beneath the flagpole and sound reveille. For the first few mornings the sleeping campers were woken promptly at seven. After a few days seven o'clock passed without a bugle note and those who were awake called Hirsch who crawled reluctantly out of his bed to sound reveille. At the end of his two weeks in camp he merely raised the flap of his tent when they called him, blew the bugle and fell fast asleep again.

He was happier in the kitchen cooking meals, but he wasn't amenable to discipline. Nahum, the leader of the movement, warned, 'There's too much monkey business. Next year there'll be no camp for you.'

The summer camp, a hundred miles deep in the Transvaal countryside, was a paradise to Hirsch, and he turned heaven and earth until Nahum relented.

In Hashomer Hatzair he studied the history of socialism and eventually wrote an essay on Keir Hardie, the Scottish Labour Party leader. The leaders of the movement hoped that when the boys and girls reached eighteen they would emigrate to Palestine. But it was only a handful who went. The majority, who had no stomach for pioneering, gave in to their parents, resumed their studies, got married or joined their father's businesses. Hashomer Hatzair endeavoured to nurture a sense of independence, even a revolt against parental control. Jews in South Africa were prepared to give money to the movement, but when the time came for their sons and daughters to leave for Palestine most parents regarded their departure as a tragedy.

The life style of the movement was based on the Free German Youth Movement, the *Wandervogel*, but it also attempted to alter Jewish customs and the leaders dreamed of creating an independent Jewish state in Palestine. They laid stress on simple living. Girls should not wear silk stockings, boys should not wear ties. Smoking was not encouraged, nor ballroom dancing. Youth life should be wholesome and creative. Young Hirsch protested bitterly about the ban on ballroom dancing. He liked dancing; in his opinion, it didn't contradict the aims of the movement.

When his brother and sister-in-law left for Palestine he grew more restless. Nahum accepted that their mother was a stormy, even a domineering, woman, and to Henya young Hirsch could be stormy in his own way. Ber Skikne had such a tranquil personality that anyone could get along with him; Mrs. Skikne, in contrast, was difficult and temperamental. Hirsch became so independent that when he ran away and joined the Navy under the name of Larry Hopkins he refused to recognise his mother when she came to Capetown to bring him home.

He told the naval officer when confronted with her, 'I've never seen this woman in my life, sir.'

His mother paled at his assertion. 'Hirschki!' she cried, 'I'm your mother! How can you say such a thing?'

'That's enough, sonny boy,' the officer told him. 'Pack your bags and get along home.'

Back in Johannesburg the fourteen-year-old Hirsch wrote in careful handwriting on a small sheet of lined notepaper to his brother and sister-in-law:

Dear Nahum and Henya,
I hope you are all well and happy. I am well as far as health is concerned, but sick as far as life is concerned. I will be gone away by the time the next letter comes so don't bother to write. But I will write separately to you wherever I will be and you can write to Ma about me. After returning to J.H.B. from Cape, life was so monotonous and with no meaning. Please forgive me about not taking your advice, but somehow there is a better life waiting for me. I have nothing more to say, so goodbye.

Chazak Veematz!
And may God bless you.
Ztvi.

He signed his name in Hebrew letters. *Chazak Veematz!* meaning 'Be strong and of good courage,' was the greeting of the youth
movement.

On his second attempt to run away he was taken off a train to
Durban by his father and sent to an aunt, Rachel Perkus, a sister
of his father's, who lived some fifty miles from Johannesburg. She
had a calming effect on young Hirsch, who later returned to
school in Johannesburg before joining an architect's office where
he learned the rudiments of quantity surveying. He spent six
weeks canvassing for a book club which a family friend, 'Jock'
Falkson, had started, and in the evenings acted with a semi-
professional theatre group, for South Africa had no real professional theatre.

In one play, *The Man Who Ate Popomack,* he was a mandarin.
A particular speech stayed in his mind: 'I do not believe that love
is anything more than a pleasure, like eating or drinking. One
likes some women more than others as one likes some food more
than others. But too much of any of them will take the appetite
away.'

'Jock' Falkson gave him the complete set of his course on
physical culture and sex education. During those months he
dreamed of leaving South Africa to find the 'better life' he felt was
waiting for him elsewhere.

SID JAMES WAS a sergeant in the Union Defence Forces Entertainment Unit during the Second World War. He was the
associate producer of the UDFEU concert parties whose groups
staged shows in service camps throughout South Africa, the
Middle East and Europe. Unlike ENSA, UDFEU was not a
professional unit, but an amateur organisation composed of
members of all the services.

Sergeant James auditioned the aspirants. If they were successful
they had to join the Army before they could become members of
the Unit. Hirsch Skikne, calling himself Larry Skikne, turned up
one morning and presented himself to James.

'He was a tall, lanky boy, full of cheek and confidence. We put on some music and he was off. He did a jitterbugging act which was fantastic, unbelievable. He was leaping about like a mad mosquito.'

James signed him on and put him into a concert party straight away. Each member of the unit was expected to exploit his or her particular talent for singing, dancing or acting. Olga Lowe, who was producing and choreographing the shows, found the new boy from Lithuania as endearing as a young puppy, but shy. And, for all his jitterbugging, he really couldn't dance.

'That new one,' she complained to Sergeant James. 'I can't teach him to dance. He's got two left feet.'

So they decided to make his jitterbugging his speciality solo in the show.

'He was always asleep', James recalled. 'We used to find him asleep under tables and benches. We had trouble keeping him awake.' They had trouble, too, in making him get a haircut. And after they had signed him on they discovered he had given a false age, but by then it didn't really matter. To many in the unit he seemed effeminate. Fellow service-men teased him and asked him when he was going to shave. There were plenty of girls in the Unit, but he didn't bother with them. At one point the army psychiatrist was consulted, but young Skikne explained that so far as girls were concerned he wasn't interested.

IN 1945, AT the end of the war, Sergeant Larry Skikne was stationed at a base camp outside Cairo. The Army authorities, recognising his agile brain, had promoted him and he travelled with an entertainment group through Italy and Austria. Now, crossing from Egypt into Palestine, he was able to see Nahum and Henya who were living on a settlement near Nathanya. Under the British Mandate it was difficult for Jews to buy land from the Arabs, so although the kibbutzim lived a collective life in tents and wooden huts they earned their living by working in nearby towns in factories, trades or on building sites.

Nahum had tried many jobs. He had even swept the streets of Nathanya and done washing at the house of a German Jewess who had given him nightshirts, petticoats and lace to launder.

When Larry arrived at the kibbutz Henya was pregnant. 'What do you think now, Larry?' she teased him. 'You're going to become an uncle.'

He looked at her and blushed.

He was just eighteen, with the smooth skin and boyish complexion for which they taunted him in the Army. But Henya noticed he had outgrown his brother. He was tall and good-looking, just like his mother.

With Nahum, he went to Jerusalem and they prayed at the Wailing Wall. They visited a cousin near Haifa and stayed with him and his family for four days. On his last night in Palestine Larry put on a one-man show in the room which Nahum and Henya occupied in the kibbutz. All the kibbutzim from South Africa crowded in to see him and when no one else could be squeezed into the cramped space the doors and windows were opened so that others could watch from outside.

Young Skikne jitterbugged, pulled faces, impersonated Hitler, Mussolini and Hirohito. He made everybody laugh. Nobody was tired on the kibbutz that night; they stayed up talking and reminiscing until three in the morning.

It was only a matter of months before the members of the entertainment group would be demobbed. 'We were all saying what we would do,' Olga Lowe recalled, 'but Larry said nothing. We were wondering what he was thinking,' To Nahum and Henya, however, he confided that he hoped to go to London to become an actor. As soon as he got back to South Africa he laid his plans. By May of the following year he was able to write to them from Johannesburg:

May I apologise for not having written sooner, but as you have probably heard I am going to England at the end of this week to study at the Royal Academy of Dramatic Art, and I have been so busy arranging things and running up and down from Jo'burg to Pretoria to see the military authorities that I don't know where I am.

I got out of the Army three weeks ago and they have given me a grant and loan of £717.2.0 to study and live in England, and might I add that I am the first person in South Africa ever to receive such a loan to go to the Academy. The idea is that they pay me £17,10.0 a month to live on, so that's not a bad deal at all, is it?

Ma is a bit *unhappy* at me leaving her again, but I have tried to impress upon her the importance of my going and the chance I have, because it isn't the easiest thing in the world to get into the Academy and, as I have said before, it's a chance in a lifetime, and anyway England is a step nearer to you and if I have enough time and money I shall definitely come and see you.

I plan to work and study in England for about three years and then if everything goes well I shall go over to America and probably stay there.

How are you all and how especially is Henya? Give my best regards to Dave, and I can't remember all the names, but I mean everybody.

Write soon and don't let the paper shortage worry you.

My love to all,
Love,
Larry.

4 | 'I hereby grant you power of attorney over my son.'

LARRY M. SKIKNE WASN'T THE ONLY NOBODY IN THE LONDON OF 1946. He shared a common anonymity with thousands of other demobbed servicemen, all of them hoping to find a career in civvy street. With his Jo'burg accent and light-brown teddy boy quiff the odds were weighed against the lanky boy. When he arrived in England that June his papers were stamped, *Entitled to land at Southampton on condition that the owner of this certificate does not enter any employment, paid or unpaid.*

His haversack, slung over his shoulder, contained a sweater and a couple of shirts. His only suit was the Army uniform he was wearing. His light voice belied his build. He had the physique of a boxer or an athlete and was handy with his big fists in a punch-up. But his ambition was to become an actor. He pushed through the crowds from the boat to the waiting train. There was no relative or friend to greet him. That didn't worry him; he was too eager to reach London and start a new life.

The warm, sunny capital into which he stepped at Waterloo was not the London through which he had passed as a child immigrant in the summer of 1934. He remembered the bright red double-decker buses, but not the bomb devastation. And the hurrying crowds were intent on building a new life, just as he was. He found a room in Chelsea; he was told the address was good, and if he was to be an artist he might as well live among artists. The rent was three pounds a week, more than he could afford. It left him with less than ten shillings for food and fares, but he was prepared to ignore the proscription stamped on his immigration papers. He took a job washing dishes in a restaurant and lived on buns and cups of tea. At a bakery near his flat fresh buns were twopence, stale buns a penny; he settled for the stale buns. He smoked cheap cigarettes, drank beer in the pubs when he could afford it and kept his eyes and ears open for any way to earn a few pounds.

He found a Slav flavour in the theatre to which he aspired. He sat in the cheapest seats that summer to see Gielgud in *Crime and Punishment* and Alec Guinness in *The Brothers Karamazov*. He went to the cinema and saw Michael Wilding, the new screen discovery, in *Piccadilly Incident*. At night he returned to reality in his sparsely furnished room.

On the first morning he walked through the narrow doors of the Royal Academy of Dramatic Art in Gower Street, Bloomsbury, he was still only seventeen. Through those same doors that first term walked John Neville, Adrienne Corri and another demobbed serviceman who was to become a successful film producer and restaurateur, Leslie Linder. When Linder discovered the Lithuanian was living on buns, dry toast and tea he brought him home and cooked him omelettes and scrambled eggs.

To Linder, Skikne was a self-possessed student, yet beneath the self-possession he sensed a nervous man. His class-mates remarked on his self-consciousness, but if there were better actors than Larry Skikne in that class few of them had such good looks or such a single-minded personality.

During the mid-term production of Oscar Wilde's *A Woman of No Importance* he caught the attention of scouts and agents who came searching for new talent at such performances. Gordon Harbord, a tall man with a military moustache, was one of the best-established agents. It was his custom to ask permission of RADA to interview any students he thought promising. He approached Larry Skikne, whom he thought was American, and

Skikne, excited at the idea of having an agent, agreed to go on his books.

From his office in the theatre area of St. Martin's Lane, by Trafalgar Square, above which he and his wife Eleanor kept a smart flat, Harbord cabled Skikne's father in Johannesburg for permission to manage the career of his son. The reply came back:

I HEREBY GRANT YOU POWER OF ATTORNEY ON BEHALF OF MY SON LARRY M. SKIKNE STOP B SKIKNE FATHER STOP SEND DETAILS OF AGREEMENT.

EDWARD WOOR OF Carr, Son and Woor was surprised when the young man in a dyed uniform walked into his tailoring establishment on Savile Row one morning. Skikne stood confidently in the long room lined with cutting tables and easy chairs and demanded to be fitted for a dark grey three-piece suit.

Woor was not the first tailor Skikne had approached. Some had told him that material was difficult to obtain and it would take a year to make up a suit; others that they wanted payment which he couldn't afford. But Woor agreed to make him a suit in a couple of months and was prepared to open an account and accept payments of ten pounds a month. The suit was to cost £27.10.0.

It was unusual for Edward Woor to take such a step, but he couldn't help thinking that a Savile Row suit would look splendid on the tall figure of this self-confident young actor. He hesitated when Skikne asked for an Edwardian cut to his suit: draped shoulders, slanted pockets on the jacket, the trouser legs as narrow as possible. He finally agreed. Extreme, he thought, but he'll be able to carry it off.

WARNER BROTHERS GAVE Skikne an interview and later a screen test. He went into a café in Old Compton Street beforehand and spent three shillings and sixpence on a three-course lunch, thinking that a proper meal would give him confidence. The lunch made him so sick that, waiting his turn in the film offices round the corner in Wardour Street – London's film row –, he had to rush out to the men's room and throw up his food.

When Warners interviewed him he was white-faced. But they liked him and promised him a contract.

ANDRÉ VAN GYSEGHEM first saw Skikne in the mid-term play at the Royal Academy of Dramatic Art. He saw a young actor who hadn't an idea how to play Wilde.

'His South African accent stood out a mile. He was all arms and legs, a great, big, bumbling boy with a weak voice. But he had wonderful teeth and a fine figure. I could see why they had cast him in the play.'

In February, 1947, the newly-formed Manchester Intimate Theatre staged its first production in the Central Library in St. Peter's Square. *The Seagull* by Anton Chekov was directed by the industrious Van Gyseghem, the company's founder. Halfway down the list of actors in the first-night programme was the name *Larry M. Skikne (by kind permission of Warner Bros.)*. Skikne was playing Constantine Gavrilovitch Treplev, the young poet. He hadn't been prepared to spend another term at the Academy. He wanted to become a professional actor, and was tempted by Hollywood, but he needed immediate experience and he was hungry. He jumped at Van Gyseghem's offer to join the new company.

The actors were recruited in London and rehearsed for three weeks in a room above the Duke of Argyll pub in Soho. When they reached Manchester Skikne, in addition to his Savile Row suit, had been able to replace his dyed uniform with a casual jacket and denims.

He confided nothing to Van Gyseghem or his actress wife Jean

Forbes-Robertson about his early life. But in a spare half hour he
wrote an air letter to Nahum and Henya in Palestine, congra-
tulating them on the birth of their son, Nachshon:

*At present I am in a dreary city, Manchester, playing the juvenile lead
with a new theatre company. The first play is* The Seagull, *by Chekhov.
I am playing Constantine which is both a difficult and wonderful part.
We open on Tuesday, the 11th. I am working all day and all night and
practically live in the theatre, except sleep there. In fact I am writing this
letter between rehearsals. If I could sleep here I would. I love my work.*

*I have at present very little outside interest as I have no time. I am also
living on the meagre sum of £4 a week, but when we open and start
playing for audiences I will be getting £8 a week and then I will be able
to order the newspapers for Nahum.*

*The season is to last four months and we are doing three other plays
called* Amphitryon 38, The Beaux' Stratagem *and* The Kirby Fortune.
*They are all works of the highest intellectual quality and they will be of
great value to me. My thoughts for the future are those of the highest form
of achievement in the theatre and films; both acting and producing and
possibly writing. But I am setting myself the task of absorbing as much
knowledge about the theatre as possible.*

*The weather here is cold, snow, etc., freezing of water, etc., and in
general things are not as one would like them to be. But I will survive.
As I have probably told you in my previous letter I am not going to
Hollywood for a long time yet and have therefore set that out of my mind
at present.*

*Prices here are at present terrible and nothing can be bought without
coupons or ration books as everything is rationed. Anti-semitism, where I
am personally concerned, is nil. So far I have not come in contact with it.
You will have to excuse me if I don't write regularly because I am so busy
and have so many letters to answer. Mother keeps asking me to write more
often, but she just doesn't want to understand.*

> *Love,*
> *Larry.*

Keen to learn, Skikne badgered the other members of the
company. How should he say this line? How should he make that
move? What would happen if he made such an entrance: 'His

claws were out in all directions,' Van Gyseghem noticed, 'gripping hard on every scrap of knowledge and experience.'

'You're such a bloody inquisitive bastard, Larry,' the other actors swore at him. 'Why don't you go to hell?'

At least, Van Gyseghem thought, he had the right approach. He was proving an asset to the company and they found him convincing in *The Seagull.* Skikne thought the passionately ambitious artist was akin to himself. In April he wrote again to Nahum and Henya:

> *Firstly, I would like to say how much I enjoyed reading your letter which to me is really a source of inspiration. I am proud to be part of a family who have each taken upon themselves work of the highest possible ideals, and although our paths are somewhat different, there is a bond which links us together which can never be broken.*
>
> *We opened with our new play* The Kirby Fortune, *by Neil Grant, on Tuesday and it has been received extremely well by both critics and public. It is a new play which has never been done before anywhere else and it therefore comes under our experimental programme. The next play is* The Beaux' Stratagem, *by Farquhar, a Restoration comedy. We start rehearsals tomorrow and I am to play one of the principal roles, that of Aimless.*
>
> *By the way, Nahum, I must apologise for not sending you those papers which I promised, but I can't seem to get hold of them in Manchester.*
>
> *The weather here has been very good in the past week. Even the sun has come out. I got a letter from home yesterday and Isaac will soon be leaving for England with his wife Anne. They expect to be here by the end of May.*
>
> *I am pleased to hear about the way Nachshon is getting on. By the photographs he certainly looks a beautiful baby. Tell the chevra in the kibutz I am delighted to hear of their interest in me and will you give my love (that is all the girls, the* men *my best regards). Well, I must fly and get some lunch and then get back to the theatre as we have two shows today.*
>
> *Love to you and write soon.*
>
> *Larry.*

It was during rehearsals for Somerset Maugham's *The Circle,* in which he was to play the young Edward Luton, that Skikne

showed his first trace of pronounced arrogance. Eric Uttley, a
short, dapper colleague of Van Gyseghem's was directing the play.
He remarked to Skikne, 'You don't look terribly English, Larry,
and you're playing a very English character. We *know* you're a
bloody foreigner, so the best thing you can do is get yourself a
blond wig.'

Harvey flushed. 'Never,' he said.

The director was determined. 'You are *not* going to appear with
that quiff of yours.'

'I shan't wear a wig.'

'You will, my boy, you will. Whether you like it or not.'

On the morning of the dress rehearsal Harvey walked onto the
stage with his hair dyed blond. He had been to the best hairdresser
in Manchester.

ROBERT LENNARD WOULD sometimes make a week-long
journey between London and Manchester, spending a night at a
time in towns with repertory theatres. Just after the war Lennard
had become a casting director for Associated British Pictures, the
complex of companies which owned studios at Elstree and the
only corporation able to compete with the massive Rank Organisation. He took his job seriously and interviewed every actor
and actress who caught his eye, talking to them, assessing their
prospects for the screen, searching for a talent that was out of the
ordinary.

Experience had shown him that it was difficult to sign an actor
with unusual looks because studio heads weren't able to identify
them with the charisma of established stars, yet Lennard knew that
when such performers achieved success it was because their unique
qualities had put them head and shoulders above their colleagues.
At least, that was his view.

On the night he first saw Larry Skikne on the stage of
Manchester's Library Theatre it was the outrageous quiff that
caught his attention. Skikne's accent didn't impress him, nor his

voice which seemed four or five tones higher than it should have been. But the unusual structure of the boy's face and his enthusiasm on the stage attracted him. He decided not to approach Skikne after the performance, preferring to wait until he got back to London. Then he wrote a letter, telling him he would like to meet him whenever he was free.

The meeting didn't take place until the end of the Manchester season and it was arranged through Gordon Harbord. The staff at the Pastoria restaurant off London's Leicester Square ensured, as usual, that Lennard had a secluded corner table. Skikne arrived better dressed than most actors, if a little spivvy, Lennard thought. There was a nonchalance about the way he fingered a long cigarette holder. Both men fenced a little until they found themselves mutually sympathetic to each other's ideas. Lennard needed Skikne's trust, and the actor, hoping to earn some badly-needed money in films while continuing to learn his craft in the theatre, was ready to give it.

Lennard had no doubts. He saw Skikne's future in terms of the American market. He didn't want any more prissy girls or men with crimpy hair and Oxford accents. What he wanted was an actor who would be accepted by American audiences. Now, here, unexpectedly, was Larry Skikne, an actor with, he thought, balls and a transatlantic accent.

The two men had several meetings over a period of months before a contract with Associated British was finally signed. It was a seven-year contract, giving Skikne a starting salary of twenty pounds a week, a pittance for a potential star.

5 | 'It's regrettable – they have changed my name.'

SKIKNE WAS ALMOST BROKE WHEN HE ARRIVED BACK IN LONDON FROM Manchester in June, 1947. It was Gordon Harbord who came to his rescue, paying him an allowance of ten pounds a week until his first film part came along and the contract with Associated British was signed.

House of Darkness was to be his first film, a low-budget melodrama directed by Oswald Mitchell, who had made such modest films as *Old Mother Riley* and *Danny Boy*. British Lion would release the film for one of the new small companies then mushrooming in London, International Motion Pictures. Skikne played a Victorian paranoiac who slumped dead over his piano keyboard at the end of the film, having played the opening chords of George Melachrino's *First Rhapsody*.

He had been considered for the part of the boy marooned with Jean Simmons on a desert island in an ambitious version of *The Blue Lagoon*, but it went to Donald Houston, and nothing had come of the Warners' offer. But the opportunity to work with the big companies would come again, he knew. When he wrote to Nahum and Henya for the Jewish New Year he reported, 'I'm well now and am working; that I feel is all that matters.'

He hadn't forgotten the proscription stamped on his immigration papers the previous summer. In the light of his future, which looked promising, those words began to worry him. Towards the end of the year International Pictures advanced him the fare to fly to South Africa to arrange his parents' naturalisation. By Christmas Ber and Ella Skikne had become South African citizens, which meant that their son Larry was also a citizen and entitled to work in Britain.

Back in England he wrote to Nahum and Henya:

Ma and Daddy are not looking as well as they should; especially Dad who has deteriorated quite a lot because of recent illness and Ma's undue neurosis and constant worry and bickering. Maybe I am being a little cruel by making the above statement, but unfortunately it is true. My coming home did, however, help a great deal.

Isaac is at a point where he feels frustrated, depressed and almost stagnant. He wants so badly to get over here and continue his work in which I have the utmost faith and confidence and which will one day carry him to great heights.

The rest of South Africa has degenerated to an inexplicable degree of laziness, exploitation and has now even lost any foundation of culture and art that it might have had, and the mad scramble for financial power and wealth has more than ever become the chief object in people's lives.

The conversation of the few people I met seemed to be, 'So you're a rich boy now,' which blatantly shows up their ignorance and stupidity.

By February *House of Darkness* was almost completed. Knowing the ill-feeling of the Middle East Jews towards Britain, he wondered if the film would ever be screened in Palestine. Theoretically the war between the British and the Jews had ended, but a new conflict had flared up between Jewish Palestine and the seven countries of the Arab League which Britain supported. He hoped his brother and sister-in-law and their child were safe.

'I feel helpless in my desire to participate,' he told them. 'I condemn this Government and their policy of starting chaos and destruction wherever they leave. I am now in a state where I want to leave here and go to America when it is possible to do so.'

IT WAS GORDON Harbord who changed Larry Skikne's name to Laurence Harvey. The film company and the distributors had decided Skikne wasn't a suitable name for a new British leading man. Harbord was inclined to agree. Skikne was much too continental. Larry should be Laurence and they would find an English surname to go with it.

Harbord enjoyed inventing new names. He used to type lengthy lists of names to see how they would look on paper. He had changed Adrienne Ricoboni to Adrienne Corri. He had given Diana Fluck the name Diana Scarlet, except that Miss Fluck didn't like being called Miss Scarlet and it was changed to Diana Dors.

He always asked players their mothers' names or the names of their relatives. Larry Skikne's mother's name had been Zotnik. That would never do. The most English name he could think of was Harvey, as in the solid Knightsbridge store, Harvey Nichols. Not so English as Harrods perhaps, but they could hardly call him Laurence Harrods.

Harbord was quite pleased with the name Laurence Harvey. 'But we have to be careful,' he told Skikne. Together they searched the pages of the theatrical directory, but they found no other actor named Harvey.

ROBERT LENNARD DIDN'T agree with the change. He would have kept the name Skikne. An unusual name was an asset, so were Skikne's good looks and his ability, as Lennard put it, 'to play the whole piano.' He could plumb the depths and scale the heights and had the capacity to convey a range of emotion on the screen.

But Lennard was more concerned about the Skikne quiff. They had a hairdresser try to coax it into a different style.

'It's my cow's lick,' the boy insisted. 'It's the only way I can wear it.'

LARRY SKIKNE, TO BE KNOWN in future as Laurence Harvey, didn't protest to Harbord at the change of name. But to Nahum he wrote:

In approximately two weeks' time I start work on another film. The story of the first film was bad enough, but the next story is even worse and although I openly refused to do it I am afraid I am bound by a sheet of paper known as a contract which I bitterly regret.

Another regrettable thing has happened over which I have no control: this time it is something more personal – they have changed my name because it was suddenly decided by the distributors that is wasn't commercial, so I am now known as 'Laurence Harvey'. O, this too, too unfortunate society!

I dream and long for the day when I can break these chains which bind me to a society which through its own folly and stupidity is heading slowly to destruction. This pseudo world of art and culture is so heart-breaking that I am more determined than ever to work and learn and then guide and teach the true principals of art and culture.

Harvey was now living in Shepherd Market, a quaint, tumbledown area of tiny squares, narrow streets and cramped houses, though he told friends he lived in Curzon Street, the long elegant street off Park Lane, behind which the Market nestled. Most of the accommodation in the Market was in rooms or tiny flats above small shops that housed grocers, antique dealers, newsagents, bakers, fruiterers and fishmongers.

His flat was on the corner of a courtyard, busy in the daytime with people who worked in the area and almost as busy at night with pub drinkers and young whores of both sexes. It was the unconventional world in which Harvey was learning to live.

By August he had completed a small part in the unpretentious *Man on the Run,* a film in which Kenneth More had an even smaller part. *House of Darkness* was due to be released in a few weeks and in both films he would be billed as 'Laurence Harvey'.

His brother Isaac and wife Anne had arrived in London from South Africa. Isaac's wife was a writer and soon afterwards Harvey went to Paris for a couple of weeks to research a screenplay which he and Anne hoped to adapt from a short story by Balzac. He thought it a beautiful love story and a subtle satire on the upper classes, with a perfect part for himself as a young and innocent lover. He was now telling Nahum that the cinema was the greatest medium of expression the world had known, but for the present, and from a practical standpoint, he had to compromise and accept certain ideas and forms which were manifest in the industry.

'One is surrounded by crude, base, unreliable and ruthless moguls (the combined weight is by no means an easy burden). I have nevertheless sufficient energy and strength left in me to continue to fight for what I believe is a true expression of one's feelings in this particular field.'

Less idealistically he added: 'I have just completed a small but important principal role in a film for 20th-Century Fox called *The Black Rose* with Tyrone Power and Orson Welles. The story itself is an early 13th-century adventure which should be very exciting. The company, as you are aware, is a Hollywood unit which is here making films. The experience has been invaluable and, who knows, it may lead to bigger things and eventually America. I play the part of Ty Power's brother, cruel, jealous and a coward (character part, of course). Ty is really a very nice and charming person whose only talent lies within those two qualities, and Orson is a completely brilliant character on his own. The film will not be released before next year, but when it is it is sure to come to Palestine.'

IN OCTOBER, 1949, Harvey left by air for Cairo to begin seven weeks' location work on *Cairo Road,* an Associated British film about hashish smuggling in which he was to play a young police officer who helps break up a narcotics gang. He saw the film as not only helpful to his film career, but also as an opportunity to be with his brother and sister-in-law in the new state of Israel. But when he returned to London after the location filming had ended, he wrote to Nahum and Henya of his 'terrible unhappiness' at not being able to keep his promise.

It seems absolutely ridiculous being so near and yet, through stupid and unnecessary restrictions, I was completely helpless. I tried every possible way and made enquiries, but there seemed nothing one could do except go to Italy and then to Israel, which of course was out of the question.

We were kept working all the time, especially as I am playing a very big part. We start work at the studios on Monday for another two months before it is completed.

In this picture (which is my best part to date) I am an anti-narcotics officer. I think it will be a very exciting film, both for its authenticity and dramatic qualities. This part is quite a strain for me and I am working and trying my best to make the character both interesting and real.

Eric Portman, who is about 45 and an excellent actor of great repute here in England, has proved a valuable study and I am learning a great deal.

Eric Portman wasn't so enthusiastic about his young co-star. Gordon Harbord met him at Elstree studios during the filming. 'Never, never,' fumed Portman, 'will I make another film with that little shit. All he does is upstage me.'

LEWIS GILBERT, a promising young director, had never seen a boy so full of self-confidence. The producer of a projected new film, *There is Another Sun,* had turned him down as too young and inexperienced to play a fairground boxer. When Gilbert told Harvey of the producer's decision he went to Bloom's gymnasium and had his picture taken in boxing kit with prize fighter Freddie Mills.

The producer changed his mind. Pretty astute, Gilbert thought.

Gilbert had directed Harvey in the film that followed *Cairo Road, The Scarlet Thread,* a thriller set and filmed in Cambridge. The unit had no permission to film in the colleges, so they sneaked in and filmed at opportune times. They worked staggered hours and stopped filming when there were too many people around.

One free afternoon Harvey asked them, 'How would you like to see my latest film, *Cairo Road?* It's showing in town.' Half a dozen members of the unit, including Lewis Gilbert, trooped into the foyer of the local cinema with him and went to the box office to buy their tickets.

'Just a moment,' said Harvey to them. 'No friends of mine are
going to pay to see my film.' He turned to the girl in the
box-office, 'Please get me the manager.'

The small group waited, but no manager appeared. Harvey
walked over to the box-office again. *'Please* tell the manager that
Laurence Harvey, the *star* of the film, is *waiting* in the *foyer.'*

Gilbert was embarrassed. 'Larry, you don't need to do this, you
know. We can all afford to pay our one and sixpence.'

Just then the manager arrived and Harvey said, 'I'm Laurence
Harvey, the star of your film. If you don't mind I'm bringing
these friends of mine to see it.'

The manager, quite bowled over, ushered them to the best seats.

Amazing, thought Gilbert. It was such a poor film and Harvey's
performance was pretty awful, but he didn't seem at all crushed.

The fan magazines were taking notice of the new film actor.
One of them reported: 'There's no danger of Laurence Harvey
getting a swollen head over the generous Press and the quite wide
popular acclaim he has received over *Cairo Road.* To him it's just
another performance that he could have done better. He judges all
his work very shrewdly from the actor's point of view. As yet, he
hasn't the touch of the film star about him.' Another magazine
published his photograph in their Postcard Series. 'This picture,'
they informed readers, 'can be cut out and pasted on a postcard.'

AT THE END of 1949 Harvey's mother was able to visit Nahum
and Henya in Israel. She was by now reconciled to the marriage
and was delighted to see her first grandchild, Nachshon. When
Harvey wrote to his mother she suggested in her reply that she
might visit him in London. The prospect didn't elate her son, who
quickly replied:

Mother dear,
   I should have been delighted for you to come and see me on your way
back, but I strongly advise you against it now for many reasons.

I am very busy and we will have little or no chance at all of seeing each other. I get up at 5 a.m. every morning and come home about 8 p.m. in the evening, have something to eat and study my script until I fall asleep. That is my routine and nothing must distract me, and it would be impossible for me to do anything else if I am to make any sort of success.

Another reason is I could not possibly be able to accommodate you in any way and my financial position being as it is makes it even less possible – so please try to understand.

I will, however, make every endeavour to come to South Africa soon to see you all, and one day, when I have any money and have achieved what I am aiming at, all the present barriers will be eliminated and you will be able to do as you please and more.

He had moved to another tiny flat in Shepherd Market on the opposite corner to the first flat. In White Horse Street, the cul-de-sac outside his window, he parked an old green Morris saloon which he polished until it looked almost new.

His first landlord in the Market recalled afterwards:

He wrote to me and I asked for references. One was, I think, from his bank, another from a friend. They appeared satisfactory. He took possession (there was no lease) and all went well for some time. Then the rent fell into arrears, a letter was written and in due course the arrears paid off. Then the arrears started again, and there was no answer to any letters.

As the amount increased – certainly it would be over one hundred pounds – I placed the matter in the hands of my solicitors. Subsequently he left (I have no idea where to) and eventually the arrears were met.

Personally he seemed the nicest of people. The rent business was just unfortunate. Obviously he must have been short of money.

Harvey told Nahum of his predicament:

I wish I could answer all your questions in detail, but try to understand I am so rushed here and living under such terrific pressure that writing letters for me must always be a very hurried affair. Besides working extremly hard and living on one's own, where I have to be my own mother, wife and secretary, I must always spend a good deal of time meeting various producers, etc., socially in order to discuss future plans.

To make things even more worrying I am absolutely flat broke and am continually paying out large sums of money in debt. To live and work in my profession is most expensive and I just cannot do so on my present salary.

Since completing Cairo Road which is extremely successful commercially I have played Cassio in Othello on television and have just completed the leading part in The Scarlet Thread, a spiv with a phoney American accent. I am now busy trying to line up something else to do.

The shortage of money here has brought, as you may know, production of films to a standstill and compared to 18 months ago we are making exactly one-fifth of the films. The American film companies are coming over to spend their frozen dollars but they bring with them their own stars, so the only parts available for English actors are small or insignificant.

We have very few international star names, and of course, the only way to do it is to go to Hollywood.

I think I am wiser though if I stay here a while longer and gain more experience. When the time is ripe I will certainly try and make my way there.

6 | 'That lady,' said the young man, 'is Hermione Baddeley.'

HERMIONE BADDELEY HAD MARRIED INTO WEALTH AND ARIS-
tocracy at the age of eighteen. Many of her friends were *chic* and
titled. But instead of choosing a life of privilege she decided to
continue with her acting career. In March, 1918, at the age of
twelve, she had made her debut at the Court Theatre in London
and from then on had not stopped working in theatre and films.
Her older sister Angela had made her debut as the Little Duke of
York in *Richard III* at the age of eleven.

Film publicists, searching for new words to write about Hermione, invariably ended up repeating themselves: 'Hermione can
be called a trouper . . . a director's dream . . . a character
comedienne adept at blowsy roles . . . She brings out the
uninhibited in audiences . . .' They listed her interests as 'music,
the arts, people living in the East End (because she often plays
Cockneys) and cultivated eating.'

Hermione Baddeley could be seen in restaurants like the Ivy or
the Caprice where she dined with many of the theatre's famous
names. She was at home in this sophisticated London scene, yet she
could explode pretension with a sharp wit. Honey-voiced, doll-
like, intelligent, her colleagues remarked on her prodigious
memory for names and faces. Known affectionately as 'Totie' to
her friends, she was brilliantly versatile and had starred in some of

the best and most biting revues on the London stage in the thirties
and forties.

In the autumn of 1950 she was at Walton-on-Thames studios
filming in *There is Another Sun,* as Gypsy Sarah, a fortune teller
in a fairground booth where Laurence Harvey worked as a boxer.

Nothing occupied her mind that first day at the studios except
her new role. The morning began with a session in the make-up
department. She pulled a face at her gypsy disguise in the big
mirror. Terrible, she thought. She scarcely recognised herself.
Even the hairdresser who came into the room at that moment to
fit her gypsy wig didn't know her. He enquired, 'May I ask your
name, please?'

'Do you mean to *say*,' came a carefully-modulated young man's
voice from the back of the room, 'that you don't *know* that *famous*
lady?'

The hairdresser hadn't noticed the young leading man waiting
his turn in the make-up chair.

'That lady,' the young man went on, 'is *Hermione Baddeley.*'

The hairdresser was embarrassed. He continued to fit the shiny
black wig, murmuring an apology.

'You say my name so beautifully,' remarked Hermione. 'But I'm
playing such a blowsy fortune teller, my dear, I really wouldn't
expect anybody to recognise me in this mess. Thank you for the
thought, just the same, young man.'

'Harvey. Laurence Harvey.'

'But of course. You're one of the young men in my film. Oh,
yes, I've heard about you. And you say your name beautifully,
too.' She appraised him in the mirror. 'You look such a strong
young man. You must be playing the boxer.'

He had boxed in the Navy, he told her, the South African
Navy. He looked as if he had just come from a gym. He had.

Wherever she went on the set in the days that followed,
whenever she relaxed for a few moments in her canvas chair, his
tall figure was always nearby.

Leslie Dwyer, who was playing the fairground boss, asked her,
'Have you noticed how that young man keeps following us?'

2. *Above.*—Harvey as a baby in his mother's arms on the steps of the family home in Joniskis in Lithuania with brothers Nahum (left) and Isaac.

3. *Above:* Harvey as baby Hirsch Skikne (front) in Lithuania with his brothers Nahum and Isaac and aunt Rachel.

4. *Below:* Harvey at kindergarten school in Joniskis. He's the boy on the right, third row from front, already showing individuality – with a child's spade in his mouth.

5. *Left:* Harvey (on right) with his brothers Nahum and Isaac soon after their arrival in South Africa.

6. *Below:* Harvey the musician – on the left of picture at his Zionist youth camp in South Africa.

7. *Below:* Harvey as a Johannesburg schoolboy with his dog Rexy.

8. *Above:* Harvey in swim trunks at the Zionist youth camp in South Africa.

9. *Below:* Harvey the boy bugler in his Johannesburg youth movement uniform.

10. *Below:* Harvey as Sergeant Skikne on a visit to Palestine in 1945.

11. *Above:* Harvey, a youthful film actor in the late 40's.

12. *Above right:* Harvey the aspiring actor in London in the 40's.

13. *Right:* Harvey with his parents during a return visit to South Africa in 1955.

14. *Left:* Harvey in Israel in 1967. Beside him are his mother and father. Also in the group his brother Nahum (with beard), nephew Nachshon (third from left) and sister-in-law Henya (extreme right).

'Yes, but one doesn't really mind,' she admitted. 'He's frightfully intelligent, don't you think?'

It would have made more sense if Harvey had shown the same interest in his young co-star Susan Shaw, a blonde, peachy girl in the English style. Hermione Baddeley tried to encourage a friendship between them, but he wasn't interested. Although puzzled by his sullen and curiously detached attitude towards young girls, she had to admit it was an unusual experience for her to be so favoured at forty-four with the attentions of a young man more than twenty years her junior.

One evening her chauffeur couldn't be found. As she waited impatiently to be driven back to London, Harvey offered, 'Let me drive you up to town. Mine is just a small car, I'm afraid. But I'm a jolly good driver.'

Such clipped English, she thought. Not a trace of accent. Or perhaps the words were a shade *too* clipped? She and Susan Shaw sat in his small Morris saloon and he drove them to London, talking and joking impulsively.

Every morning afterwards Harvey, with chauffeur-like punctuality, arrived at her house with the pink door and leaded window panes near the corner of Chester Square, in London's Belgravia district. As he drove furiously to the studios, she would remark, 'Such a sweet little car, Larry. But why the hell must you drive so fast?'

He was such fun, yet strangely reticent about his background. His Lithuanian origins were known to her, though he had spoken only of South Africa. Come to think of it, she decided, he did look slightly Litvak with those high cheekbones, well-defined in spite of his chubby face, and his narrow grey eyes.

On the last night of filming *There is Another Sun* they went together to an informal party for the cast and technicians in a pub near the studios. It was after midnight when they got back to London. For the last time, Hermione reflected, this strange but amusing young man was driving her home. In a way she was relieved that the film was over and she could return to her work in the theatre and drive her own comfortable Jaguar without Harvey thinking her ungracious.

As he drove the Morris past the bare trees of Chester Square to her house near the corner of Eccleston Street, he suddenly remarked, 'I've done such a foolish bloody thing, darling.'

'What's that, Larry?'

'I've lost the keys of my flat,' he said, drawing the car to a halt outside her pink door.

Afterwards she decided she had been too credulous that night. Her son was at Eton College and his room was empty. She made the offer without thinking. 'My son's at school. You could have his room.'

'That's sweet of you, Totie, my love.' He grinned and kissed her on the cheek. 'I hate to be such a nuisance.'

Within a few days, almost before she realised what was happening, he had moved his belongings and his furniture into her house, as though it were his own. The rent he owed the landlords of Shepherd Market could wait.

He obviously found the elegant area of Chester Square to his taste. He didn't tell Hermione how long he planned to stay.

ROBERT LENNARD HAD faith in Harvey. He believed he had star quality, but convincing his austere directorate was difficult. The publicity department of Associated British organised a cocktail party at the Savoy Hotel at which the heads of Associated British Pictures could meet their contract artists.

Harvey knocked back vodkas in the bar before the ordeal of coming face to face with the film financiers and accountants who, like their counterparts in the Rank Organisation, were hardly the best judges of good scripts or fine acting.

Lennard was telling his bosses what talented artistes they had under contract when Harvey walked into the room, drunk. Embarrassed, Lennard said, 'Sir Philip, may I introduce Laurence Harvey, one of our most talented leading men?' And to Harvey, 'This is Sir Philip Warter, the chairman of our company.'

Harvey missed Sir Philip's proferred hand by six inches and fell face forward onto the carpet.

The buzz of conversation in the room stopped. Lennard was mortified. Everybody looked at the young man on the floor who was now rising unsteadily to his feet. Harvey got up, glanced behind him as though he had tripped over the carpet and grinned apologetically.

Such indiscretions could be glossed over, but it was difficult to pacify the accountants when Harvey, through his agent, sent the company a large bill for wines and another bill for more than £200 for Savile Row suits. Lennard made excuses to the accountants, but lost no time in telling Harvey that Associated British would provide the wardrobe for his next film.

Gordon Harbord advised the actor, 'Please don't do it again, Larry. Take their clothes or we'll have trouble just as we had the last time.'

Harbord and his wife Eleanor would ask Harvey to lunch at their flat in St. Martin's Lane where Eleanor listened sympathetically to his problems. Her husband, watching the young actor toying with a salad, would remark, 'That's not giving you much strength, old chap, is it?'

Harbord was paying doctors' bills for him. Harvey complained of constipation and had irrigation treatments sometimes once a week.

Intensely conscious of his body, he had noticed his adolescent chubbiness turning to adult fat. Aware that actors look ten pounds heavier on the cinema screen, he and Hermione began dieting rigorously, eating mainly fish and salads and drinking white wine. His narcissism had fed on the post-war cult of the body beautiful which had spawned picture magazines filled with male torsos. When Harbord looked for publicity photographs Harvey produced a set of near-nude studies of himself.

'But we can't show *these* to anybody,' Harbord exclaimed.

Harvey's broad mouth broke into a grin. 'Why not? There's not much to be seen, is there?'

If Bob Lennard saw these photographs, thought Harbord, he'd have kittens.

But Lennard was more worried about Harvey's expensive escapades which were unpractical on his second year's salary of £30 a week. When Harvey had money in his pocket he liked to fly to Paris. One weekend he flew to Le Bourget Airport, collected a hire car and drove towards Nice for a meeting with Orson Welles; he was hoping Welles would give him a part in a film he was making in France.

The meeting never took place. In Grasse, in the hills above Cannes, a French driver opened his car door unexpectedly and dented Harvey's hired car. The row that followed between the two drivers became so abusive that a gendarme was called. When he tried to separate the pair Harvey swung a punch at him. Instead of meeting Orson Welles he landed in the local prison. He hated the discomfort of his filthy cell which had no toilet. He swore at his jailers, shouting at them to contact his lawyer, his agent, his casting director, his brother Isaac in Paris. It took ten days to bail him out of prison, and only then because Isaac had friends who were influential with members of the French Parliament.

By the time he was released Harvey was feeling uncomfortably close to the criminal classes. The best-known crook in the prison had offered him a job with his gang when he got out.

When Associated British Pictures decided to drop the third-year option on his contract it had nothing to do with his French escapade or his indiscretion at the Savoy. The accountants had discovered that his profitability to the company was unsatisfactory in relation to his cost. Associated British were often shortsighted; they also decided to drop Brigitte Bardot's contract.

Lennard broke the news to Harvey over lunch. Harvey arrived at the Pastoria Hotel in a white drophead Chrysler which he drove ostentatiously with the hood down, smoking a Passing Cloud, 'the gentleman's cigarette', through a long holder. He had borrowed money from a friend to buy the car. American cars enjoyed a brief boom in Britain after the war; now they could be bought cheaply off the kerb in the car merchants' coterie of Warren Street. They were costly to run and Harvey never got more than ten miles to the gallon. Hermione, who had come to believe that his creditors thanked him for borrowing, was upset. She had preferred his smaller cars.

'It's silly of you,' she told him, 'to try showing off too soon.'

At a corner table in the restaurant Lennard told him of his directors' decision. Money, they had hinted, was scarce in the British film industry, but he had persuaded them to agree to renegotiate Harvey's contract at the second year's salary of £30 a week, certain that if he held onto the actor, despite his company's 'lack of faith', he could arrange an American deal eventually. But Lennard was not his own master. Robert Clark, the studio head, now a property millionaire, had obviously laid down the terms.

Harvey was shaken. He promised, however, to consider the 'offer'. Probably he would have agreed to Lennard's terms if he hadn't read in a newspaper two days later that Associated British profits had topped two million pounds. He concluded that Lennard had double-crossed him, not knowing that Lennard hadn't seen the financial report before its publication.

He instructed Gordon Harbord, 'Send the newspaper cutting with my compliments to Associated British and tell them to tear up my contract.'

His sense of disillusion was reflected in the letter he wrote to Nahum and Henya:

I have just completed my third film this year, tentatively titled There is Another Sun. *I am starring in it and playing a boxer in a fairground. It is quite an exciting, unpretentious film and I should be very popular with the cinema audiences.*

I have also at last broken my contract with Associated British Pictures. They have treated me rather badly and have made a huge profit out of me last year by sub-letting me to independent productions for ten times the salary they paid me. They are without doubt the biggest and widest organisation in England and breaking away from them was both foolish and brave, but I have proved that I have the ability and am already established as a rebellious, vital individual.

I have caused in many circles much controversy and am now at this early stage going to fight alone. The battle will be more gruelling, vicious and, with the present depressing state of everything, even more uncertain, but one must be prepared to suffer for what one believes in. I have no definite immediate plans and am desperately looking for somewhere to live. I am staying with friends until I find a flat.

I must confess to being slightly rundown and overworked. The weather here, of course, doesn't help any and I am trying to get over my third bout of flu this winter. Everything is in such a financial state that I can't afford a rest and must carry on for the moment until I see my way clear.

7 | 'Now that the night before our day is ending.'

HARVEY SETTLED INTO THE HOUSE IN CHESTER SQUARE AS THOUGH TO the manner born. He and Hermione Baddeley, the handsome boy and the vivacious, middle-aged woman, were seen together in the best restaurants and fashionable night clubs. 'He became one's lover, of course', she said afterwards.

Young men did not usually attract her, but he worked on her like a charm. She had to admit he had a marvellous sense of humour and made a great fuss of her. Although he rarely talked about his background he displayed the natural graces of someone brought up in the utmost comfort, endearing himself to her grand friends.

When she took him to a peer's castle in Scotland he fitted in with such ease that one debutante, convinced that he had blue blood, became wildly infatuated with him.

The peer invited Harvey to come grouse shooting. 'My God,' thought Hermione, 'he *mustn't* go. He's bound to shoot my friend.'

But Harvey set off with the rest of the party, his gun tucked confidently under his arm. That evening they all returned unharmed and with braces of grouse. She was as much astonished as relieved when the peer said, 'That young friend of yours shoots damn well, Totie!'

Grouse-shooting was one skill, paying his bills at the Caprice another. He had to rely on the generosity of the restaurant's genial manager, Mario Galati, who was ever ready to help young actors. He was so impressed by Harvey that he gave him credit that stretched from months into years.

Harvey revelled in the atmosphere of the fashionable Caprice, eager to capture the attention of the many celebrities who dined there, and Hermione introduced him to lots of them.

He began to camp it up in a setting where producers and actors greeted each other unashamedly with kisses and *'darlings.'* When Olga Lowe, his choreographer from South African Army days, opened in London in *Golden City* Harvey spotted her in the Caprice after the first night. He came over to her table, kissed her hand and enthused, *'Darling,* I'm so *pleased* you had such a *fabulous* first night!'

Good for you, Larry, she thought. He was almost unrecognisable from the gawky, jitterbugging boy who had entertained the troops.

There were less harmonious times in the lives of Harvey and Hermione. His jealousy, born out of a sense of possessiveness, was most disquieting when he had been drinking brandy. Hermione recalled going to a 'frightfully funny queer party with him where practically everybody was gay as gay.

'This sailor was talking to me when Larry came over and practically beat me up. I threw my hands up to cover my face. It was *awful.* I left the party, but he followed me home and beat me again. He was the only person who ever beat me up.

'I was making a film at the time and my face was bruised. But he was so terribly sorry the next day he sent for three doctors.'

She forgave him and for a time life was wonderful again. But his moods changed. He used to park his car in the mews that ran beside her house. Once, after angry words, he stormed out, climbed into his car and, as she went to join him, steered the car straight at her. She flung herself against the wall to avoid him.

'Another time he was utterly furious with me about something and he started to kick me around the room. Really rough stuff. I tore on to the bed and he came at me. I must have been thinking quite quickly. He was wearing a beautiful silk shirt and I clutched at it. He was so startled for a moment that I was able to slip from under him and dash downstairs for help.

'For the rest of the night Larry was hugging me and crying.'

Hermione thought that was the Slav in him, the quality that made this 'rather animal-looking man' so attractive ordinarily.

His brother Isaac said later, 'I saw Larry and Hermione Baddeley together. Larry was sometimes extremely cruel to her. He used her. He had a serious Oedipus problem in being attracted to older women. But he used them.'

Hermione began to think of 65A Chester Square as an unlucky house. When she and Harvey went night-clubbing thieves broke in. When she went to bed early Harvey would 'phone in the middle of the night to say, 'I'm at Les Ambassadeurs. Why don't you come on over, darling?'

'I'm in bed, Larry.'

'Come on, Totie, my love. Get up and come out.'

HE DIDN'T CONCEAL his disappointment with the low-budget films he was making.

'I hate these messy little films,' he told Hermione.

She knew that James Elroy Flecker's *Hassan* was to be revived in the West End. The director, Basil Dean, was having problems casting the play; most of London's actors had already been engaged for the ambitious Festival of Britain. Dean and Hermione were old friends; he had made her a star when she was sixteen and he was ready to listen when she called him up and suggested Harvey for a part in *Hassan.* She was aware that Larry had no West End experience, but Dean, with a high regard for her theatrical judgment, agreed to give him a private audition.

ON A SUNNY day in early May, 1951, Harvey walked into the Cambridge Theatre, needing Hermione's reassurance to face the audition by Dean, whose stern professionalism had earned him a somewhat frightening image as far as young and inexperienced actors were concerned.

Groping his way onto the stage through the darkness of the wings Harvey tripped over a large ash tray. It rolled down the stage, narrowly missing the footlights, and fell into the orchestra pit with a loud crash.

He stood on the stage, searching the stalls for the powerful Basil Dean. He could see nobody, and nobody spoke.

'I'm terribly sorry about that', he apologised to the rows of empty seats.

From somewhere in the circle a voice answered:

'Shut up and get on with it.'

Harvey tried to speak his lines from the play, but dried. 'I'm terribly sorry', he repeated nervously, 'I'll have to read my lines.'

There was no answer. It's like talking to God, he thought. I don't even know where he is. He began:

'Now that the night before our day is ending, and the Wolf's Tail is already brushing the eastern sky; now that our plot is ready, our conspiracy established, our victory imminent, what is there left for me to tell you, O faithful band? Shall I say, be brave? You are lions. Be cunning? You are serpents. Be bloody? You are wolves . . . '

The voice from above broke in curtly:

'Thank you very much.'

That night Hermione was able to tell him he had the part of Rafi, King of the Beggars. Harvey felt his career in the theatre was now assured. Basil Dean was an exacting director and had given *Hassan* its first production in 1923. He listened to all that Dean and Hermione could tell him about his part. He repeated the big speeches over and over again, striving to capture the rhythm of Flecker's poetic language.

The notices were good, but *Hassan* did not repeat the success of its original run and Harvey was soon looking for work again.

Robert Lennard was still convinced of Harvey's potential for

America. Lennard's choice of Richard Todd as a contract artist was justified when Todd was accepted by American filmgoers after *The Hasty Heart.* He saw similar promise in Harvey and suggested him to director David Butler for a musical version of *Charley's Aunt.* Ray Bolger was to play Charley and Butler wanted an English actor as the straight man.

'I told Larry I had put him up for the part', Lennard recalled. 'It was a singing role, but I trusted him enough to know he wouldn't make a fool of himself'. Butler's interest waned when he went back to Hollywood and Warner Brothers' chiefs showed no enthusiasm. Robert Shackleton got the part.

Lennard had also suggested Harvey to Warners' talent scout Sophie Rosenstein when she came to England. 'We've got plenty of young men like Larry Harvey in America', was her verdict. 'He'll do much better if he stays in England.'

THERE IS A camaraderie in the theatre. Eric Uttley, who remembered Harvey from his Manchester days, gave him a part in a Sunday night play of his own, *Uprooted,* an English family story in which he played one of the sons. The play didn't travel, although *The Daily Telegraph* decided Uttley was an author to be watched.

Uttley, who was running a try-out theatre with two co-directors at Kew, near London, offered him a part in a new play by Hugh Hastings, the author of *Seagulls Over Sorrento.* The play wasn't long in rehearsal when people connected with the production realised Harvey didn't know his lines and asked Uttley to sack him.

Uttley recalled, 'They used to take Larry out at night and get him tight and then complain the next morning that he didn't know his lines.

'But I knew he'd be all right because I had produced him in a play before. I told them so, but I suspected these queer people were after him and he wasn't playing along. Well, you know how the theatre is. Apart from being a rat race, it's sex and everything.'

The theatre at Kew paid its actors around eight pounds a week. The directors, like the actors, lived in hope that the plays would be transferred to the West End or that the critics would come along. Harvey was aghast when Uttley told him he was being dropped from the cast. He went on his knees in the theatre office.

'For God's sake, Eric, keep me on,' he implored.

'I'll try', Uttley promised, 'but you shouldn't have fooled around so much.'

He knew that Harvey preferred to feel his way carefully into a part and by the first night he would be word perfect. He made a further attempt to save the actor's job, but by now others had convinced the directors that Harvey would never do. Uttley was outvoted and he felt badly. 'Larry was desperate. Nearly in tears, I would say. But I couldn't get him back. Perhaps Lithuanians are emotional; he was the only Lithuanian I ever met. In any case, he was an actor and actors are rather emotional.'

Eric Uttley never saw him again.

HARVEY, ANGRY AT what he considered the world's rejection of his talents, drove down to Cornwall with Hermione. Urging the big Chrysler along the winding road that led to Par he thought of his enemies who were throwing up their hands in horror at his friendship with Hermione, suggesting she was old enough to be his mother. To hell with them. She was the only person he had met since he arrived in England who had shown him true kindness, and she believed in his gifts as few others did.

From an old house above the seaside village of Par he wrote to Robert Lennard:

Dear Bob,

I heard the news from Gordon today much to my surprise, and, I confess, my disappointment. Knowing that I could have played a light comedy role I have been practising singing and, much to the surprise of everyone, I had discovered a good baritone voice.

I cannot express my gratitude to you for the interest you have shown
and although I have blundered my personal life I have, with some
suffering, tried to prove that I have a talent crying to be exploited.

I am absolutely broke and thinking of selling my car and going to
America with the proceeds. I would appreciate it if I could see you and
have a little chat and discuss it. I think you are probably the only person
I can turn to for advice.

> *Hoping to see you soon,*
> *Always,*
> *Larry.*

Eric Portman, who had become a friend in spite of their skir-
mish during *Cairo Road,* had introduced him to the strange house
at Par where he would spend week-ends with his male friends. It
created much local gossip, yet he never neglected Hermione. Even
when she was having her hair styled in the village *salon* he would
sit beside her, holding her hand and chatting amusingly.

When he returned to London he got the part of a tough teddy
boy in the film *I Believe in You.* He felt confident again, still
convinced he could be a big movie star.

He had walked away from Associated British; he was now ready
to change his agent.

THE ACTOR EDWARD CHAPMAN had met Harvey during
the making of *Man on the Run.* He considered him arrogant and
pushy in the way he interrupted conversations to read aloud his
press cuttings. When a group of players were discussing great
actors of the past over lunch in the studio restaurant and Chapman
recalled a particular performance he admired, Harvey rudely
dismissed him.

'What would you know, you beat-up old ham?

He apologised later.

Although Chapman detested Harvey's conceit, he found his
personality extraordinary and mentioned him to his wife Cons-

tance Chapman, who ran Connie's Agency, one of London's leading theatrical set-ups.

'There's a perfect pest on the set,' he told her, 'badgering everybody with his press clippings. But he's a very good-looking boy and determined to be a star. Why don't you come down and meet him?'

A few days later Connie Chapman was introduced to Harvey at Elstree. Yes, she decided, he's quite attractive. She gave him her office number, and told him, 'Do ring me. I may be able to help you.'

He reached into his inside pocket and drew out a handful of press clippings.

'No, no,' she said, 'I've heard all about those. I don't really need to read them, thank you.'

In 1951, with his Associated British contract dropped, Harvey called to see Mrs. Chapman at her office and asked her to take him on. She arranged for his five-year contract with Gordon Harbord to be taken over and for Harbord to be paid the commission for the remaining period.

Harbord was disappointed. 'If you think they can do more for you than I can, then right-ho, Larry. Go along with them.'

The boy's a madcap, he concluded.

HERMIONE BADDELEY TOLD Edward Chapman that Harvey would make the finest stage Romeo. During his lean months she ensured he was seen at the Caprice and Les Ambassadeurs. Her friends said, 'Poor Hermione! He's using her money to get there.' She shrugged off such remarks. If she was silly about money it had nothing to do with Larry Harvey. They were jealous of her real-life Romeo. What did it matter if he sometimes camped it up, kissed men and called them 'darling'? She didn't think he could actually live with a man, but then the gay line was a very thin line.

She joined him in a treasure hunt organised by a newspaper to publicise a new film. They rushed round the West End, finding all the clues, including a hair from Tallulah Bankhead's head which they seized when they traced her to her mews cottage.

When they arrived at the Caprice they were presented with their prize by a dark, soft-voiced man who was rapidly becoming a leading independent producer in British films. His name was James Woolf. The prize was a jeroboam of wine, much too heavy for Hermione to hold. So Woolf placed the jeroboam in Harvey's hands.

ONE OF THE giants of the British film industry in the twenties and thirties was C. M. Woolf. His sons James and John had started their own production company, Romulus Films, in 1948. John, the older, was reputedly the business brain, James the artist. Their first venture was *Pandora and the Flying Dutchman,* starring Ava Gardner and James Mason. 'A beautiful film to look at', James used to say later, 'but too full of symbolism.' They were more confident of success with their second film which John Huston had just directed for them, *The African Queen.*

The Woolfs were seeking new talent. That evening at the Caprice James said persuasively to the winners of the treasure hunt, 'Congratulations – and now you must both have dinner with me.'

Harvey replied eagerly, 'We'd be delighted.'

Over dinner Harvey gave the performance of his life, drawing on all the accents, all the mimicry, all the wit at his command and displaying them for his influential host. Woolf was slightly dazed by the performance. He said to Hermione, 'I think Larry here is just the sort of young man my brother and I are looking for.'

When *The African Queen* was due to be premièred a large invitation card arrived for Harvey and Hermione at 65A Chester Square. After the première James Woolf introduced his brother John to them. By now he had seen *There is Another Sun,* which Lewis Gilbert had screened for him in a preview theatre in Wardour Street. The Woolf brothers were ready to sign a contract with Harvey.

Hermione thought, 'I'm like a lucky coin to this young man.' Her brother-in-law Glen Byam Shaw, who had been appointed co-director with Anthony Quayle of the Shakespeare Memorial Theatre at Stratford-on-Avon, had invited Harvey to join the company. Hermione recalled, 'I think by now my family was saying, "We don't like this young man. Hermione is not bothering about her career." '

But her perceptive brother-in-law said, 'I think Harvey has a most wonderful voice. I'd like to have him at Stratford.'

Harvey was cockahoop about the Romulus contract and talking in terms of a Hollywood career. Byam Shaw met him and asked, 'When do you go to Hollywood?'

'Oh, my films won't start for another year.'

'Well, then, come up to Stratford.'

Harvey's salary with the Stratford company was £50 a week, which James Woolf augmented with money from Romulus. Woolf grumbled to film director Brian Desmond Hurst, 'I can get £30,000 a film for Larry and there he goes, off to Stratford for £50 a week.'

'Jimmy,' said Hurst, 'you should be happy he's at Stratford. Because after Stratford you'll get £90,000 a film for him.'

THE SEAGULL *by*

𝕾𝕾𝕾𝕾𝕾𝕾𝕾𝕾𝕾 𝕾𝕾𝕾𝕾𝕾 𝕾𝕾𝕾𝕾𝕾

Characters in order of appearance :

Masha	LUCIELLE GRAY
Daughter of Shamraev.	
Simeon Simeonvitch Medvedenko	NORMAN MITCHELL
Jacob	GEORGE FORDE
Peter Nicolaevitch Sorin	ALFRED BURKE
Constantine Gavrilovitch Treplev	LARRY M. SKIKNE
	(By kind permission of Warner Bros.)
Nina Mihailovna Zarechnaia	JEAN FORBES-ROBERTSON
Young daughter of a wealthy landowner.	
Evgeny Sergeitch Dorn	KEITH CAMPBELL
A doctor.	
Paulina Andreevna	ANN STEPHENSON
Wife of Shamraev.	
Irina Nicolaevna Arcadina	CHRIS CASTOR
An actress.	
Ilya Athanasievitch Shamraev	PETER FRANKLIN
A retired lieutenant, managing Sorin's estate.	
Boris Alexeyevitch Trigorin	ANDRÉ VAN GYSEGHEM
A writer.	
Cook	DELLA TURVEY
Maidservant	JOANNA JONES

☙

The Play Directed by ANDRÉ VAN GYSEGHEM

Assistant Director, ERIC UTTLEY

Décors and Costumes by ANTHONY MENDLESON

16. *Left:* As Larry M. Skikne he made his first professional stage appearance in England in Chekov's *The Seagull* at Manchester's Library Theatre, February, 1947.

17. *Below:* Gordon Harbord, the well-known agent – intimately connected with the early career of Laurence Harvey.

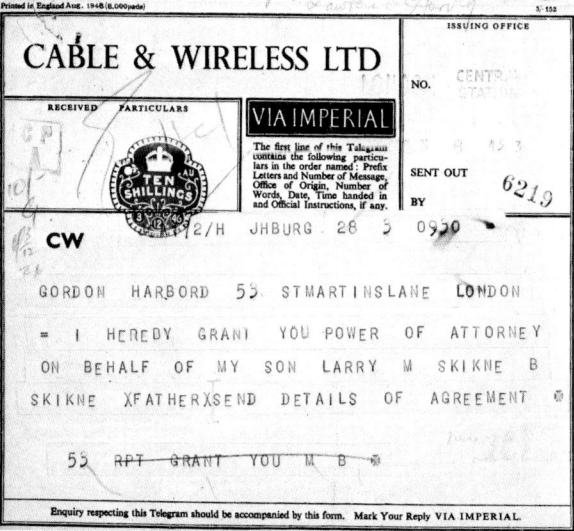

15. *Left:* The telegram that Skikne's father sent from Johannesburg to Harvey's first agent, Gordon Harbord.

18. *Left:* In *There Is Another Sun.*

19. *Right:* At London's Waterloo Station en route to New York for the Broadway production of *Island of Goats* in 1955.

20. *Left:* Harvey in the make-up of the Cobbler in *The Wonderful World of the Brothers Grimm.*

21. *Right:* Harvey (right) in *There Is Another Sun* with Leslie Dwyer, Hermione Baddeley and Susan Shaw. It was on this film that he first met Hermione Baddeley.

22. *Left:* Harvey (centre) as the young policeman, with Joan Hopkins and Edward Chapman, in *Man On The Run.* As a result of this film he was contracted to Associated British Studios, Elstree, near London.

23. *Right:* With Eric Portman in *Cairo Road* which dealt with narcotics smuggling.

24. *Above:* Sylvia Sims, singer Cliff Richard and Harvey in the film of *Expresso Bongo* in which he played a pop artistes' unscrupulous.agent.

25. *Below:* At London's Lyric Theatre (left to right) Paul Scofield, Peter Ustinov and Harvey rehearse for a midnight show for an actors' charity in 1956.

26. *Below:* Harvey and first wife Margaret Leighton rehearsing for a charity performance at the London Palladium in 1956.

8 | 'They said you were too old for me.'

IN THE SPRING OF 1952 HARVEY ARRIVED FOR HIS FIRST SEASON IN Stratford-on-Avon with a reputation as a promising, if outspoken, young actor and the man in Hermione Baddeley's life. He sensed resentment among the established Shakespearean actors in the company.

'I think they're accepting you, but they hate my guts', he said to Siobhan McKenna, the redhaired Irish actress, also there for her first season.

Siobhan had the idea that English theatre people were free and easy, but when she went along with Harvey and the other new-comers to the rehearsal hall on that first day they were given a lesson in behaviour. The reputation of Stratford must be upheld, they were told. No excessive drinking, no late nights, exemplary moral behaviour. My God, she wondered, am I really back at my convent school again? Afterwards Harvey invited the twenty-nine year old actress to coffee in the green-room.

'What did you think of that, Siobhan?'

What could she think, she replied, except that it was an extraordinary introduction to Stratford.

'The funny thing is, darling,' Harvey grinned, 'nobody takes any damn notice of these sermons.'

He was rehearsing the role of Aufidius in *Coriolanus* and would later play Orlando in *As You Like It* and Malcolm in *Macbeth*.

The approach to acting by the young man who parked his Chrysler outside the Swan Hotel was more committed than his flashy image conveyed. After the day's rehearsals he would sometimes ask Glen Byam Shaw to be allowed to rehearse again in the evening.

He drank and talked late into the night and introduced Siobhan to the town's restaurants.

'Larry taught me how to drink wine. We both liked crusty bread and we'd buy one large loaf, scoop the middle out of it, fill it with butter and ham, and share the loaf and a bottle of wine between us. The inside of the loaf we fed to the swans on the Avon.

'Larry was the only person I've ever known who dared send back the wine in a restaurant. When I told him how embarrassed I was, he'd just say, "You mustn't be. You see, my love, you must *impress* them from the start. And there's no point in tipping waiters when you are leaving a restaurant. The time to tip is when you arrive. Then you're assured of absolutely marvellous service." '

She found him a breath of fresh air in Stratford's inviolate atmosphere. He hated to lose touch with London, and on one of his journeys he invited her along. They called at Hermione Baddeley's house in Chester Square.

Hermione was not pleased to see Harvey with the redhaired Irish girl. She looked at Siobhan, then asked Harvey imperiously, 'And *who* is this?'

MARGARET LEIGHTON drove into Stratford in her Jaguar soon after the opening of the season. She, too, was to appear at the Memorial Theatre for the first time. A tall, willowy blonde of thirty she had started her theatre career in her native city of Birmingham. 'I was brought up by my parents in a very proper manner,' she recalled. 'I attended a church school until I was fifteen.'

From Birmingham she went to the Old Vic in London and later played in the commercial theatre. Women's magazines described her as one of the most beautiful women in England.

In 1947 she was given her first screen test and chosen from 900 aspirants to play Flora McDonald to David Niven's *Bonnie Prince Charlie*. The film was calamitous, but she scored a personal success. In the same year she married publisher Max Reinhardt and they went to live in his London flat, but later moved into Albany, the exclusive apartments on Piccadilly. They also kept a country house near Guildford.

Although she was a beautiful woman many of her colleagues found her aloof. She was shy, was not a late-night partygoer and drank only an occasional glass of wine. Her agent arranged that she should meet the young actor playing Orlando in the hotel outside Stratford where she had a small suite. The actor didn't wait for introductions.

'Laurence Harvey is the name,' he announced. 'I hear we've just missed playing together in *The Deep Blue Sea*.'

'Really?'

'They said you were too old for me.'

That's good for openers, she thought. It was true she had been named for Terence Rattigan's new play, but the part was taken by another actress, Peggy Ashcroft, and she had come to Stratford instead. She wasn't used to men introducing themselves in such an offhand manner, but she accepted his handshake with grace. As they sipped wine and talked about the season, she decided he was quite uninhibited, a type she had not met before. And so young and debonair.

Their subsequent relationship had a curious beginning. She recalled, 'Larry relied on the fact that I would drive out of Stratford and pick him up in my Jaguar when his car broke down, which was often. I always seemed to be driving out at night to rescue him.'

Siobhan McKenna would say she could see the pair falling in love on stage, though it was difficult to know whether it was Rosalind falling in love with Orlando or Leighton falling in love with Harvey. 'Their love affair brought something special to the play.'

Harvey was not put out by the disparity in their ages or their different backgrounds. They rehearsed together for *Macbeth*, in which Margaret was playing Lady Macbeth, and began to be seen together. Although they were discreet about the affair, the relationship was talked about in Stratford, a setting for many affairs. Together they seemed happy, even carefree, and Harvey, who had known months of frustration, was enjoying the experience. Margaret Leighton was a member of the theatrical establishment; he had yet to be accepted, but at Stratford he was working beside Gielgud and Richardson, actors who were held in esteem, if not reverence.

Margaret was embarrassed when he spoke too freely in company. He always needed an audience, she soon decided. But she admired the way he spoke his mind at a time when people in her own circle thought it bad manners. She regarded their relationship as an adventure. Every day with Larry was different.

Harvey defined his taste for older women:

'I like them provided they have beauty, are slim and dress well. I like them a bit showy and I adore the mother image.'

In Margaret Leighton he had discovered a cool beauty with an elegance characteristic of certain young Englishwomen, and he began to suggest the clothes she should wear. When they went to a fête near Stratford she dressed in a patterned summer dress and hat which she thought appropriate for the occasion. But he frowned. 'That's a frightfully dimity old maid hat, my love.'

He talked to her about his past, about his Army and Navy days, but not intimately. He preferred to live for the day, discussing film projects and plays and the money he needed for all the luxuries he dreamed about. She found him too practical to be a romantic.

He made no secret of the fact that he had come to Stratford for experience as an actor. Most of the time he worried about money, but he didn't worry about his relationship with Margaret Leighton until her husband came to Stratford to give a party for the Shakespeare company.

Max Reinhardt arrived earlier than expected. Harvey made a swift exit through a back window, only to return later through the front door as one of the guests.

It was the season in which the London critic Kenneth Tynan savaged John Gielgud's production of *Macbeth*. It left him 'unmoved to the point of paralysis.' Only Harvey as Malcolm and Siobhan as Lady Macduff came through unscathed. Margaret Leighton said to Siobhan, 'What a lovely review for you, but how shattering for the rest of us.'

'I don't read reviews when I'm working, Mag. Look at the effect they've had on you.'

Harvey was more pleased that James Woolf had brought John Huston to Stratford to see his performance as Orlando. Later he wrote to Nahum and Henya at the kibbutz in Israel:

'Our days are taken up completely with the theatre. We live, eat, breathe, sleep Shakespeare and there is little time for anything else. The experience one gains here is invaluable to oneself as an actor and to one's future. I have already been approached to do a film with Katharine Hepburn which is to be directed by John Huston, but I can do nothing until the end of the season which is 30th October.

SO LONG AS THE CHRYSLER held together he drove to London regularly. He continued to call on Hermione Baddeley who by this time had struck up a friendship with an Irish businessman. One evening Brian Desmond Hurst had brought some friends to her house in Chester Square and Harvey joined them for drinks. The unexpected arrival of the Irishman changed the cosy scene.

'There was the most awful fight, one of those real fights, and Larry knocked my poor Irish friend out,' recalled Hermione. 'He was an older man than Larry and not as tall, but very broad. Nobody knew quite what to do. I didn't like such incidents at all.'

The Irishman was carried into a spare room more drunk than

unconscious and laid on a bed. 'It was like some ghastly murder story,' said Hermione.

But to Harvey it was simply a petty annoyance.

HE DROVE BACK to Stratford preoccupied with his need for money. He was earning £50 a week and living like a star with four times that salary. He would have to make a decision soon between theatre and films. In August he wrote to Nahum and Henya:

> I cannot remember now if I did write to you to tell you about the great decision that I had to make – whether to continue working with this theatre for the next three years and play great parts, or to go into films. I have chosen films because of economic reasons, as you can imagine, and as I am so steeped in debt at the moment I will try and clear it all up next year. Being of a family of idealists makes one rather regret this course, because to be the ideal and great actor it has been proved that Shakespeare and playing Shakespeare is the only way. I must confess I have had my moments of loathing it, but when one thinks about it one finds what a great source of inspiration and truth there is in his writing.
>
> I am delighted to hear about Nachshon's great progress as a child, and would very much like to meet him one day.
>
> It has been definitely established that I am going to Capri to make the film with Humphrey Bogart, and we don't start there till January 1st, so it will probably be early next year when I am able to come over, and not before. I have to go straight over to Hollywood when I finish here on November 1st, and return in time for the film. I cannot at the moment say anything as to publicity you spoke about regarding my visit, because it is such a long way off and everything is so uncertain, but when the time does arrive I will definitely make a point of letting you know all the details, as you requested.
>
> I have told you before about Bob and there is nothing that can be done about it. I think he has a chip on his shoulder and is a very complex character, which makes for the type of person that he is. I understand full well what you mean in your letter about him and have had a similar experience with him. Unfortunately there is nothing I can do.

'Bob' was his brother Isaac who had changed his name to Robert Sinai. Nahum had also taken an Old Testament surname, Sneh, meaning 'the burning bush', but he had done it by the simple expedient of dropping the 'kik' from Skikne.

Harvey hadn't time to worry about Isaac or his problems for, in addition to his worries about money and his career, there was the question of his continuing relationship with Margaret Leighton. He said to Siobhan McKenna, 'If you have an affair with a woman and her husband divorces her, then you have to marry her. Maggie and I aren't sure whether we will eventually want to get married.'

Towards the end of the season at Stratford, though determined to carry on the affair with Margaret when they both got back to London, he was preoccupied with making good the money he had lost during his eight months at Stratford.

He was so confused that he repeated to Nahum and Henya the story of his difficult decision:

'I don't think I ever told you that I was offered a three year contract by this theatre and star parts including Iago, Romeo and Hotspur at star salary and most of all the opportunity of developing into a really great actor. They compared me to a young Laurence Olivier and Gielgud and said they needed badly in this country someone to take their place. I believe also that this is the first time in the history of this theatre that such a contract has been offered.

At the back of all this the big film companies were wooing me with promises of MONEY and international fame. But above all I had to consider my domestic problems and responsibilities. For three weeks I went round like a drunken lunatic unable to decide and eventually turned down the theatre offer and the possibility of a great and distinguished future – for MONEY.

The directors of the theatre told me I had ruined my career and for their part could go and sell myself and be sucked up and destroyed by the film moguls and as far as they were concerned I was finished.

My sacrifice is a really great one and one I regret very much at heart if the truth be known. So far I have had to borrow money to exist because this theatre pays no money and the cost of living here is something terrible. All this because of Mom and Dad. I will do everything in my power and

*give, give until it hurts. As much as the income tax will allow me. I do
not start earning any money till I start my first film and am at the
moment doing all I can.*

*If you can arrange a little private cottage for them I will pay the rent
and send some money to help support until such time as I am able to look
after them properly.*

9 | 'These Hollywood parties are positively sleepmaking.'

JAMES WOOLF WAITED IMPATIENTLY FOR THE STRATFORD SEASON TO end. He was anxious to get his protégé away from the theatre to test Brian Desmond Hurst's prediction that Harvey could earn him £90,000 a film. The flight to Hollywood from Heathrow took thirty-three hours. It was raining when they stepped out of the terminal building into a waiting limousine on a November day in 1952.

Woolf looked lugubriously at the weather; he would have looked lugubrious even if the sun had been shining. Harvey was disappointed. The glittering city of his dreams was rainwashed and the palm trees, as they drove along Sunset Boulevard to the Beverly Hills Hotel, were sodden.

Unlike the young man beside him, Woolf didn't care for sunshine. Woolf never used swimming pools; he hated sunbathing. He was only nine years older than Harvey, yet though they both wore draped suits and white shirts with spread collars they could have passed for father and son.

Woolf liked Hollywood for its efficiency and its people. The telephones worked, his laundry came back and clients arrived punctually. Still, he preferred to make films in England and his career in Hollywood had been undistinguished. Before the war he had worked in the publicity department at Universal, not because they wanted him, but because his father had arranged it; he was the favourite son.

After the war, during which he spent six years of what he considered misery in the Royal Air Force, never airborne and never posted further than the Orkney Islands, he went back to Hollywood on a boat filled with war brides. The crew locked him in his cabin to protect the brides, allowing him out for half an hour each day. They need not have bothered. Woolf wasn't interested in girls; he was thinking of the beautiful films he was going to make in Hollywood, a Hollywood untouched by war, where the sheets on his bed would be silk and the restaurant steaks king-size. But the films he produced at Universal were, by his own admission, 'tiny nothings'. He returned to England to start Romulus films with his brother John. Laurence Harvey was the first actor the company put under contract and Woolf prided himself on his astuteness in signing a young man of such good looks and talent, an actor as ambitious to become a star as his mentor was to make him one.

Woolf was welcome in Hollywood after the success of *The African Queen*. Romulus had proved that by hiring Humphrey Bogart and Katharine Hepburn, director John Huston and producer Sam Spiegel they could package a movie as neatly as the Americans.

Unfortunately, few of Harvey's eight films since 1947 had been seen in the United States. The young men Hollywood was fêting were Brando, Clift and a Welshman named Burton. Undaunted, Woolf paraded Harvey from party to party. There was nothing else to do in the evenings except go to parties. Hostesses lavished hospitality on the two men until it became embarrassing. Harvey found he was just a pretty face to them. He tried hard to attract attention. He went to a Favourite Person party at which celebrities appeared in disguises ranging from Napoleon to Mickey Mouse. Harvey arrived in slacks, sports shirt and a cashmere sweater.

'If one is truly honest,' he informed his hostess, 'one turns up as oneself.'

The sun came out and the pool parties resumed. Harvey

plunged in and swam around with the other guests, helping himself to drinks from floating trays. He noticed Bogart sitting fully clothed by the poolside, making sure his whisky didn't get wet.

'How wise of you, old chap,' Harvey told him, 'My wine tastes like vintage chlorine.'

It was hardest to succeed at parties where the guests performed a party piece. For obvious reasons they were the most popular. But how could one follow a guest like Garland or Sinatra? If people were to notice him he would *have* to shock them. He took the floor with an impersonation of a singing nun performing a striptease. Nobody laughed. The crowded room fell silent. Hollywood's religious conscience had sentimentalised its nuns in popular films.

'I'm sorry if I've shocked you,' he apologised.

He felt the tension ease. Then he added, 'I didn't know this was a Sunday School treat.'

Woolf cautioned him as they drove back to the hotel.

'Okay, Jimmy, love, I'm sorry. I shan't do it again. But these bloody parties are positively sleep-making.'

He was terribly nervous when he made the first screen test. As he had done before that first interview in London, he ate a large lunch. Sydney Guilaroff, who had styled his hair for the test at MGM, saw him put his finger in his mouth in the men's room afterwards and throw up the lunch in the washbasin.

THE BOGARTS GAVE a party for Woolf and Harvey when they were leaving Hollywood. Bogart was the king of Hollywood; Harvey hadn't even got the small parts he had tested for. And the promise of a part in the John Huston film had come to nothing. Woolf was talking over a four-picture deal for him with Fox, but in Hollywood you are only as popular as your last film.

Harvey moved among the guests, across the black and white tiled floor where a negro band was playing for the dancers. He said 'hello' to the James Masons, the Van Johnsons, the Sam Goldwyns, even if few of them recognised him. He hated to go to bed early, yet he left the Bogarts' soon after midnight while the band was still playing.

As a white-coated waiter opened the front door for him he saw Porfirio Rubirosa, the South American diplomat, in the hall. He was bursting balloons with his lighted cigarette end.

Harvey brushed past him into the warm night.

IN LONDON IN 1953 the Italian director Renato Castellani was searching for a Romeo for his screen version of Shakespeare's play. Determined to film the love story in his native Italy, Castellani wasn't concerned about the sacredness of the text. The film would be so ravishing he might even by-pass Shakespeare's dialogue.

He toured the English provincial cities, interviewing hundreds of young hopefuls, not really caring if they had heard of Shakespeare. The Rank Organisation, producing the film, were worried. The neo-realist Castellani could use an inexperienced girl he had found in Derbyshire, Susan Shentall, for his Juliet, but they insisted on an experienced and professional Romeo.

Woolf suggested Harvey for the part and Castellani accepted him. The film began shooting on Italian locations and Harvey's casting caused a small *frisson* of excitement in England, even at Stratford. From the Hotel Bauer Grünwald in Venice Harvey wrote to Nahum and Henya (who had just had a baby girl) and his father who was with them in Israel:

Dearest Daddy, Nahum and Henya,

Thank you for your letter and your very kind invitation to come and see you. I am so sorry to hear that your baby girl was so ill. It must have caused you all great anxiety and all my sympathies are with you. I wish her a speedy recovery.

I have been hard at work here on this film for the past ten weeks. It is progressing slowly, the task being made more difficult than it would be in a studio because everything is being done on the spot. We finish in Venice at the end of this week and go to Verona for two months. I would so love to come to Israel to see you all, especially at this particular time, but am afraid I will have to disappoint you.

You must realise and understand that I am here to do a job of work to which I am contracted and cannot possibly just take a few days off at will. Being on location we are made to work twice as hard. I am up at 4.30 a.m. every morning and work till 8 p.m. every evening.

I did manage to get three days off two weeks ago and had to go racing back to England where I had to make an important decision. I have signed a contract to go back to Stratford-on-Avon next year for ten months and then go to New York for a four months season and a tour of Canada and America for three months.

I had discussions with the directors of the theatre who want me to go back there as the STAR and leading man of the season, which is a great honour as they believe in me to the extent of following in the footsteps of Laurence Olivier and John Gielgud. I, on the other hand, have had to sacrifice and get a release from my film contract for that period and at great personal financial loss. I know I have done the right thing because I do not want to be just another film star, but a great and distinguished actor with a classical background which I can only get in the theatre, and now that I have reached a position where I am in demand in both spheres I want to maintain it on the highest possible level.

I am going to play Romeo again, Oberon in A Midsummer Night's Dream *and Troilus in* Troilus and Cressida, *parts that no other actor of my age has ever been asked to do before, here or in America. If I am a success then there will never be any dispute as to my position as one of the leading young actors in the world today.*

This is a very proud moment in my life and the work in hand and in the future will take all one's time and energy and concentration. Naturally in the next two years I will make little or no money, but will maintain as much as possible the allowance to Mother and Dad, but I cannot be called on to make any great financial gestures. I want to do everything in my power to secure both my own future and that of Mom and Dad's, but it is a slow and arduous process. I would love to have come to see you, but you do, I hope, understand my position here. If, of course, it is at all possible I will come most definitely.

I am thrilled that Daddy is being looked after so well and tell him to enjoy himself and relax. My love to all.

Love,

Larry.

Harvey considered Susan Shentall, his screen Juliet, naïve, but with the polish of a girl who had been put through a good school by her well-to-do grocer father. He took her to dinner one evening to a restaurant noted for its roast chicken dishes. The dieting he had begun with Hermione Baddeley was extreme. The girl watched horrified as he discarded the chicken meat and chewed the bones. She glanced round the restaurant to see if anybody had noticed.

'Larry,' she whispered, 'one doesn't *do* that sort of thing.'

'Nonsense,' he said.

Wherever she went she was chaperoned by one of her parents. Harvey found her mother a handsome woman, understanding of actors and apologetic for her daughter's lack of experience. The columnists did what they could to create the illusion of an off-screen romance between the screen's Romeo and Juliet, but Susan's interest was for the son of a Leicester Lord Mayor who came to visit her on location.

Castellani worked his actors hard. For months they sweated it out in the hot sunshine. Harvey had seen little of Margaret Leighton who was now playing in Eliot's *The Confidential Clerk* in London, and she forgot his twenty-fifth birthday. No card, no telegram, no 'phone call that first day of October.

After the day's filming he got into his new Jaguar and drove furiously into the hills, throwing the car into fast bends, feeling the tail slip as he accelerated into a straight. One bend came at him too quickly. He tried to pull out of it, but the rear wing swung into a low stone wall.

His anger turned to tears. Next to himself he loved his cars. His old cars had been polished until they shone, and now this £2,000 worth of Jaguar, bought on the strength of his film with Castellani, was damaged.

Just before *Romeo and Juliet* was completed he heard that Henya had lost her baby girl. 'All one's faith and courage and determination,' he wrote her, 'must come forth in order to survive this terrible ordeal. I know so well what it means because I suppose I too have experienced it my way.'

ON A JUNE MORNING in 1974 the actor John Ireland was
flying to Washington D.C. from Los Angeles for a special
screening to Congressmen of a film he had made back in 1950, *All
The King's Men*. He was in a window seat, first-class. An hour out
of Los Angeles, having read the *Los Angeles Times* and finished
breakfast, he became uncomfortably aware of the empty seat beside
him. He thought of the many trips he and Larry Harvey had made
together and of their long friendship which had begun because
Larry had gone to see him in *All The King's Men* and asked Jimmy
Woolf to sign him for the film *The Good Die Young*, which
started shooting two days after Castellani had finished *Romeo and
Juliet*.

He remembered the party at Les Ambassadeurs in London to
announce the film. Woolf had assembled a large cast of established
players, some American like Gloria Grahame and Richard
Basehart, others English like Larry and Margaret Leighton, and
one Canadian, himself.

The wittiest man in the room that night was Larry Harvey. By
comparison everybody else seemed dull. Ireland and Harvey hit it
off from the start. That had been more than twenty years ago.

Good God, he thought, looking at the empty seat, I've never
embraced any other man, ever. I don't embrace my own sons, I
shake their hands. But when he and Larry met, it was different. If
Larry had been away for a month they embraced as though they
hadn't seen each other for years. They had both gone through
several wives, some of whom had tried to separate them and not
succeeded. A woman can be jealous of her husband's ordinary
friendships with other men and Ireland believed he had seen
extreme examples of such jealousy. He looked out of the aircraft
window and suddenly saw Larry's face quite clearly.

'You might like to know, folks,' came the Captain's voice over
the intercom, 'we are now flying over a ghost town in Arizona.'

'Right on cue,' thought Ireland. 'I must be psychic.'

LEWIS GILBERT, WHO had directed Harvey in *The Scarlet Thread* and *There Is Another Sun,* was brought in to direct *The Good Die Young.* James Woolf had bought the book, which told of five ex-army men blowing up a bank safe.

Gilbert decided Woolf might just as well have thrown the book away. The original American story had been given an English setting which made it implausible. The production was an attempt to film in the American style, but the censor would not allow the film-makers suggest that the British police carried guns.

As for Harvey, Gilbert thought he had improved as a screen actor and Woolf had given him the best part in the film, but he had become too self-conscious about dieting. An actor, if he is to play another character, must forget his looks on the screen, and Harvey found this difficult.

AFTER *ROMEO* AND *The Good Die Young* Hollywood was ready to give Harvey a break. Warner Brothers cast him as a Crusader in chainmail in *The Talisman* with Rex Harrison, George Sanders and Virginia Mayo. The director was the same David Butler, noted for his Doris Day musicals, who had not been able to use Harvey in *Where's Charley?*

Brian Desmond Hurst hadn't been far wrong. Woolf negotiated a five-year contract with Warners for half a million dollars.

The unit filmed for a few weeks at the Warner lot at Burbank before Butler took them into the Californian desert to El Centro, near the Mexican border, which became the setting for Palestine in the Middle Ages. A self-assured guy, Butler thought Harvey. When he was directing him Harvey would say, 'Fine, David, but why can't I do it this way?' Warners saw him as a new Errol Flynn and on horseback he rode just as confidently as Flynn had done in *The Charge of the Light Brigade.*

He invited Butler and the film crew to a Mexican restaurant in El Centro and ordered quail. The restaurant owner didn't raise an eyebrow.

'How many?' he asked.

'A bevy,' said Harvey.

Filming in the desert Harvey sweated in his imitation chain mail, a crochet replica which the studios had created. Virginia Mayo stepped before the cameras in a flimsy dress which stirred provocatively with the slightest desert breeze. Butler called for Harvey to take her in his arms. When the actor's chain costume made indentations on her body, she complained.

'I assure you, darling,' said the Crusader, exchanging his lance for a cigarette holder during a break, 'that my armour weighs only ten pounds. If I were a real Crusader I would crush you with ninety pounds of chain mail.'

In one scene he had to lift George Sanders, complete with armour, from a chair to a couch. Sanders, who was a heavy man, helped him during rehearsals by distributing his weight evenly so that Harvey could lift him without much trouble. But when Butler called, 'Okay, let's shoot it,' Sanders sagged like a sack of corn.

Harvey struggled until he had raised him in his arms. Then he dropped him heavily on the studio floor.

'Next time,' he snapped, 'please co-operate.'

His sudden acceptance by Hollywood was earning him space in London's Fleet Street newspapers and reports of his success had reached Israel. He found it necessary to tell Nahum and Henya:

I am palling slightly with all this publicity about my contracts and fabulous earnings and millionaire talk.

This money which I will get only when and if I make films here over the next five years, will be split up between four other people, the Chancellor of the Exchequer and myself. Ten per cent to my American agent, ten per cent to my agent in London, 50 per cent of the profits over and above my basic salary to the company to which I am under contract in England, plus the million and one other people whom it is necessary to employ as an evil necessity. Super tax at 19/6 in the pound leaves me almost nothing, plus the fact that for every pound I send home I have to pay that again in tax.

I admit I am not poor, but if I were asked to produce any sum of money

*in cash I couldn't, and I have to live from week to week earning it and
spending it.*

I have also had to pay the Stratford theatre £10,000 to get out of A
Midsummer Night's Dream *in order to do this picture, so when I get
back to England and start my season there I will be working until the end
of October for NOTHING.*

*Warners have dangled and enticed me with every possible financial
and golden promise to do four more films for them, including Paris in*
Helen of Troy, *have offered to buy my contract from Stratford, but I have
turned them all down with a flat, fat NO. Everyone thinks I am a
lunatic, but I know what I am doing, even with this terrible financial
sacrifice which I cannot afford because I will have to pay my way there
with my own money.*

*So you see we all have our problems and with success it seems to get
worse, the responsibilities greater, the nervous system doubly tense.*

*I am sorry to hear you are both not very well and I sincerely hope you
are on the road to recovery. I haven't had a day's rest since I have been
here. Working in a highly-efficient technical atmosphere is most exciting
and very exhausting.*

HARVEY ARRIVED BACK in London at the end of February
1954 after a stopover in New York. He carried six pairs of
specially-tailored blue jeans in his luggage and predicted that all
his English friends would soon be wearing Westerner clothes. But
for London he continued to favour suits with draped jackets and
narrow trousers, part Edwardian, part Manhattan, part Italian, but
tailored unquestionably in Savile Row. His cufflinks were gold,
his cigarette holder gold-tipped, his watch brushed gold and
nine-jewelled, his shoes silver-buckled.

He was wearing the luxuriant blond hair and the blond goatee
from *The Talisman*. His right index finger was splinted as a result
of a fight scene in the film. 'That, dear hearts,' he explained to
reporters, 'is CinemaScope for you. Far too much leeway to leap
around in the long shots.'

James Woolf was planning Harvey's every professional move.

He had given him an apartment adjoining his own in the private block of expensive flats in Grosvenor House on London's Park Lane. Number 36, which was Woolf's, had a living room, bedroom, bathroom and a small kitchen with a large fridge. Harvey moved into the connecting flat which had a bedroom and bathroom.

The apartments were furnished with antiques and costly prints. 'All rather val.' Harvey would tell friends. 'Val' had become his private term for valuable.

Now he could drive his white Jaguar into the forecourt behind Grosvenor House on Park Street and abandon it among the other expensive cars parked there, knowing that the top-hatted commissionaire would garage it for him.

Hollywood, he told journalists, had offered him half a million dollars to stay and make more films. Rather flattering, and rather humbling, to know they wanted him so badly. But he was ready to resist their advances; he would settle for one film a year and go back to Stratford to play Shakespeare.

What he didn't say was that the Stratford contract had been negotiated while he was still making *Romeo and Juliet* in Italy. His fee for *Romeo* was £30,000, so Stratford shouldn't expect him to work for seven months for £50 a week. But they would make no concessions.

Fifty a week was their rate, even for Laurence Harvey.

10 | 'Relax, dear heart, Romeo is here.'

HE TOLD THE CORONER AFTERWARDS THAT HE HADN'T SEEN THE cyclist until he came in contact with his car.

'He was practically on top of me. He came towards me without giving any signal.'

Harvey had been pushing the Jaguar hard along a dual carriageway that May afternoon in 1954, dashing back from London to Stratford for a performance of *Romeo and Juliet,* when he struck a Ministry of Civil Aviation policeman near Northolt airport. The man was still alive when they lifted him into the ambulance.

The police asked Harvey to accompany them to the station at nearby Ruislip. It was his first time inside a police precinct since Grasse. He produced his insurance and licence and gave them the phone number of his solicitor. They returned the Jaguar to him. As he left the station he looked at his watch and realised he was eighty miles from Stratford with less than three hours to curtain up.

The grille and front bumpers, so carefully polished that weekend, were dented. The impact had been greater than he imagined. He could only hope that the cyclist would live.

By the time he reached the A40 again he was calmer, but worried about the time. He took the road through Banbury as far as the Jaguar works at Coventry, where they agreed to give him another Jaguar until his damaged car was repaired. Twenty minutes later he was parking outside the Stratford Memorial Theatre.

He pushed through the stage door fifty minutes before the curtain was due to go up. His understudy was ready to go on.

'Relax, dear heart,' he told him. 'Romeo is here.'

Then he asked the manager to 'phone Ruislip police station to enquire about the injured cyclist.

The curtain went up on time in the great theatre. Minutes after Harvey stepped on to the stage the cyclist was dead. The management kept the news from him during the intervals; it was not until the end of the performance, after he had taken five curtain calls, that they told him.

It wasn't going to be the happiest season. The golden days of 1952 when he played Orlando to Mag's Rosalind, when he and Siobhan eked out their salaries on crusty bread and red wine, were gone. He knew that established actors were sneering at his extravagant life and his Hollywood contracts. The doors of Hollywood were open to him like the gates of Babylon, they said, and he was ready to walk through.

The critics called his Romeo 'a mechanical, clockwork lover crying crocodile tears.' It was, said one critic, as though a swimming club idol had leapt out of his sports car into Shakespeare's Verona. They had called his screen Romeo 'theatrical', now they were saying his stage Romeo was 'suburban'.

He told Nahum and Henya that the critics had attacked his performance because he had given the character of Romeo a strength, a Latin excitement and a madness they were not used to or had never seen before. Still, all the theatre's seats were sold out to the end of the season.

Nahum and Henya had now decided to leave the kibbutz and move into their own apartment. 'Your decision', he told them, 'came both with shock and expectation. I can only by imagination compare it to the idealist form of existence which, after years of toil and struggle and hardship, bears little or no fruit and the life of the individual and family is gradually eaten up. It is the same in every way of life, only different in degree and environment.'

Troilus and Cressida had been attempted only three times in seventy-six years at Stratford. The theatre considered this savage tangle of a tragi-comedy too difficult to stage. If the critics disliked his Romeo, they disliked his Troilus even more. He couldn't play a lover nor could he manage Troilus in a play that mocked at love. His self-confidence might be wonderful, they agreed, but as an actor he was back where he started. His voice was an inaudible, low-pitched croon, more suited to a night club than the tents of ancient Greece. A performance that should have been witty, cynical and profound was simply dim, brash and shallow.

One critic said it was the worst performance in a leading role he had seen at Stratford. It was suggested he had reached the parting of the ways. Either he could coast to Hollywood and wealth or stay in England and learn the actor's disciplines.

Before the season ended he had sent his greetings for the Jewish New Year to Nahum and Henya.

'This year', he told them, 'there has been nothing but controversy, filth, praise, and every other imaginable thing written about me in the Press which has unnerved and upset me very much. In spite of it, however, one manages to survive and fight it. I suppose when one really becomes a public figure of note and importance one must expect everything whether justly or unjustly written.'

The romance between Harvey and Margaret Leighton continued. Max Reinhardt, understandably hurt by the gossip about his wife and the young actor, had left Piccadilly's Albany and moved to a flat in Chelsea. Harvey observed, 'People love me or hate me. I obviously don't foster detached emotions.' By the end of the second Stratford season the newspapers reported that Reinhardt was seeking a divorce. By the New Year the divorce court had granted him a decree nisi on the grounds of misconduct by his wife with the twenty-five-year-old actor. Neither Harvey nor the actress denied the allegation and Reinhardt was awarded costs against Harvey.

Despite the new freedom they now enjoyed Margaret Leighton

didn't see enough of her lover. He was playing the screen's Christopher Isherwood to Julie Harris's Sally Bowles in *I Am a Camera* at the film studios by day and when he came back to London in the evening she had gone to the theatre to appear in Rattigan's *Separate Tables.*

Early in 1955 he packed his bags and flew to Egypt to play Durrance, Ralph Richardson's old part, in the re-make of *The Four Feathers,* for which the Woolfs loaned him out to Alexander Korda. The new version was titled *Storm Over the Nile.* The cast and crew filmed in the desert around Khartoum for six weeks, 'six weeks of hell', Harvey told Mag, living in tents which were often blown away at night. She would rather he devoted himself to the theatre. The savagery of the Stratford reviews were proof enough that he was neglecting his craft and that the critics, never kind to him at the best of times, were alienated by his Hollywood trappings. She knew the idea of becoming accepted by the British theatrical establishment appealed to him. When he said, 'Well, I'm young and when one is full of energy and vitality one can afford to make mistakes,' she wondered if he was really shrugging off the hurt of those reviews.

Before returning from the Sudan he flew to Johannesburg for the opening night of *Romeo and Juliet* at the city's biggest show house. The delinquent of the forties had become the star of the fifties and the African Consolidated Theatre group arranged receptions and interviews for him. He had achieved what he had promised his mother as a boy: he was a film star and had flown home to see her. But he wasn't ready to consider taking her back with him. Instead he made his parents a cash gift. He wrote in March to Nahum and Henya:

> *My very short visit home did cause great excitement, but the nervous and physical strain of trying to cram everything into those few days was very exhausting.*
>
> *I have, apart from the money I am sending them every month, given them £3,500, which I have told them they can use as they please, as they now have very strong feelings about coming and settling with you.*

I do not want you to mention this to them, but I hope you understand that it has meant a great drain on my financial resources, and as I do not get this off income tax, I have to earn about five times as much in order to pay it off, but I am thrilled and delighted if it brings them any happiness, as then, I suppose, one would have achieved something.

I am still working on the re-make of The Four Feathers *and should be finished sometime near the end of April after which I shall be going back to Hollywood.*

I am very pleased you all enjoyed Romeo and Juliet, *and Nachshon's mimicry sounds quite enchanting.*

I must say that Ma and Daddy both looked extraordinarily well, and simply by overpowering her, I managed to keep Ma rather in a less nervous condition than usual! Everyone else of course has grown up, some unrecognisably hideous, and others quite enchanting, but Johannesburg itself as a city is splitting at the seams and has grown and developed to an extent which is quite unbelievable. The buildings, apartments and motor cars get larger and larger, and the mentality of the people smaller and smaller.

In August, 1955, he took the boat train from Waterloo, prepared to face the critics on Broadway in a play by Ugo Betti. He sailed from Southampton and before crossing the Atlantic the liner called at Cobh to take on passengers from Ireland. Just like an emigrant scene, he thought, watching the tender chock-full of passengers and their luggage chugging towards the liner. Along the waterfront groups waved to the departing passengers. It was like an American wake.

On the tender Siobhan McKenna waved at the fading figures of her husband, actor Denis O'Dea, their young son and her sister on the quayside. It was shortly after her mother's death and she hated the prospect of this separation from her family. Before she had stepped aboard the tender her six-year-old son Donncha covered his face with his hands. Noticing his gesture, Siobhan had suddenly decided, 'I'm not going, Denis. I can't.'

'You had better go', said her husband, 'or they'll sue you.'

She was about to make her first Broadway appearance in Enid Bagnold's *The Chalk Garden.* On board the liner a steward told her:

'The Captain, madam, would like you to be his guest at dinner this evening.'

'Give the Captain my thanks. Tell him I don't feel well.'

She looked out of her stateroom window and saw people from the little houses in Cobh waving as the liner moved into the bay. She threw herself on the bed, sobbing. She was so unhappy at leaving her family that she hoped *The Chalk Garden* would flop.

A voice at the door said, 'Mr Laurence Harvey is on board, madam. He says would you care to join him for drinks before dinner.'

Oh, my God! she thought. Larry Harvey. He would be so extrovert, so cheerful. She dared not tell the steward that Harvey was the last person she wanted to meet. 'Please give him my thanks,' she called. 'Tell him I'm sorry, but I'm not feeling well and can't join him this evening.'

A few minutes later there was a loud knocking at the door. 'It's me. Larry.'

'Go away, Larry Harvey. I just want to bawl my eyes out.'

'What a Mother Machree way to carry on,' said the voice outside the door. 'Save your tears for the stage, darling.'

Siobhan opened the door warily. The young man was dressed in a blue blazer and white ducks as though for a cruise. She looked down at his feet. Yellow slippers trimmed with fur.

'Where in God's name did you get the slippers?'

'From Greer Garson in Hollywood. Aren't they divine?'

She found herself laughing.

'Larry Harvey, they're just too much!'

'Come on, Siobhan, he said, 'stop behaving as though you're on a coffin ship. Let's turn this trip into a cruise.'

Harvey entertained the guests at the Captain's table. He banished the monotony from the chef's life by asking him to prepare special dishes. He introduced Siobhan to two elderly ladies who owned a chain of American newspapers and had been sailing round the world. The four of them went drinking in the evenings. 'Divine little dears', he called them.

When the liner reached New York Siobhan had become

enthusiastic about her play. Celebrities and reporters came on board when the liner docked. She was so nervous on this first visit to America that when Cary Grant was introduced to her she asked him, 'Are you playing the butler?' Harvey laughed. Grant just smiled and said, 'I'm standing by in case the actor playing the part doesn't work out.'

Harvey began to have doubts about the Ugo Betti play, *Island of Goats*. He was staying in a suite in the Sherry Netherlands Hotel overlooking the Grand Plaza; Siobhan McKenna was in a smaller hotel on 58th Street. They compared notes in the evenings as to how their rehearsals had gone. Usually Jean-Pierre Aumont joined them. He, too, had a play opening on Broadway that autumn.

The Chalk Garden was having a pre-Broadway run out of town when *Island of Goats* opened at the Fulton Theatre. Harvey received thirteen curtain calls from an enthusiastic audience. Afterwards his leading lady, Ruth Ford, gave a party at her apartment at the Dakota.

The play must be a success, he told himself, encouraged by the curtain calls; yet he was tense despite the party atmosphere. At four in the morning he went out and bought the papers. The reviews were bad. He sat down on the kerb and thought, 'What a great Broadway debut!' He dropped the papers in the gutter and wondered if he had come all this way for nothing. For a lover of life he was too often dissatisfied with it.

Next morning he was surprised to find a large queue outside the theatre. He went up to his dressing room and called the manager. 'How can they close the show when people are queueing for tickets?'

'They're not queueing for tickets, Larry. They're looking for their money back.'

Siobhan called him from out of town. She had heard the news.

'Don't worry, darling,' Harvey said, 'Now I can come to your first night.'

He arrived with Noël Coward.

'Splendid, splendid,' he said. 'Better than your Saint Joan.' He was as pleased as if the show had been his own.

MARGARET LEIGHTON WAS at London Airport to greet him when he arrived from New York on a grey November morning in 1955. She was wearing the large sapphire engagement ring he had given her. As they embraced he forgot about his Broadway flop. Driving into the West End they discussed what he could do to retrieve his reputation in the theatre. Their friend John Clements, she said, had joined the board of the Saville Theatre and was presenting a series of plays. There would be a part for him.

After Christmas he began rehearsals for Clements in *The Rivals*. He had studied the part of Jack Absolute carefully, talking it over with Mag. He was all that Absolute should be – tall, handsome and rakish, but it remained for him to make the character an engaging hypocrite.

The columnists were still writing of him as a particularly unEnglish celebrity, an egotistical young man with a wardrobe filled with expensive suits and invitations from Hollywood to write his own cheques. John Barber, the London *Daily Express* critic, told him bluntly:

'I have always hated you on the stage, so have my colleagues.'

But on the first night of *The Rivals* Barber and his fellow-critics decided that Harvey's talents had at last caught up with his off-stage performance. They admitted he had always had talent; now they conceded it had been schooled, and in Jack Absolute he had created his first real stage character.

Harvey knew that if his Jack had flopped his career would have been set back ten years. But he had confidence. No other young actor of twenty-seven, however successful in the theatre, could have driven to his first night in a new sable and sand Rolls Royce, with Mag beside him, wrapped in her furs against the February night.

He bought a mews house at Bruton Place, a cobbled laneway off Berkeley Square. He had the interior gutted and rebuilt to his taste. A pink front door opened onto a living room, in which an ottoman and chairs were covered, like the walls, in black velvet. A white, black and gold marble dining table stood in the centre of the purple-carpeted room. The bedroom of mauve and white was dominated by a four-poster bed.

The bathroom was styled in shocking pink.

He gave interviews to the papers about his impending marriage and provided guided tours of the cottage for his friends, padding through the rooms in his gold-embroidered slippers, flourishing his ten-inch cigarette holder.

He tried to sound sincere when he talked to columnists about women.

'They're divine, wonderful, mysterious creatures. One cannot live without them.' And, he added, they had the greatest gift God gave a human being, which he envied hopelessly: the ability to bear a child. He and Margaret had a great longing for a child, he said. It seemed a pity that a woman so beautiful as she should not produce anything more endearing than a stage performance.

Margaret Leighton had remarked of her previous marriage, 'I married before a matinee and spoiled the marriage and spoiled the matinee'.

But of marriage to Harvey all she would say was, 'We have no wedding plans.'

11 | 'I have no idea what contribution I made to his life.'

MICHAEL WILDING WAS WAITING ON THE PLATFORM AT CHICHESTER station on a sunny spring morning in 1974 as the train from London pulled in. At sixty-two he bore little resemblance, except for his smile, to the urbane and handsome young romantic star of British films of the late forties, *Spring in Park Lane* and *The Courtneys of Curzon Street*. Herbert Wilcox, who discovered him, described him then as 'an extraordinary and talented young actor.'

Now, in semi-retirement, he was dressed in a sober dark suit and looking older than his years. He drove a small black saloon car to a pub overlooking a sea dotted with white-sailed yachts. He talked of the old days and about Hollywood, where he had been married to Elizabeth Taylor. He didn't miss Hollywood, but sometimes he wished he could go back to visit old friends. 'I've so many friends there, but with Margaret not well my visits are few. The farthest we can go is up to London occasionally.'

After lunch, in an alcove of the pub overlooking the sea, he drove the car a couple of miles along narrow roads, through green countryside, to Gauntlet Cottage, a single-storey, whitewashed cottage by the roadside. An estate agent had found the cottage for the couple. They had driven down from London one evening to view it and bought it at once.

Wilding's wife Margaret Leighton, tall and graceful and still beautiful at fifty-two, walked slowly into the ornate sitting room filled with books and paintings. She was not well, but held herself erect as on a stage. 'I'm sorry you've come on one of my bad days,' she said in a compelling voice.

Wilding fixed drinks. At the mention of Harvey's name he recalled meeting him for the first time in the late forties. 'He was a round-faced young chap. Pleasant. But obviously very ambitious, though not in an aggressive way.' He smiled. 'I wasn't ambitious.'

He looked across at his wife, seated on a wide sofa.

'Do you feel up to talking about Larry, darling?'

She hesitated.

'It's all so private, Michael. Should I really talk about him now?'

He lit a cigarette for her.

'If you feel well enough, darling.'

She began to talk, cautiously. Her husband listened attentively as she recalled her first meeting with Harvey in Stratford twenty-two years before. 'It was a curious friendship for both of us. What I mean is, it was new for both Larry and me. I found his company engaging, and he was so very courageous, determined you might say. I did think our liaison would work out, though at the beginning I was unsure. There was no uncertainty in either party about getting married. But I have no idea what contribution I made to his life.'

She rose from the sofa, sighed and walked into another room and returned with an album of photographs. She turned the pages until she came to the photographs of her wedding to Harvey. The groom was bearded and blond, his bride smiling, her blonde hair carefully arranged, her bare arms suntanned. Her dress, she recalled with pleasure, was pale pink. She began to reminisce about the wedding.

SHE HAD FLOWN from London in August, 1957, to join him in Gibraltar. She had finished the run of *Separate Tables* on Broadway, in which she had scored a great success. Harvey had flown over to be with her after she had fallen on the stage and broken several ribs. He had by now grown a beard and dyed his hair blond for the role of frogman Commander Crabbe in the film *The Silent Enemy* which he was making on location in Malta and Gibraltar.

They both agreed it would be a good idea to marry on the Rock. They could marry in the local register office, but when they went along to take a look they found the place so depressing they dropped the idea at once.

They turned for advice to friends who introduced them to Commander William Diamond on board the British frigate HMS Ursa. A splendid idea, Harvey thought, to get married on board ship. But Margaret was worried. She told him she didn't much care for the publicity that had surrounded their engagement. 'And I don't think the Admiralty would take too kindly to this idea.'

One morning when he was filming she went along to Bill Diamond. 'Do you realise,' she asked him, 'that if you allow this wedding on board your ship it's going to be all over the newspapers? I think you ought to let your powers-that-be know about it.'

The Commander contacted the Admiralty. The Admiralty were firm in their reply. On no account should the wedding take place on board the *Ursa*.

She broke the news to Harvey when he came back to the hotel after filming. 'Then let's find another ship,' was his reply.

Friends found them a ferryboat and the town registrar came aboard at eight the next evening and married them. John Clements, who was in the film, and William Fairchild, the film's director and screenwriter, were the witnesses. Afterwards they went ashore for a champagne party at their hotel.

There was no honeymoon. Harvey returned to work next day, strapping on oxygen equipment to dive five fathoms for the film's underwater sequences.

When the couple got back to London workmen were still busy on the mews house. This annoyed the bride. She hoped they would leave quickly, but she was beginning to learn that Harvey the architect had taken control and his handiwork was never finished. 'It's such a pretty home, Larry. But you're turning it into a Chinese tea house.'

Those early days of marriage were memorable. 'I can't say how happy Larry was; all I know is I was very happy. There was an interesting story every day. Every day was special. It was good or it was bad, and when it was good it was very good and when it was bad it was awful. One had to be on one's toes to meet a continual stream of the unexpected. I was working in the theatre most of the time, so I had to fit my acting career somehow into this extraordinary life.'

Harvey had his own ideas about the clothes women should wear. He took his bride to the best couturiers and became cross if she bought prudently. He'd say, 'Why buy such a load of rubbish, Mag? Come on, let's fly to Paris and get something chic.'

He bought her jewellery and was pleased when she wore shoes decorated with diamonds, particularly if they were in the heels. He made no fuss when her jewellery was stolen by burglars when he was in America.

'They've taken everything you've given me, Larry.'

'Darling, don't worry about it. It's heavily insured.'

He never allowed her to drive his Rolls, but she could drive the Jaguar. When she told him one morning she was going to walk across Berkeley Square to Moyses Stevens, the florist, he insisted, 'I'll drive you.'

The florist's was a hundred yards away. She saw no point in arguing with him, but sat in the back of the Rolls while Harvey drove her to the shop. When he pulled up outside the florist's the doorman asked, 'Would you mind parking around the corner?'

Harvey enjoyed the idea of being mistaken for the chauffeur. 'Certainly, mate,' he replied, and drove into adjacent Fitzmaurice Place.

The wardrobe space in the mews house was filled with his suits and shirts. The bathroom shelves held his own bottles of perfume, mainly Prince Gourelli. As the months went by Margaret discovered a characteristic about her husband that annoyed her. Contrary to her own preference, he didn't much like eating at home. Both of them were dieting, but he always wanted to dine at a restaurant, usually the Caprice. They had an Italian couple looking after the mews house, so when they ate at home they had Italian food. Occasionally Harvey might cook a meal, usually a cheese dish, never anything English like roast beef.

She was disturbed to find he suffered frequent illnesses. He was moody at home, and this she attributed to his stomach pains. She didn't know if he got these pains from the white wine he drank, but as long as she had known him he had been reluctant to take advice from doctors. When his sinusitis troubled him he became depressed. Most painful of all was an abscess on his sinus; he had no option but to allow a doctor draw it under morphia. After the treatment he was in abject pain. In the evenings the pain would go away, but during the day drugs gave him no relief and in the end he had to consult a specialist.

He came home ashen faced. The specialist had told him that the pain from an abscessed sinus was one of the worst imaginable. For days he lay on the bed with the curtains drawn. He would not go out until the pain had passed. Nobody except Margaret must see him in this state.

She, for her part, began to realise how complex their marriage relationship was. Just as her parents had been shocked at her divorce from Max Reinhardt, not believing that one of their children could contemplate such a step, she was shocked to find her husband unable to settle down in the conventional sense. He rejected any moment in the day that was, to him, a waste of time. It was as if he had a compulsion to live out every minute to the full. Having dinner at home was a waste of time when he could be meeting fellow-actors and producers in a restaurant and perhaps talking himself into a new part.

Marriage mattered a great deal to her, and she didn't like to think that she and Larry were solely concerned with their own careers. She was sure that love and affection meant more to him than he admitted and that despite his restless nature he did like to have a home.

IN HER CHICHESTER sitting room in 1974 Margaret Leighton
rose, closing the wedding album. She had made a new life for
herself as the wife of Michael Wilding; they were planning to sell
their London flat and settle for good in the peaceful Sussex
countryside.

Before she left the room she said, almost as an afterthought,
'Larry had an inadequacy in his make-up. But I can't tell you, or
anyone, about it. It's too personal.

'But he was, oh yes, he certainly was aware of it.'

12 | 'Harvey's an exotic butterfly', said Braine.

IN A COTTAGE BEDROOM IN YORKSHIRE THE YOUNG JOE LAMPTON LAY beside the sensual, but older Alice Aisgill. During their love-making he suddenly expressed his repulsion that she had once posed nude for an artist. His jealousy sprang from his growing air of ownership. Alice belonged to him.

She thrust a thigh in his face. 'That's what you like, Joe, isn't it? Leg show and lingerie?' He grabbed her by the shoulders. 'You stupid bitch. It isn't like that at all. Can't you see it's the idea of other people looking at your nakedness that I hate?'

The director said, 'Cut.'

Harvey and Simone Signoret separated. A moment of physical passion in a British film was over. Such a scene had never taken place before in the conservative British film studios. In later years the Woolf brothers maintained it had never been repeated.

John Woolf first heard about *Room at the Top* when watching a television discussion between Yorkshire housewives on BBC's *Panorama*. Politician and businessman Woodrow Wyatt had been questioning the women about a novel which their local librarian, John Braine, had written.

Next morning he asked his secretary to 'phone the publishers. Before lunch the galley proofs of the book were on his desk. He read them through that evening and called his brother James. He had found a fascinating subject for a film, he told him, the story of a young man clawing his way to the top in a provincial town.

'A marvellous part for Larry. And I think there's also a good part for Heather.'

Heather Sears had been first cast by the brothers in the Joan Crawford film, *The Story of Esther Costello,* and she and Harvey were the only two artists under contract to Romulus Films.

James Woolf read the book and agreed with John. They both found the author's treatment and exploration of sex unusual, and daring by the standards of the time. They had no hesitation in buying the film rights and setting up the production. They called in Jack Clayton, the young chief production executive with Romulus. He had worked as an assistant director for Alexander Korda, but wanted to direct his own films. The Woolfs had given him *The Bespoke Overcoat,* and this had won a Hollywood Oscar and awards at film festivals. They felt he was ready to make a full-length feature film.

'How would you like to direct this book?', John Woolf asked him.

'Very much,' Clayton said.

At the reception given by the Woolfs to announce the film at London's Savoy Hotel, Clayton was nervous of the publicity. He was a sensitive man, reticent about his film-making. He was not planning to make a romantic film. Realism was what counted in Braine's story, and he could achieve it by taking his actors and crew on location to the actual setting of the story, the area around Bradford and Halifax where the smoke-filled skies would lend authenticity.

There was a surprise in film circles at the casting of the experienced French actress Simone Signoret as Alice, the second woman in Joe Lampton's life. Clayton was ready to defend his choice in the teeth of arguments that the woman in the novel was English. Alice to him was highly sensual and Signoret was ideal so far as he was concerned. She herself admitted that she didn't want to play sweet young girls any more; she was a mature woman of thirty-seven and ready to play a woman of forty.

Clayton knew Laurence Harvey and considered his special

qualities as an actor came from what he was as a person. He found him generous, not in terms of money, but in his emotions. Whether or not he thought him right for Joe Lampton he had to take him; that was the Woolfs' decision. They had been casting round for a role for Harvey and this was to be it. The slight, unobtrusive Clayton wasn't prepared to make any claims for the proposed film of *Room at the Top;* he didn't even share the Woolfs' belief that the story was particularly daring. In his opinion it was a satisfactory rendering of an ordinary situation that had been treated in many novels, but he had jumped at the chance to direct a film dealing with a period he found fascinating, and through which he himself had lived. The novel described a crucial moment of history when men had come back from the war, and England was changing politically and socially. Joe Lampton was the pushy young man who represented a mood of liberation in a people who had lived through five years of war. And Clayton agreed with the Woolfs that the film could make a decided step forward in cinema history.

At the Savoy Harvey talked amusingly about the part, a glass of wine in one hand, his cigarette holder in the other. Both props seemed incongruous, for his brown hair had been shorn to a spiky crew-cut for his new role.

When he arrived at the Victoria Hotel, Bradford, in June, 1958, he checked in unnoticed, arousing less curiosity than a foreign wool merchant. Bradford was to wool as Mecca is to a Mohammedan. In a town in which the soot and grime of belching chimneys had long obliterated any architectural grace its buildings may have possessed the talk was of wool deals, not films.

Harvey decided how he would play his film role. Lampton would be a cad whose aim was to reach the top and stay there, caring little about the methods he used to achieve his ambition. Good looks and a deadly charm were his weapons of attack against his women victims. 'The world is full of challenging questions,' Harvey said of the film. 'Isn't it time the cinema illustrated them and encouraged people to get on with living, not dreaming?'

Clayton, James Woolf and most of the sixty members of the

unit were also at the Victoria Hotel. Clayton was aware that almost every page of the story could have been filmed at Shepperton studios, but he reassured himself that sooner or later he would have to face the problem of atmosphere, an essential ingredient in the film. When he read the book he knew how much the cold, gritty environment of the North of England had conditioned the hero to fight for a place at the top in the fictitious city of Warley. Talking over the film with Harvey and the Woolfs he emphasised how the Yorkshire locations could be integrated into the film to become an integral part of the story.

One of Clayton's first visits was to the Little Theatre group at Bingley on the outskirts of Bradford to find extras for the film. He sat in on rehearsals for *The Queen and the Rebels.* Afterwards he talked to the members of the cast and engaged them on the spot at three pounds a day, including meals. John Braine was a member of the group, playing the small part of a revolutionary; he was not included in the deal, but he was to be employed as an adviser on the film.

Harvey created less interest among the local community than the wayward sons of the wool millionaires, yet in London the papers never failed to notice him. During his last appearance on the West End stage in *The Country Wife,* petrol rationing had kept his Rolls off the road. He had bought a motor scooter on which his chauffeur drove him to the first night. A publicity stunt? Not at all, he said. 'I don't pay mỳ chauffeur to sit at home all day.'

There was no Rolls for him in Bradford; the company sent him north in a studio car. After the quiet of his mews house in Bruton Place the hotel was as noisy as a railway siding. Trains shunted in and out of the station all night. In the small hours he 'phoned the night porter to ask:

'Can you tell me what time this hotel gets to King's Cross?'

Yorkshire people were friendly, if not much interested in film stars. To the extras he was polite, ingratiating himself with them. But they thought him theatrical and the local Press found him elusive and difficult to interview.

Clayton did not believe that the violent sequence in the film involving the beating-up of Joe Lampton should be any different from a fight in real life, and he admitted he had been in a few fights himself. He filmed the sequence as it would have happened, not according to any film-making tradition.

Harvey refused to allow a stuntman take his place in the scene. At three o'clock in the morning a group of Bradford citizens, wakened by the noise outside their windows looked out to see a young man being beaten up and thrown in the canal. They called the police and a squad car came dashing to the scene only to find the man emerging sodden from the dark waters was Laurence Harvey. Three toughs had been brought specially from London to toss Harvey in the canal for the sequence. One of them turned out to be a bird breeder, the second made voluntary collections for an animal welfare organisation and the third said he loved babies.

Donald Houston, the big, affable Welsh actor, who played Lampton's office friend, was more to the liking of the Bradford people. He could talk to the locals on their own terms. Yet Bradford was committed to making money just as much as Harvey was. Local shopkeepers took exception to Clayton arriving with the unit to film street scenes on a Friday, their busiest day. So the filming had to be changed to Sundays. The city was living up to its reputation of being ruled by the ethic of material successes.

To Bradford and Halifax people the exploits of Joe Lampton were perhaps too close to the bone, and Clayton was trying not to hurt local feelings. The passionate love scenes between Joe and Alice would be filmed in the studios, but the seduction of the boss's daughter, Susan, had to be filmed on location in a local quarry. Heather Sears as Susan was sensitive, too. So the assistant director asked the assembled extras if they would mind leaving the location. They walked away and waited patiently at a distance to be recalled, slightly curious at what these film folk were up to.

But if the locals were looking for scandals, there were none. The actors and the film crew lived discreetly at their hotels. Only Harvey, anxious not to be outshone by Simone Signoret, an established star in international films, asserted his status by shouting at the hotel porters. He shocked the extras by quoting the bawdiest lines from *The Country Wife;* local ladies winced at his four-letter words; and Heather Sears, afraid of his caustic tongue, kept her distance from him when they were not filming together.

If Harvey had been honest with himself he would have admitted that the real star of Bradford was the city's own John Braine.

SIXTEEN YEARS AFTERWARDS John Braine remembered Harvey as 'an exotic butterfly.' How Harvey would have assessed Braine to-day is another matter, for the novelist who talked was not the £13 a week Bingley assistant librarian who had written *Room at the Top.*

The middle-aged Braine had settled into a large detached house at Woking, twenty-eight miles from London in what the newspapers referred to as stockbroker territory. Despite the setting he had few of the trappings of the modern successful writer. No casual clothes, but a sober brown suit. He was still class conscious, although he had moved to the affluent south and become a member of the right-wing Monday Club, and he still spoke with a broad Yorkshire accent. A friendly man, sturdy and chubby-faced, he was a compulsive talker, holding emphatic views about politics and the tax system and hinting that he was disenchanted with the Socialist Government.

He scanned his bookshelves.

'Yes, *Room at the Top* is there somewhere. I can't get away from it, even if I wanted to.' Most films before *Room at the Top,* he said, were made to a formula, and when a producer bought a best-selling novel he tailored the novel to that formula.

'But with my book the only real changes were to make it work as a film. The guts of the story were all there and most of the dialogue was mine. If you look at the script you will notice wherever the dialogue is poor it isn't mine.

'The new dimension of the film was in presenting a boy from the working classes not as a downtrodden victim, but as he *really* was. It wasn't important that Joe Lampton was honest about sex, what was important was that Joe was honest about the whole business of class. Most ambitious working-class boys want to get to hell out of the working class. That was a simple truth that had never been stated before. The English working classes are the least politically-minded in the world; they always have been. Give the English working class man half a chance and he becomes a bourgeois.'

Braine first met Harvey in the lounge of the Victoria Hotel. He thought him an exotic creature, suave, smiling, drinking wine, waving a cigarette holder. His clothes, for Bradford, were avant-garde. Hardly the actor to fill the shoes of the no-nonsense Joe Lampton. He had never been consulted about the choice of Harvey for the part; Romulus made that decision and Braine's first reaction was negative; he would have preferred Donald Houston, although he knew that British juveniles were thin on the ground and probably none of them was capable of playing Joe. At least he and Jack Clayton had agreed that the Bradford locations could not be filmed in Shepherd's Bush, with bit players struggling to master the Yorkshire accent.

When Braine had ordered a scotch Harvey remarked that he should try vodka, the purest spirit in the world. Then he said:

'I hear your book has become a bestseller.'

That was all. He went on to talk about other subjects. Braine was slightly disappointed. He had hoped Harvey would have asked his advice about the portrayal of Joe, but he realised Harvey had made his own mind up about the character. Could he really do it? The man talking to him was tall, slim and reeking of cologne. He must have taken a bath in the damned stuff. His crew-cut was obviously a special job that no ordinary hairdresser could have managed, and his accent was pure RADA. To Braine he looked outrageous.

The Woolfs had called in dialect experts to coach Harvey in the Yorkshire accent, but when Braine heard the accent on the set he thought it was too broad for his Joe. In other respects, as the filming proceeded, he had to concede that Harvey seemed a good choice for Joe because there was a lot of Joe's character in him. He wasn't Joe in reality because Joe was basically very English, but as Harvey was a ruthless man Braine could not see him fail in the part.

It was really character casting.

When Braine and his wife asked him to their house outside Bradford, Harvey was surprised to discover they had no car. 'But, John', Harvey said, 'you must get yourself a car. Even when I was poor I always had a car. I always believed in buying the biggest car I couldn't afford.'

Braine thought it pleasant to have stars like Laurence Harvey around who didn't have to live like the rest of men. He enjoyed his company as a creature of the stage. He was as he believed actors should be. He distrusted actors who wanted to be serious and responsible citizens; he expected them to be like Harvey, living in style and spending extravagantly. Around Bradford he noticed Harvey never grumbled about signing autographs. In the hotel lobby after a long day's filming, however much he wanted to get to his room to take a bath, he signed for the autograph hunters.

'The time to complain, John, is when they stop asking me.'

Braine had the impression he considered writers were not important. He could be polite to a writer, as he could be polite to anybody else, but respect was missing. He wasn't interested in what Braine was writing; he was preoccupied with his own projects. He had acquired the film rights of a book about a Polish refugee's journey across Asia. 'It doesn't much matter', Harvey said, 'whether it's true or not. It's a damned good story.'

It would take five years to film. He would penetrate not only the Gobi desert but also Tibet. It would be an epic on which the actors and technicians would be faced with hardship. 'I'll make it, John, because I don't think every technician in the industry is averse to a little dust in the desert. Men are meant to accept challenges!'

Braine let him talk. He decided Larry Harvey loved an audience. When he had finished he commented; 'I'm all for people escaping from prison camps.' He didn't add that he knew damned well it wouldn't make a marvellous film.

Most men, Braine observed, when they caught sight of a good-looking woman betrayed a flicker of desire, as though saying to themselves, 'I wouldn't mind *you*'. With Harvey he never saw that reaction. Harvey gave the impression that sex was something calculated and tied to his own advancement. He wouldn't play a dirty trick for its own sake; that would be foreign to his nature; but he might play a dirty trick if he thought it would advance his career.

He detected in him a rare attitude of cold indifference to sexual relationships, male or female. Sex was something to be used. The fact that Larry camped it up was simply the Noël Coward influence; Coward had a lot to answer for.

He watched James Woolf fuss around him like a mother hen. The small man with a mouthful of bad teeth, wearing expensive clothes that looked cheap on him, nervously chewing cigars, was rather pathetic.

One night Braine was sitting with a group of film people in the bar of the Victoria Hotel when Harvey said he was feeling tired and went upstairs. Half an hour later Braine looked up to see him walking towards them wearing silk mandarin-style pyjamas. Harvey solemnly kissed each member of the group goodnight. A stage kiss, on the cheek. God knows what the other people in the lounge were thinking, but Braine supposed one got used to such behaviour if one mixed with show people.

Harvey was making sure he held the stage. There would have been no room in such a scene for Margaret Leighton. Braine knew she was his wife, but he had never seen her in Bradford.

HERMIONE BADDELEY had not forgotten *Room at the Top* in her sunny eighth-floor apartment, adorned with flowers and objets d'art, at Westminster in the summer of 1974. She was still petite and vivacious and busy with plays, films and television performances on both sides of the Atlantic. She recalled that it was Harvey who had suggested her for the part of Elspeth, Joe Lampton's confidante, in *Room at the Top*.

'Jimmy Woolf rang me and said Larry was very keen for me to play in *Room at the Top*. "It isn't a very big part, but he's frightfully keen to have you."

'My agent was strongly against my doing it because it was such a small part. I'm essentially a stage actress and if I make a film I like to have a good part in it.

'So we first of all turned it down. Then Larry finally persuaded me to do it. I thought he was very good in the film, didn't you? He was very professional and worked so hard.'

It had been almost six years since their affair had ended.

'When he was at Stratford working for my brother-in-law he kept 'phoning me and being furious about my Irish friend. He was very jealous in those days. He had wanted to marry me, but I was clever enough to tell him, "I'm twice your age, so don't marry me. You're not the marrying sort, anyway". When he was keen on anyone he was painfully jealous. He also had a terrific ego, you know. *Such* an ego! And he was working on his own career, so I didn't think he could ever have a happy marriage.

'When he was drinking he lost his temper and became violent. That was rather tiresome.'

IN LEEDS ON a cold, dark midnight in January, 1959, *Room at the Top* had its première at the Ritz Cinema. Harvey was in America and Simone Signoret in France, but Heather Sears and Donald Houston went to the screening. John Braine told the audience that the film must have been the first which, when seen on the screen, completely satisfied its author.

The Archdeacon of Halifax, the Reverend Eric Treacy, was less complimentary. He said later, '*Room at the Top* is a story of sordid, sexual filth.' In response to public demand the film had enjoyed a fortnight's showing in the town. 'It may have made a lot of money for the producers and exhibitors', the Archdeacon said, 'but it may have done incalculable harm to the enormous number of young people who saw it.'

13 | 'Don't waste your breath, Duke. Just sign him.'

HARVEY WAS IN HIS HOTEL SUITE IN BOSTON WHEN JAMES WOOLF 'phoned from London to tell him he had been nominated for an Oscar as Best Actor of the Year for *Room at the Top*.

He had studied the role of Shakespeare's *Henry V* during the last weeks of filming and as soon as the final scene was shot flew to San Francisco, re-reading his part on the plane journey and arriving just in time to join the Old Vic company for the opening night.

The Americans loved him. 'The most stimulating actor in the Company,' Brooks Atkinson called him. 'His Henry V was a performance of classic size.' If the English critics considered him a *parvenu*, the Americans decided he was in the best Old Vic tradition.

And now, more than halfway through his six-month tour, came the news of his Oscar nomination. Even John Braine ought to be pleased, he thought. The critics found that he had created a complex character out of Joe Lampton, though the author thought his hero straightforward. The screen Joe had a social awareness and beneath the opportunism they sensed a hidden warmth.

To Gordon Harbord, his first agent, and his wife Harvey wrote:

Dear Gordon and Eleanor:
Thank you so much for your cable. It was so kind and thoughtful of

you to think of me these many thousands of miles away and I suppose I
must have done something dreadful again to deserve it.??? Am so pleased
for the company that the picture has been so well received and also that
your initial faith and promise for me has not been in vain.

The tour has been an absolute triumph and a thrilling experience for
me. It's a wonderful company and I adore Michael Benthall [the director
of Henry V]. Is one ever going to get these sort of subjects again?? One
keeps asking oneself. Oh, well!

Bless you both.

> *Love,*
> *Larry.*

Margaret Leighton had considered him brave to have taken on the
role of Henry at such short notice. She liked him as the King, for
the role suited him, whereas he had overstretched himself as Joe
Lampton.

Married life at their Bruton Place house was far from conventional. Harvey was often away, and even when he was in London
he ate out, and sometimes when he was in the house he didn't eat
at all. This annoyed her, but what could she say to a man who
never stopped working and counted every other activity as
secondary?

Harvey didn't stop to consider the realities of the situation. He
seemed dissatisfied with the cottage mansion and the period
furniture.

'Of course it's all junk,' he said on one occasion.

His object in building a beautiful house was not to live in it; it
had been sufficient for him to create it. He had already lost interest
in *Room at the Top*, though he would have to live with the Joe
Lampton tag for many years. Once he had executed a project there
was always something in the realisation that didn't accord with his
concept of what it should have been. Marriage had been another
enthusiastic project. At one time he had wanted to marry Hermione Baddeley, but she had argued, 'No, Larry. I'm just a little
patch in your life.' Now he was beginning to think that marriage
to Mag wasn't what it might have been.

IN HIS SHEPHERD Market days he had met a young writer, Wolf Mankowitz, who thought him at the time an arrogant post-RADA punk playing hard at being the Young English Actor. But later, as Harvey grew more confident, they became good friends. Mankowitz, whose family had come from the same area in Lithuania as the Skiknes, believed that Lithuanian Jews shared certain characteristics and that Harvey's humour, like his own, was mordant.

Jack Clayton had directed the film of Mankowitz's play *The Bespoke Overcoat* and had asked him to write the screenplay for *Room at the Top*. Mankowitz, a citizen of cosmopolitan London, was out of sympathy with regional writing, so he declined the offer. But he began to see more of Harvey in those days, usually at James Woolf's apartment at Grosvenor House.

When Harvey returned from the tour of America the book about the Polish refugee's walk across Asia was gathering dust on the shelf. He now talked about a film version of Mankowitz's musical play *Expresso Bongo*. He badgered the Woolfs to make it.

'I don't like it for you, Laurence,' said James Woolf, 'It's not your sort of film.'

'It's a marvellous part, Jimmy.'

'Tell me, Laurence, why should you want to play a Cockney spiv?'

If Woolf didn't like a property nobody could persuade him to buy it. Harvey by now had a stake in Romulus, but although he talked like a producer he wouldn't make a business decision. At executive level the real producer was John Woolf, who was becoming a powerful man in the world of British films.

John Woolf thought Harvey magnificent as Henry V. He knew that if Harvey were content to stay with the Old Vic he could have a fine career as a Shakespearean actor; he also knew that Hollywood was waiting for him. *Room at the Top* had opened to rave notices across America and his brother James was ready to manage his career in California.

Mankowitz suggested to Harvey that if he really wanted to star in *Expresso Bongo* he should buy the show. But he guessed he

27. *Right:* Screen wedding for Harvey and Heather Sears in the film version of *Room at the Top.*

28. *Below:* Harvey the star at Cannes. *Room at the Top* had been shown at the Cannes Film Festival. Behind his shoulder (left) is Robert Fevre le Bret, director-general of Cannes Film Festival.

29. *Above:* John Braine, author of the book *Room at the Top.*

30. *Left:* Jack Clayton. He directed Harvey in *Room at the Top.*

31. *Left:* Harvey (right) rocks Michael Craig in a boxing scene from *Life at the Top.* Shooting of Craig's scenes in the film had to be re-arranged when the actor suffered a bruised mouth.

33. *Below:* On location in Yorkshire for *Life at the Top* – Harvey with Honor Blackman.

32. *Above:* Terence Stamp and model Jean Shrimpton call on Harvey during the filming of *Life at the Top* in London.

34. *Right:* With Simone Signoret, the 'other woman', in the film *Room at the Top.*

35. *Above:* Zena Walker plays Juliet to his Romeo at Stratford-upon-Avon in 1954.

36. *Above:* The young actor at Stratford-upon-Avon. Harvey with actress Zena Walker on the banks of the Avon.

37. *Below:* Harvey at Stratford-upon-Avon in 1954. Muriel Pavlov played Cressida to his Troilus. Anthony Quayle (right) was Pandarus.

38. *Above:* King Arthur smokes a king-size cigarette. Harvey during a break in rehearsals for *Camelot* in London.

39. *Above:* Harvey makes a recording of songs from his first stage musical, *Camelot,* before the show opened in London.

40. *Below:* Harvey and co-star Elizabeth Larner (right) get a backstage visit from Mr and Mrs Jack Hylton at the first night of *Camelot* in London's Theatre Royal, Drury Lane. Hylton, a theatrical impresario, presented the musical.

didn't have the courage to make the decision alone; he depended on the guidance of the Woolfs. So Mankowitz made a deal with producer-director Val Guest before *Expresso Bongo* ended its run at the Saville Theatre and they talked about giving the role of Johnnie, the pop singer's promoter, which Paul Scofield was playing on the stage, to Harvey.

'We can't afford him,' said Guest.

But Mankowitz knew that Harvey was so keen to play the part that they could come to an arrangement.

The Woolfs agreed to loan him out. According to the terms of their partnership with him they would share in his income from the film. Harvey's enthusiasm was tempered with disappointment because Guest was directing. He wanted to direct *Expresso Bongo* himself. But it needed an experienced film-maker to turn out a film musical in six weeks on a budget of less than £130,000.

It was to be one of the last black and white musicals; there wasn't enough money to make it in colour.

Once filming had begun Harvey entered into his role with verve. They filmed in the studios and on the story's Soho locations. Mankowitz himself walked through the opening titles as a vagrant carrying a sandwich board which read, 'The End of the World is Nigh'.

Harvey worked so hard at his part that in his fast-talking exchanges of dialogue with Sylvia Sims his wide boy accent, which was an incredible mixture of Cockney, Yiddish and mid-Atlantic, lapsed into the broad South African of his youth.

Mankowitz had first seen Harvey at a party in his Shepherd Market days telling extended jokes like a music hall comic who didn't know when to stop, and his act fell flat. But over the years he had perfected his mimicry and polished his story telling. At the Caprice on New Year's Eve, when the guests made their own entertainment, Harvey would provide the funniest turn of the evening. His Russian emigré *persona* was the most hilarious. A little of it had crept into his *Expresso Bongo* role.

The film proved extremely popular and was to have a long life. But Harvey and Mankowitz believed that if only the Woolfs had backed them with another £50,000 it could have been one of their most successful ventures.

It was one of Harvey's favourite films. He loved to run it for his friends and, like many comics viewing their own work, fell about laughing when he saw it.

HARVEY DIDN'T WIN the Hollywood Oscar which dropped into the toga of Charlton Heston for *Ben Hur.* Nevertheless Hollywood producers realised that Harvey had almost slipped through their fingers. Everybody was talking about Joe Lampton, even John Wayne.

Woolf rushed his protégé into the first of a television series Hitchcock was producing and while he was working on the TV film Wayne called him. He reckoned he had a part for him in *The Alamo,* an epic film of the 1836 Texas siege in which Wayne was not only going to play Davy Crockett, but also produce and direct. He wanted Harvey to play Colonel William Barrett Travis who had died commanding the garrison.

Wayne was taking a gamble in attempting for the first time to direct his own film and, although his name was insurance at the box-office, he wanted a bright new star to make his film more attractive.

Harvey was shocked to discover that Americans were wondering where the screen's Joe Lampton had come from.

'It's hideous to think they are asking me about my experience,' he said to James Woolf. 'Don't they know I've made all those films? Don't they know I've emerged from a sweatshop of theatrical experience? Is all the work I've done lost to them? Or are they just idiots and morons?'

Woolf reassured him. 'That doesn't matter, Laurence. What matters now is that you can write your own meal ticket in dollars.'

Harvey went along to the meeting with Wayne as nervous in his stomach as he had been during his early screen tests at MGM and Fox. He had not learned to talk like an American. His reflexes

prompted a flow of RADA-accented boasting about his ac-
complishments at Stratford and the Old Vic. Wayne knew all
about the actor's *Henry V,* but he said in a voice deeper than
Harvey's, 'Don't give me all that manure about art. I'm up to my
shoulders trying to get this picture together.'

There was a growl from an elderly man wearing a black
eyeshade. John Ford, as much Wayne's mentor in earlier days as
Woolf was now Harvey's, was ensuring that he made a good job
of his first attempt at direction. 'We haven't got much time, Duke.
Don't waste your breath talking to him. Just sign him.'

Wayne wondered afterwards if he should have played Travis
himself instead of Davy Crockett. Harvey's Colonel was tight-
lipped and high-keyed. He was trying hard, perhaps too hard, but
he knew he must identify with audiences across America and
quickly consolidate his success in *Room at the Top.*

Even Wayne had to admit he was an incredible worker. When
a cannon wheel rolled over his foot on the location he went white
with pain. They got his boot off. No bones broken, but the foot
was swelling.

'Get him to hospital,' ordered Wayne, worried about delays on
the film. But Harvey refused to go.

'Just bring me a bucket of boiling water and a bucket of ice.
I'm going to try an old cure.'

When they brought the buckets he plunged his injured foot
alternately into one, then into the other.

'The hot and cold treatment,' he explained.

It worked. If it hadn't, he might have been out of the film for
weeks. But next day he was back on the set.

Wayne had no social life during *The Alamo.* He found the
responsibility of producing and directing and playing Davy
Crockett a burden. He stayed sober and went to bed early. As the
days passed he became edgy. One evening after filming an argument started and the cowboy star picked on Jim Heneghen of
The Hollywood Reporter. Heneghen wasn't able for the Duke.
Nobody was. But Harvey flung his slim figure between the two
men. The powerful Wayne, angry at the intervention, grabbed

Harvey in his big hands. The small group of film people stared in astonishment as he lifted Harvey off the floor and flung him through the plate-glass window.

Wayne said nothing about a hospital.

When the others rushed outside Harvey was getting to his feet, shaken but, incredibly, unhurt.

When Wayne retired to bed in the evenings Harvey went out dining. On the location at Fort Clarke, which Wayne was renting for the film, the stars had been given the officers' comfortable quarters. But it was as difficult to find a good restaurant as it was to find good wine. Harvey, who refused to drink liquor because it would make him fat, sent a 'plane to Dallas for supplies. When he came in from filming that evening he could hardly get into his quarters. The rooms were piled high with cases of Pouilly Fuissé Louis Latour. They blocked the light from the windows, but he didn't care.

'My God,' he exclaimed, 'I'm the happiest man in south-west Texas!'

Wayne sometimes called him a miserable sonofabitch, telling him that if he wanted to stay a star he should emulate him and cut out the acting junk. Harvey found it difficult to think of anything he and Wayne had in common. He believed in the art of acting, Wayne in re-acting. They never discussed politics together. 'If we talked politics, Duke,' Harvey said, 'I'd shoot you.'

But still they insisted they were 'buddies'.

On Wayne's birthday Harvey ordered two cases of champagne as a present. Wayne was on location that day and the cases were left in his quarters.

Before he returned Harvey suddenly thought, 'What a waste of gorgeous bubbly on a man who prefers hard liquor!' He told one of the crew to go to Wayne's quarters.

'There are two cases of champagne in there, one vintage, the other non-vintage. Bring me back the vintage.'

In some circles he had the reputation of spending two hundred pounds to earn a hundred. But John Wayne's birthday present didn't cost him a cent. The bill went to the production office. And Harvey got himself a case of vintage champagne.

EVERY TWO YEARS the novelist Richard Condon, a former film publicist, moved with his wife and children and dachshund to a new country. They had just settled in Mexico, having lived in France and Spain, but they had been sitting around for months waiting for their furniture to arrive from New York.

The furniture was eventually found in a railway siding at Laredo in Texas. While he was arranging to send it to Mexico City Condon was invited by Jim Heneghen to visit *The Alamo* unit, eighty miles north of Laredo. It was there he met Laurence Harvey for the first time. He thought it odd that such an elegant English actor should be playing an American army officer, even though he was behaving like a Texan.

As they talked, Harvey asked him about *The Manchurian Candidate,* Condon's new novel about an American Army traitor. He wanted to make the film and play the traitor. But the bids were already out for the book and Condon knew that although Harvey's career was about to zoom he didn't yet have that kind of money.

Anyway, as Condon was to learn, 'he wanted to play everything that came along.'

BY THE TIME Harvey left Texas the liquor-drinking film crew members were sampling Pouilly Fuissé Louis Latour. 'What a super lot of winos you make,' he told them.

He returned to Hollywood and joined James Woolf in the restaurants he had discovered during his *Talisman* days, restaurants which could produce his favourite food and where the waiters didn't raise an eyebrow when he ordered them to bring his favourite bottle of wine in a bucket of ice.

He and Woolf dined with friends at the Interlude on St.

Valentine's Night, February 14, 1960. His sinusitis was troubling him. He went to the men's room until the worst of the pain was over.

On his way back to the table he met a San Francisco friend dining with a fair-haired, beautifully-groomed woman. The woman didn't join in their conversation. She seemed offended at Harvey's bad language.

As he left them he placed a finger on the woman's bare shoulder and traced an imaginary line down her arm to her wrist.

'I see you've been in good company,' Woolf said to him when he returned to his table. 'You know who that woman is, of course?'

'No. Who?'

'Harry Cohn's widow. The wealthiest woman in Hollywood.'

He had no sooner said the words than Harvey was back at the other table. He took Mrs. Cohn's hand in his.

'Dear lady', he said, 'do forgive me for not recognising you.'

'I thought his whole speech a little too much,' Joan Cohn said afterwards, even though she had been conditioned to actors' behaviour by her late husband.

'Would you have dinner with me tomorrow?' Harvey asked her.

She didn't think so.

'Then how about lunch?'

'I'm sorry, my diary is filled for the next two weeks.'

'Then may I have your 'phone number, dear lady, and I shall call you when you're free?'

'You can get my number through Columbia Pictures,' she said, ending the conversation.

She was not impressed by the young man, least of all by his crude language never before used in her presence. She admitted he was attractive, but he seemed just another actor.

Next day he 'phoned her. And the next. After ten days she agreed to have dinner with him. They went to La Rue, and as they walked into the dining room they saw the columnist Louella Parsons sitting in the most prestigious booth. They sat at a table not far from Louella's and ordered *coq au vin* and a bottle of

Pouilly Fumé. When the waiter left the table Harvey said to Mrs. Cohn, 'You remind me of my wife. I love her very much.'

She was forty-five, he thirty-two.

From La Rue they went on to a couple of night clubs. When they reached Joan Cohn's mansion on North Crescent Drive after midnight she invited him in for a drink for the road. He surprised her by saying quite casually, 'Let's get to beddies.' At that point he hadn't kissed her.

She said afterwards: 'I declined, and the next day he apologised. We became friends before we became lovers.'

14 | 'This divorce has practically ruined me.'

EARLY IN JANUARY, 1961, THE LONDON *TIMES* CARRIED THE NEWS item that Mrs. Margaret Skikne (otherwise Harvey) had been granted a decree nisi against Mr. Larry M. Skikne (otherwise Harvey).

Harvey wasn't in London to read the prosaic paragraph. He was at the home of Mrs. Joan Cohn in Beverly Hills as master of ceremonies at the launching of a fashion collection before an audience of her wealthy friends. It wasn't the clothes that stole the show, but Harvey.

Champagne glass in one hand, cigarette holder in the other, he commented on the creations. 'Marvellously stunning, don't you think? And so loose! If there's anything I adore it's loose women.'

When the models got caught in their zippers in the ante-room he smiled lasciviously. 'Can anybody see what's going on backstage?' The designer decided she was losing sales when he described her favourite garment as 'Wonderful, wonderful! If you have a neck as big as your waist you could wear it.'

When the guests had drifted away in embarrassment he sank down on Joan Cohn's emerald green carpet.

'That, *liebchen,*' he decided, 'was my first and last fashion show.'

He was enchanted with Mrs. Cohn's mansion of thirty rooms in period French chateau style set in ten acres of gardens on North Crescent Drive. Moss Hart once told him he didn't believe he was a Lithuanian refugee but a prince who had stepped out of a castle. Joan Cohn's home, the legacy of her late husband, Harry Cohn, the multi-millionaire king of Columbia Pictures, was indeed a castle, filled with beautiful furnishings and expensive paintings. Chandeliers lit the ornate rooms and the Renoirs and Van Goghs on the walls. There were loggias and cabanas, a large swimming pool, even a film theatre. Harvey felt like a Renaissance prince in such grandeur.

AT THE DIVORCE hearing in London an inquiry agent gave evidence in support of Mrs. Margaret Skikne's allegations of her husband's misconduct.

Margaret Leighton was desperately unhappy. She was alone in the mews house off Berkeley Square, alone with the four-poster bed, the Sheraton furniture and the black wallpaper. By her own admission she was almost neurotic. She had seen Harvey's career at that time advance possibly beyond her own. In the intervals between plays and films their temperaments had clashed. Sometimes there had been scenes when he decided he didn't want to eat at the Caprice where they kept a permanent table. She couldn't see why they should pay three pounds to cancel a meal; he argued that they were earning enough money not to have to worry about losing three pounds:

'What's the point of having money? Who cares if the steak gets burnt? Throw it to the peasants!'

She knew that people had thought her naïve about her marriage. She wasn't. 'I knew what was going on; I should have known. After all, I knew Larry for nearly nine years. He dominated me, of course, in every way. I was afraid of him. And in the end I was terrified of the break-up.

'I would like to think I knew Larry Harvey. I felt he was concealing a certain amount, but not totally. What he didn't tell me I guessed, and there were moments when he came clean.'

And yet she missed him. She missed his telephone calls made

halfway across the world and his sudden unannounced arrivals. Out of the divorce in January, 1961, she got the mews house and the furniture. A few weeks later she was offered £15,000 to appear in the film *Return to Peyton Place* in Hollywood. She turned it down because she didn't want to be near her ex-husband.

AFTER THE DIVORCE Harvey decided to travel the world wherever his work took him. He would be like an actor in Elizabethan times, moving from town to town and from audience to audience. More comfortably, of course. He would have his cars, his six suitcases, his seven grips and his secretary and chauffeur. He wouldn't have to worry about the plumbing because wherever he went the best suites in the best hotels would be reserved for him. Marriage was for the few, for men with nine to five jobs and the entire weekend to spend with their wives.

He knew he could never be one of those titled actors with snooty children and clipped lawns, telling their agents they can't fly to Hollywood because they are having dinner with the local gentry. Nor did he think he would be marrying again for a long time. How deeply the divorce had hurt him he revealed in a letter he wrote to Nahum in August, 1961, although he did not refer to his ex-wife or Joan Cohn:

> *Thank you very much for your letter which I received to-day. I am sorry and must give vent to the age-old excuse of not writing to you for, as you know and must be aware of, I have had so many problems of a personal nature, plus the pressure of work in these last months, that quite honestly I have had little or no time to think about anything else.*
>
> *I am afraid and I regret to say that the divorce, which is at last becoming final, has practically ruined me. The house and all its contents, which has taken me eighteen years of hard work and concentration, and what little money I had made I have now had to give up as part settlement, and the thought that all this has been dissipated in one moment and with such rapidity is something that has come as quite a blow.*
>
> *Now I have to start all over again, right from the beginning. At the*

*moment, I am without a place of residence of any kind and feel like a
wandering Jew, with no roots of any kind except the world of the theatre
and films which is fortunately giving me a haven and a home where I can
express my feelings and what little talent I have.*

*I don't know what or where I shall end up as I intend now to go
wherever my work takes me until such time as I decide to re-establish my
roots and where to do so.*

*With all these problems, I am very happy to say I saw a private showing
of the Tennesse Williams' play called* Summer and Smoke, *which film I
made here in Hollywood for Hal Wallis and I think, and I say this in
all humility, it is without question some of the best work I have done to
date and feel sure, although one never knows, that when it comes out
towards. the end of the year, it will confirm the reputation that I have
taken so many years to establish.*

*I am sending you a cheque for £300 post haste as you requested and I
hope that it will contribute to the liberation and rehabilitation of our
cousin who may, as you know, be the only remnant of our family in
Lithuania. Please let me know what progress you make in that direction.*

JOAN COHN visited him when he made *Butterfield 8* in New
York. He was exhilarated by the weather and the vigorous town,
and by the superb professionalism of Elizabeth Taylor, who played
John O'Hara's 'beautiful, tempestuous and wanton' heroine Gloria
Wandrous to his Weston Liggett, the poor boy who got rich
quick by marrying into a stuffy American family. At the city's
Gold Star studios they ticketed more incoming calls for Harvey
than for his co-star, calls from friends, agents, producers and, of
course, Joan.

With James Woolf's help he had been contracted to make
twelve films for four American studios, not counting the films he
hoped to make independently. He was behaving, they said, less
like a man than a beehive. He had headaches, hangovers and an
increasingly nervous stomach, but he was working on his own
terms.

It all went well until he made *Spinster* on location in New
Zealand. He played a war hero intent on deflowering a virginal

schoolteacher, Shirley MacLaine. The script had been re-written until he felt his part made no sense. When he saw the film he decided it was the biggest dissection since the slaughterhouse.

He moved to New Orleans to play a grubby young man living in a cathouse in *A Walk on the Wild Side,* a cleaned-up version of Nelson Algren's novel.

He came down in the elevator from his suite in the Roosevelt Hotel for his first day's shooting in his film clothes – dirty jeans, a scruffy wool shirt, a sweat-stained stetson and muddy boots. A group of businessmen sharing the elevator stared at him distastefully. As the doors opened at lobby level and the men stepped out one of them remarked within earshot of Harvey, 'I guess they let anybody into hotels these days.'

'They sure do,' Harvey agreed, striding past them to the limousine which waited to take him to the location.

There were few stars, he decided, who could match his talents or his professionalism. In his love scenes with Capucine in *Wild Side* he pulled faces at her, crossed his eyes and told blue jokes. When he embraced her he breathed garlic from his luncheon salad in her face and deliberately raised his knee as he pulled her closer to him.

His scenes with Jane Fonda were scarcely more satisfactory. She decided she might just as well be acting by herself. But she saw that Harvey was no match for his third co-star in the film, Barbara Stanwyck. Harvey kept Stanwyck waiting on the set while he talked on the telephone in his dressing room. She went to find him, calling, 'Mr. Harvey, will you kindly get your ass out here?'

Harvey hung up the 'phone and walked onto the sound stage.

'Right,' he said. 'Shall we get on with it? You know what you're going to say in this scene, Barbara?'

She eyed him coolly. 'Look, buster, I know exactly what I'm going to say. You don't have to worry about me. But if I can assume that *you* know your lines then take that cigarette holder out of your mouth and let's begin.'

Harvey didn't talk about Barbara Stanwyck to the newspapers.

But he claimed that Jane Fonda and Capucine were the best actors
he had worked with:

'Jane Fonda? She goes around as if she's in drag. And Capucine
is a ghastly woman. It's not her fault she can't act.'

When Capucine read Harvey's remarks in *Time* magazine she
wrote to the editor to point out that she had protested indignantly
when she heard he was to play her lover in the film. 'Mr. Harvey
whacks away at nearly all the heroines he has to embrace in films;
it's safer than denouncing the critics.'

Harvey also wrote to *Time's* Editor to thank him for spelling his
name correctly.

His Press quotes were diligently worked on. It was his way of
ensuring that he was given space and that the world would take
notice. He and the journalists were professionals and he reckoned
they needed each other. He behaved outrageously in public by
kissing an ex-Governor of California full on the mouth in the
Bistro restaurant in Beverly Hills and telling a girl at dinner, 'I
can't decide which one of you I like better, you or your date.' It
was easier than punching people on the nose, as some stars did, to
make the headlines.

He didn't admit to the press how unhappy an experience *A
Walk on the Wild Side* had been. Eight writers had tinkered with
the script. Charles Feldman, the producer, had fired the director
and when Harvey protested Feldman called him to his office and
jabbed a finger at him.

'We need four more weeks on this picture. And you're to
blame. Only you. You're the only person who's bad in the picture.'

Harvey knew he was giving a superficial performance, the sort
of performance he invariably gave when a picture wasn't going
well. But he asked, 'Tell me why, Charlie, dear heart?'

Feldman didn't say why.

Harvey reported as instructed for the extra weeks without being
asked to step before the cameras. The overtime earned him
100,000 dollars. Even so, he despised the film so much he tried to

have his name taken off the titles. Feldman threatened to sue him, at which point Harvey backed down.

There was one pleasant memory. On location in New Orleans he came to know a Belgian priest who worked in the city's poorest quarter. When they were filming in Basin Street cemetery the priest invited him to lunch, opened a bottle of white wine and served a Benedictine with the coffee. Charming, thought Harvey who, in return, asked the priest to dinner and told him he would send a studio car for him.

'There's no need for you to go to such trouble,' said the priest. 'I shall collect you at your hotel.'

Harvey was impressed when the priest arrived in a big white Chevrolet, more so when he got into the car and found it had a telephone. A good business to be in, he told his new friend. He lifted the receiver and asked, 'Is that You, God?'

'Don't get me wrong, Larry,' the priest said. 'Do you really imagine I could run a car on a salary of fifteen dollars a month?' No, the Chevrolet was a police car because he happened to be the local police chaplain. If he had any money he would spend it on building a community hall for his parishioners.

When Harvey got back to Hollywood he and Joan Cohn raised the money and the hall was built.

ONLY A FEW onlookers were in Central Park on one of New York's coldest February mornings in 1962 when a tall young man, hands thrust in the pockets of his overcoat, walked toward the end of the pier at the Boat House and unhesitatingly stepped feet first into the icy lake.

To the onlookers it may have seemed a suicide bid. But to the film crew on *The Manchurian Candidate* it was a key scene in the film.

Harvey, playing the brainwashed Sergeant Shaw, was helped out of the water by a shorter man, also huddled in an overcoat, his friend Major Marco, played by Frank Sinatra. The crew quickly wrapped Harvey, who was shaking with the cold, in his monogrammed robe, gave him a shot of brandy and rushed him in a studio limousine to the Sherry Netherlands Hotel across the Park. Slightly amazed, the director John Frankenheimer exclaimed:

'All in one take!'

As the dripping actor hurried through the lobby, his plastered hair stiff with ice, the guests stared curiously at him. What puzzled the film crew, and would have puzzled those hotel guests had they recognised Harvey, was why this star, now making his eighth film in two years and averaging £100,000 a part, should have decided to play the scene himself when he could have used a stunt man.

He wore no wet suit beneath his street clothes. Publicist Charles Moses thought the plunge would have killed any other man. But Harvey was no ordinary man. He was like a piece of tempered steel, with a toughness developed in his Army and Navy days. And he had a high threshold of pain.

He was totally engrossed in the complex character of Sergeant Shaw, playing the part with a conviction that was essential if he was to persuade the audience that a brain-washed soldier could commit a series of killings without compunction when the victims were his friends, his father-in-law, his wife and finally his mother.

He saw no reason to consult Richard Condon, the author of *The Manchurian Candidate,* about how he should approach the part. He had his own conception of Shaw; he found in him the insolence, the class consciousness, the ruthlessness of Joe Lampton. He also realised it was his most important film role since *Room at the Top.*

For Sinatra the role of Major Marco was crucial, too. Like Harvey he had made a series of indifferent films through which critics said he had sleepwalked. Like Harvey he was moody, arrogant and egotistical with a caustic tongue when it suited him.

The two got on well together, but Sinatra could give his co-star uncomfortable moments. He supplied a magazine writer with a number of insinuations about Harvey. His family had Communist associations, suggested Sinatra, and there was more to Harvey's habit of kissing men in public than met the eye.

When Harvey read the typescript submitted for his approval he was alarmed. He asked Charles Moses if Sinatra was serious, and was there a danger the article might get into print, even though he would veto it?

Moses went to Sinatra's dressing room.

'What have you done, Frank? Larry's got himself in a hell of a state over that article.'

Sinatra grinned. 'Okay, Chuck. Tell him it's all a gag.'

Moses hurried back to Harvey and confessed that Sinatra had just pulled one of his practical jokes.

RICHARD CONDON was living in Geneva with his wife and children and dachshund during the shooting of *The Manchurian Candidate.* Although the book had been described as a time bomb when published in 1959, Condon knew its filming was fortuitous.

A big Hollywood star had bought the book and backed out of the deal. When John Frankenheimer and the writer-producer George Axelrod were able to acquire the rights they secured a commitment from Frank Sinatra, and with this ace up their sleeve went for the finance to Arthur Krim, the president of United Artists.

'I'm sorry, boys,' said Krim, 'but I won't make this picture.'

Krim was politically-minded and was to become finance chairman of the Democratic Party. Just the same, Frankenheimer and Axelrod were surprised.

'Not only will I not make it,' vowed Krim, 'but you'll never get it made because I'm going to call every other movie company and talk to them. You're just not going to get a deal, boys.'

'But why?'

'Why . . . ?' He looked at them in disbelief.

'Do you think we're going to embarrass our President by putting all this in a movie? Are you out of your minds, boys?'

41.   *Above:* Harvey at 36. A champagne celebration on his birthday during the run of *The Winter's Tale* in London. Actress Jane Asher, in her first West End play, helps Harvey blow out the candle.

42.   *Below:* Harvey in plaster. During rehearsals at the Chichester Festival in 1970 he slipped and broke a bone in his right knee.

43.   *Below:* Despite a broken knee Harvey, equipped with walking stick, takes the lead in Shaw's *Arms and the Man* opposite Sarah Badel at the Chichester Festival in 1970.

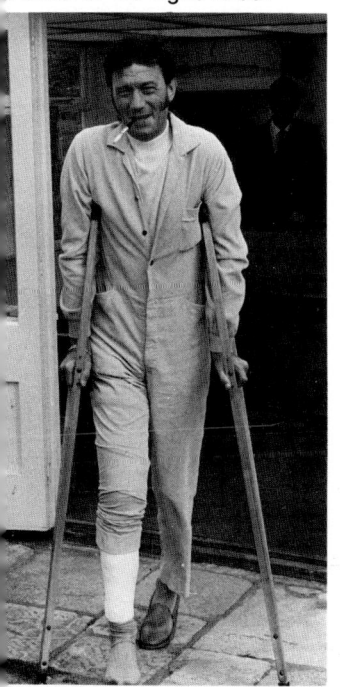

44. *Above:* Margaret Leighton with escort Harvey at a London party in 1954.

45. *Below:* Harvey in the role of frogman Commander Crabb in *The Silent Enemy*, filmed in Malta and Gibraltar.

46. *Right:* Harvey and Margaret Leighton in their London mews home shortly after their marriage.

48. *Below:* A kiss for his bride. After his marriage to Margaret Leighton in Gibraltar in 1957.

47. *Above:* After the wedding in Gibraltar Harvey carries his actress bride Margaret Leighton across the threshold of their London mews house.

49. *Left:* Wedding party in Gibraltar. Harvey and bride Margaret Leighton with John Clements (right), who gave the bride away, and screenwriter William Fairchild, the best man.

50. *Above:* Cheek-to-cheek pose with actress Elaine Stritch after the first night of *The Time of the Barracudas* in Los Angeles.

51. *Below:* Meeting the Master. Harvey with Somerset Maugham on the terrace of Maugham's villa at Cap Ferrat. Harvey, troubled about his portayal of Maugham's hero in *Of Human Bondage,* had flown from Dublin to ask the Master's advice.

The director and the screenwriter were almost convinced by Krim that a film revealing the holder of America's highest award for gallantry as his country's most deadly traitor was not perhaps the best propaganda. Krim, remembering that the author of the novel had worked for him, said, 'I don't like Condon, anyway.'

The two men walked out of Krim's New York office bitterly disappointed, but not beaten. Axelrod caught a 'plane to California and met Sinatra. When he told him of the meeting with Krim, Sinatra called John F. Kennedy at Hyannisport. The President had already read Condon's novel and liked it.

'I have no objections to the film,' he said. 'What's gotten into Arthur?'

Sinatra asked him, 'Will you call Arthur and tell him so?'

The President called Krim and said, 'Arthur, you can't be serious. Go ahead and make the picture. And make a'wonderful picture.'

Condon had been twenty-two years in the film business before becoming a writer. He was slightly weary of film studios. He didn't see the film of *The Manchurian Candidate* until it was previewed in London. Other actors, he thought, might have played Sergeant Shaw like a robot, but Harvey had found the sadness in the character and reached out for the tragedy. Condon realised the film had come at the right time in Harvey's career and he had brought his total self-confidence to it.

'Isn't it strange', Harvey remarked with self-mockery, 'that I had to jump in the lake in Central Park before people took any notice of me?'

His fee for *The Manchurian Candidate* was 270,000 dollars. He regarded his success in the film as almost mystical, and Condon became a talisman for him. He would visit him at his villa in Geneva, sometimes with Nöel Coward, more often with James Woolf, and always he would ask Condon:

'Anything in the typewriter for me, Dick?'

FAILURE, LAURENCE HARVEY told the journalists, had never entered into his plans. From the beginning he had envisaged only success. To achieve success one needed ambition, dedication, courage, self-confidence and a willingness to learn, and he had shown all these attributes.

One night in London the BBC screened an early film, *Innocents in Paris,* in which he had played the small part of a waiter. But on the television screen there was no trace of Harvey, nor did his name appear on the credits.

Film buffs telephoned the studios for an explanation. The film, the BBC pointed out, had been edited before they bought it, and James Woolf had done the editing.

Woolf had his answer ready.

'For an audience to see Laurence Harvey in an obscure part at this stage of his career would help him not at all. I decided to scissor his role right out of the film.'

NOW THAT Harvey was divorced, it was no longer necessary for Joan Cohn and himself to cable each other discreetly, signing themselves 'TUP 161,' the licence number of the Thunderbird he had bought after *The Alamo.*

He had given her expensive presents, his first a gold Fabergé cigarette case with the crest of Nicholas II of Russia in diamonds. Joan decided that her lover no longer needed TUP 161. Their first Christmas together she turned in the Thunderbird for an opalescent Rolls Royce which she tied with a huge bow and parked outside his house in Hollywood.

'I never had much interest in cars,' she said, 'but I knew he secretly wanted a Rolls.'

15 | 'I never let the noises in the jungle frighten me.'

HOLLYWOOD'S SCREEN IMAGE OF HARVEY WAS THAT OF AN ARIS-tocrat; England saw him in proletarian terms. To his friend John Ireland he was the actor who couldn't stop working. A few days before leaving Hollywood for Europe he drove Ireland to the Bistro for dinner. He reached across to move a bundle of scripts from the passenger seat of the Rolls to make room for his friend.

'It's a good job you're going away for a while,' Ireland said. 'Now maybe the rest of us will get some work.'

'Have you looked at some of those scripts, dear heart? Most of them look as if they came out of back pockets or bottom drawers.'

The exception was Terence Rattigan's play about Lawrence of Arabia, *Ross.* Producer David Merrick had flown from New York to discuss the role with him. Harvey wanted to play Lawrence, and his casting seemed certain until an embarrassed Merrick 'phoned him to say that Rattigan had turned him down.

The playwright had every right to do so, but Harvey suspected this was yet another door slammed in his face because he had divorced Margaret Leighton. Both he and his ex-wife had gone to extreme lengths to avoid meeting each other. The previous year he had signed for *Altona* at London's Royal Court Theatre when Margaret, he knew, would be on Broadway. A letter from Terence Rattigan was said to suggest that it would be unwise of him to appear on the London stage. Opinion, the playwright allegedly pointed out, was ranged against him. He would be pilloried.

Harvey had to buy himself out of his *Altona* contract. Still, if the theatres were closed to him he could make as many films as he chose. He told John Ireland over dinner he would never let the noises in the jungle frighten him. Far from it; he loved the challenge of the other beasts.

He began work on a film for Carol Reed, *The Running Man,* with locations in Spain and Ireland. An apt title, said his enemies. When he arrived in Dublin in the autumn of 1962, Harry Barr, a dark-haired young driver with a car hire firm specialising in film company work, drove him from the airport to the Shelbourne Hotel. His Spanish chauffeur, who was driving his Mark Ten Jaguar from Spain, wouldn't arrive in Ireland for a few days.

Next morning the car hire firm told Barr, 'Mr. Laurence Harvey wants to see you at Ardmore Studios.' Harvey was crossing from one of the sound stages to the old mansion which housed the administrative offices when Barr met him.

'Why the hell didn't you pick me up this morning?'

Barr was apologetic. 'I wasn't supposed to pick you up, Mr. Harvey.'

'From now on I want you to pick me up. You and nobody else.'

When the Spanish chauffeur arrived with the car Harvey found excuses for him to do any job except drive. Barr continued to collect the star in his firm's car, touring the city with him, taking him to antique shops and private galleries. In Louis Wine's Harvey bought an antique snuff box which disappeared at the studios three days later and was never found.

He soon learned that the word *gourmet* meant little in Dublin. Was there nowhere to eat in this town? he asked Barr. The driver told him that a Scotsman and his wife had opened a small restaurant in a laneway behind the Shelbourne Hotel. Harvey took his co-star Lee Remick there one night. Peter Powrie, the young owner, and his wife Kathy served them a superb meal. But they were uncertain of the restaurant's future.

'You don't have to worry,' Harvey assured them. 'As long as *I'm* here people will come.'

He was right. When Dublin society heard that Laurence Harvey and his friends were dining at the Soup Bowl the restaurant began to prosper.

Harvey offered to invest in the restaurant, as he had done with the Bistro in Beverly Hills, but Powrie's wife knew her husband would be inhibited by a board of directors.

There was no question of allowing Harvey to run up bills. The Powries were short of capital. Although they bought the best meat and fish for Harvey and his friends, stocked up with caviar and imported cases of Pouilly Fumé, they had to pay their suppliers' bills promptly. On Sundays Powrie would go to Harvey's suite in the Shelbourne Hotel and wait while the star examined the invoices.

'My God, Peter!' Harvey would exclaim, 'did we really drink all that wine?'

The bills were settled in cash, never by cheque. From a wallet containing some £500 in notes, Harvey would pay a bill of between £100 and £200.

In those first weeks Kathy Powrie risked losing the business the star was bringing them. His raw language when he had drunk too much wine annoyed her. One evening a young student was helping her in the tiny kitchen when Harvey squeezed in and began swearing. She thought his language out of character with his handmade lawn shirt, immaculately creased slacks and cashmere sweater.

'I'm quite certain,' she said, 'you can find nicer words in the dictionary – and just as expressive. I'd be obliged if you and your friends left, and we'll forget about the bill.'

She knew they could ill-afford to lose the money and least of all the regular custom of Harvey and his friends.

Harvey was surprised, but he was willing to apologise. He and his friends had no intention of leaving the Soup Bowl.

BEFORE *THE RUNNING MAN* was long in production Harvey sensed it would be an unmemorable film, like many others he had made. Carol Reed, who had shown such skill in making thrillers like *The Third Man,* had so fallen in love with the Spanish location during the first weeks of filming that he was criticised for concentrating on the setting rather than the stars.

Harvey didn't argue, though in a letter he wrote in August from the Hotel Reina Cristina in Algeciras to Joan Cohn in Beverly Hills he seemed burdened with problems:

My Darling,

Am just about to dash off to work, starting a week of night shooting. Received your two very sweet letters this afternoon and am obeying your every instruction by now writing personally. Everybody left to-day except Frank (Wells) who will be leaving the day after to-morrow and with whom I have had long talks regarding those million and one enterprises that are brewing on those distant shores.

If I sounded distant or cold or remote or whatever you said on the 'phone last night it is only because I'm beginning to find the weight of all the problems unbearable and am angry, annoyed and scolding myself for being so weak and stupid. It is impossible to even attempt to share any of it with you or anybody else and only I can and should solve them.

It is too easy to put on a cheerful front and I fail to understand why I can't behave as naturally as anybody else does.

The answer of course is that I shouldn't have called you last night and will not do so in future unless I am feeling happy, gay, on top of the world, aggressive, scintillating, sexy and generally false unto myself. I understand only too well how you must feel listening to a dull boor on the other end of the line and can only apologise for it and promise to the best of my knowledge and future behaviour that I will try not to do it again.

It was so sweet of you to talk to George Cukor for me, but I doubt if any of them are seriously considering me. Please give my love to the Frankenheimers and the R. Harris's and tell Moss (Hart) if you see him, that I will be writing to him. I have told Frank, who will no doubt be talking to you when he gets back, to get on to Ken Herman and get the whip cracking on selling the Palm Springs houses now that the season is about to start again. Please give my love to all at 1000.

My love to you as always.

Ever,

Larry.

Harvey now saw an opportunity to set up his first film as director and booked space at the Sevilla Studios in Madrid for later in the year. He remembered nights at Grosvenor House when he had pleaded with James Woolf to allow him direct a feature. But Woolf had been obstinate. Harvey's talent was as an actor; he had made his reputation; his fees were more than satisfying, and it wouldn't do to jeopardise his future.

Harvey, in spite of Woolf's evaluation, had long cherished the idea of directing his own film. He believed he had found an exciting subject in a novel, *La Cérémonie* by Frederic Grendel, the story of an attempt to rescue a bank robber from prison where he is due to be executed unjustly for the murder of a bank guard. By shooting in black and white and deferring his own fees he believed he could make the film for a budget below a million dollars. George Ornstein of United Artists agreed to put up most of the money. Harvey would produce, direct, play the leading role and contribute to the screenplay.

Before he had finished *The Running Man* in Ireland he had signed his actors: Raf Vallone, George Chakiris, Jack MacGowran, Noël Purcell, Lee Patterson, Murray Melvin and John Ireland. Oswald Morris, who was photographing *The Running Man,* agreed to join him as lighting cameraman and from Ardmore he handpicked a technical crew. His choice of leading lady was determined by the budget. He couldn't afford a big fee for a star, and anyway he regarded most of the women he had worked with in British studios as 'puddings'.

James Woolf, however, had discovered a young actress playing in English repertory at Worthing, a leggy girl with straight dark hair and a Botticelli face. He had put her in a blonde wig and cast her as a schoolgirl who gets a crush on her teacher in *Term of Trial.* The actress was Sarah Miles, just eighteen.

Harvey decided to cast her in his film. But he would show her without her blonde wig.

The crew moved into apartments and small hotels in Madrid. Harvey took a suite at the Castellana Hilton. Nothing but a suite would satisfy him, and at any rate the hotel was giving him credit.

The Sevilla studios had certain advantages. They were only ten minutes' drive from the centre of the city and the large stages could accommodate a composite prison set with its cells, corridors and halls. The lack of adequate soundproofing was a disadvantage, and even when the red light went on some Spaniards ignored it.

The vast prison set was so heavy the studio workmen couldn't 'float' the walls, which were supported by scaffolding, so they kept spraying the plaster with water; they dared not allow it to solidify or it would be difficult to dismantle after the filming.

The continuous spraying of water and the bitterly cold weather made conditions intolerable. The crew members wrapped scarves around their mouths and the actors wore ski suits under their costumes. Harvey walked around the set, cigarette holder clenched between his teeth, hands dug deep in the pockets of his sheepskin jacket, script tucked under his arm in a leather holder embossed with gold initials.

He found conditions most gruelling at night when they filmed at Toledo where the city walls served as the prison exteriors. In the afternoon he and cameraman Oswald Morris would prepare the terrain, Harvey tugging a woollen cap over his ears to keep out the biting cold. But when he was before the camera he sometimes had to appear in just a shirt and trousers. He tried not to think about the cold. Having nurtured this project for years until it was a reality he was prepared to endure every discomfort, even lack of sleep.

Years of film acting had conditioned his agile brain to know what one could or could not do with a camera and lights, and he depended now on first-class technicians for their co-operation. Whenever he joined them late at night at Casa Paco, a popular restaurant in an old part of Madrid that served charcoal-grilled steaks, chips, ice cream and as much red wine as one could drink, he enjoyed discussing the next day's filming with them.

He worked what he considered practical, if long, hours from two in the afternoon until nine or ten at night, with the crew and artists snatching a break when they could.

As Christmas approached he grew tense, hating the thought of losing five days' filming. He knew that most of the unit were anxious to fly home to their families, so he persuaded them to work longer hours. He didn't want to lose the rhythm of the film or the enthusiasm of the crew. In the past he had worked for directors who told him, 'Get out there and get on with it. We're paying you a lot of money, so don't waste time talking.' Now he was his own director and he wanted to make the most of his opportunity.

RICHARD CONDON was in Madrid when Harvey was directing *The Ceremony.* Condon and his wife Evelyn joined Harvey and John Ireland one morning in a buying spree in an antique saleroom. 'Larry was buying like it was Maples,' said Condon, who knew he was fond of money and was convinced he thought like a trader rather than an artist.

'He was interested in money for two reasons: to prove to his peers that he had made good, which was very important to him, and to indulge himself. He'd buy a shaving brush for 137 dollars.

'He had a calculating business mind. When very young I imagine he decided on the kind of life he wanted and quickly put his keen intelligence into motion. He would merchandise himself to reach the top of a profession which pays better than any other. Knowing he couldn't become the world's heavyweight boxing champion, I guess he figured acting could pay almost as much. He acquired the flash and dazzle necessary for success in show business and an absolute belief in his own ability to think his way through what is essentially an emotional business.'

It wasn't simply because of the quality of his writing that Harvey sought Condon's friendship. He was pursuing the good luck element of *The Manchurian Candidate.* To the writer the real basis of their friendship was good humour; they made each other laugh. 'Larry was one of the most gregarious persons I have ever met, though this might have been prompted by a sense of loneliness. He never stopped talking over dinner and he ate like a bird.'

Condon watched him at work on *The Ceremony*. He knew how much Harvey wanted to be a director. 'But you can't will these things – not on your first picture, anyway. Larry didn't know how the film would turn out, although he was proving irresistible to the crew and the other actors.' Condon feared he was making a mistake in playing the leading role and directing at the same time. He was taking a screwing from the backers by making the film without fees for a share of the hypothetical profits.

Harvey was so ill one morning he couldn't make the set. For a few days he had worked with a sniffling cold and the crew members had remarked on his pallor. John Quested, his assistant director, believed the emotional drain of acting and directing, of forcing himself to switch suddenly from one skill to another, was affecting his health. Influenza, the doctors said. His temperature was 102.

Joan Cohn flew into Madrid and checked into the Hilton to be with him as the doctors filled him with antibiotics.

He was a restless patient. Some of his bravura deserted him, but he knew he daren't stay in bed more than a couple of days. There would be insurance claims if the film stopped shooting, and he couldn't afford that.

On the second day of his illness the 'rushes' arrived from London. Muffled in his sheepskin coat he hurried out to view them. Many directors never get what they want on film because they cannot convey their ideas to the crew, and what they see in the 'rushes' is not what they had in mind. But Harvey had the gift of carrying his crew with him. Whether they were creating a film of quality was another matter.

Within a few days he was back at work. Trouble came when he prepared to film Sarah Miles' nude scene. The girl, obviously lonely in Madrid, was nervous. Harvey assured her that the scene would be, as he said, tasteful and filmed in low-key lighting so that her body would be scarcely visible. But she couldn't face the scene.

Shooting was delayed as he tried to change her mind. 'You read

the script,' he told her impatiently. 'You knew this scene was in
the script.'

'I can't do it.'

'You'll *have* to do it. If you don't you're out of the picture.'

While she hesitated the problem of her nude scene became
gossip in film circles in Madrid. Harvey wasn't amused; the last
thing he wanted was a scandal in a Catholic city.

He finally compromised. 'We'll cut the scene to a minimum.
We'll clear the set of everybody except the essential crew.'

He had engaged Sarah Miles because he knew she had sex and
class, a combination lacking in English actresses since Vivien
Leigh. Now the silly girl was making a fuss about taking her
clothes off. What the hell for? When she finally stripped she
looked just a skinny kid.

Without telling her he invited photographers onto the set and
positioned them behind the Mitchell camera and the lights so the
actress would not see them.

He walked away when the scene was shot. If she had a body, he
said, she wouldn't have worried about taking her clothes off.

When the photographs were published in London Sarah Miles'
future father-in-law 'phoned Harvey to complain. Her well-to-
do-parents were shocked. Even the servants were embarrassed to
see their young mistress nude. He shrugged it off. He would have
thought it an excellent way to keep one's domestic staff content.

Before Harvey left Madrid *Variety* reported that *The Ceremony*
had finished shooting two days ahead of schedule:

*Producer-director Laurence Harvey has found a backer to pick up most of
the picture's under-the-line costs and guarantee a prestige send-off in
Spain.*

HARRY BARR, while driving for his car hire firm in Dublin,
got a message to 'phone the studios at Ardmore. They asked him
if he would agree to work for Laurence Harvey as a private
chauffeur.

'Of course,' he said.

He returned his firm's car keys and went to the Shelbourne Hotel to collect a letter from Harvey inviting him to become his chauffeur. At Ardmore they told him there was a seat booked for him on a 'plane to London and from there he was to take another 'plane to Madrid.

Harvey met him in the Castellana Hilton, immaculate in a suede suit, beige polo-neck sweater and suede shoes embroidered with his initials in gold thread. He put his arms around Barr and kissed him.

'My Spanish chauffeur has damaged the Jaguar,' he said. 'I can't keep him. That's why I've sent for you, Harry. I think we'll get on well together.'

Two days later Harvey flew to Los Angeles, instructing Barr to drive his Jaguar to Dublin.

'I'm going to make another film there. Be ready to meet me in a week's time.'

16 | 'My boy prince is a genius,' said Joan Cohn.

HARRY BARR MET HIM WITH THE WHITE MARK TEN JAGUAR AT DUBLIN Airport one late February morning in 1963. Barr was to be paid £15 a week as chauffeur, plus meals and expenses. Harvey stipulated, 'Anything we say or is said in this car is confidential.' The salary paid to Barr was a tiny fraction of the money spent on the second re-make of Somerset Maugham's novel *Of Human Bondage*.

Harvey was to play Leslie Howard's old part of the sensitive, crippled medical student Philip Carey. He checked into a third-floor suite in the 19th-century Shelbourne, comprising a spacious living room and a small bar overlooking St. Stephen's Green, a bedroom and two bathrooms. His bed was arranged to face north and covered with a mink bedspread, a present from Joan Cohn. He filled his wardrobe with thirty suits and jackets and a dozen pairs of shoes handmade in Paris. In his suite he changed into a blue towelling robe monogrammed with his initials and sent Barr to buy a £250 Sony tape recorder and a selection of four-track tapes from Sibelius to Sinatra.

Late at night when the volume was turned high hotel guests, kept awake by the sounds of Harvey's music, complained to the manager. Barr knew that Harvey hated to be alone at night; he disliked even dining alone. If he went out to dinner Barr would accompany him to the restaurant and wait there until his friends arrived. Then he would say, 'Okay, Harry. See you later.'

'Dublin is dullsville at night,' he complained. 'All I can do is go to the Soup Bowl and make the best of it. And you know, Harry, I made that Soup Bowl.'

The Powries were known by now, but Harvey would still squeeze into their kitchen and make the Bearnaise sauce. He would join Irish theatre people like Micheál MacLiammóir and Hilton Edwards for dinner. Their conversation would be witty, the language blue. But no matter who the other guests were Harvey demanded to be recognised as the star. Sometimes diners asked, 'Who is that man? His language is awful.' Kathy Powrie would whisper to Harvey, 'Pack it in!'

He would turn to her and ask innocently, 'Me? What have I done?'

'Just behave.'

Film people began to frequent the restaurant. One night Peter Finch, Peter O'Toole and Harvey were at separate tables in the small ground-floor dining room. None of them was prepared to acknowledge the other's presence. Harvey retreated to the kitchen. 'Let me give you a hand,' he said to Kathy, but all he wanted was to get away from an embarrassing situation. There didn't seem to be room for three stars in one small Dublin restaurant.

He continued to ask the Powries to let him invest in the Soup Bowl. Kathy said to him, 'We don't want money from you, Larry.' Her husband did not consider they were part of his *entourage,* but they might have been if they had accepted his offer.

Once the filming began the Powries tried to get him back to his hotel before midnight, but they seldom succeeded. In the Shelbourne at six a.m. the hotel desk would call his room. Harvey would mumble, 'All right' into the receiver, and fall asleep again. At seven o'clock a room service waiter would arrive with his coffee to find him beneath the blankets. He would whip the covers from his head, announcing. 'It's a beautiful morning, sir!'

'Get the hell out of here!'

'A beautiful morning, sir, despite the time of year.'

'Stop shooting that crap!'

The waiter would persist, knowing that in the lobby the

chauffeur was asking frantically, 'Can't anybody get Mr. Harvey downstairs?'

Eventually the waiter would drag the star from the bed as Harvey shouted, 'Get your hands off me, you cotton-picking sonofabitch!'

He would stumble into one of the bathrooms, fill the washbasin and plunge his head in the water. When he came out of the bathroom, towelling his hair, he would ask, 'Well, how do I look?'

The waiter would pour him cups of cona coffee until he seemed wide awake. There was seldom time for a bath, but he showered in the studios during the day and took a bath when he got back to the hotel in the evening. He was as immaculate as his car. If you lifted the bonnet, they said, everything underneath was gleaming.

Soon after filming began Joan Cohn arrived. She fussed over Harvey at the studios, wrapping a coat around his shoulders between scenes. 'Darling, you must be frozen. And you're tired. Why don't you rest?' In his dressing room she would prepare a basket of fruit. And when she went back to Dublin in the after-noon Harvey would call the hotel when he was ready to leave the studios.

'May I speak to J. C., please?'

'Sir?', the surprised switchboard operator would ask.

'J. C.'

'I'm sorry, but there's no such person registered here.'

'Jesus Christ, of course there is! Haven't you heard of Joan Cohn?'

At the Shelbourne Joan would have two club sandwiches and a double Tio Pepe waiting for him. Frank Sinatra had ordered a dozen bottles of Tio Pepe to be delivered for his birthday when he was filming *The Running Man* in Ireland. Joan Cohn had done better. She arranged with the Shelbourne to furnish a room with antiques to create a period atmosphere, and in an adjoining room a table was laid for dinner for thirty-six guests.

Harvey returned from Ardmore studios soon after seven. Joan told him she was holding a small party for him. He took a bath, changed into a beige polo-neck shirt, beige slacks and a suede jacket. He wore suede shoes with the initials 'L.H.'. When he went down to the party on the first floor the guests stood and applauded him. A four-tiered birthday cake was wheeled in, and Joan kissed him. He cried with surprise and delight.

'My boy prince is a genius,' Joan said.

Kim Novak, his leading lady in *Of Human Bondage*, thought differently.

KIM NOVAK ARRIVED at Dublin Airport on a bleak February evening. Her fair hair was hatless and she hugged a bright red wool coat around her tall figure. She signed autographs and talked to newspapermen who had been told by the film's publicists that Miss Novak's first meeting with the Press would also be her last during the filming because her part as the Cockney waitress Mildred, first created on the screen by Bette Davis, would be extremely demanding.

Marilyn Monroe was six months dead and Kim Novak now presented the image of the sex goddess who aspired to serious acting. From the early 'fifties she had co-starred in films with Frank Sinatra, William Holden, James Stewart and Jack Lemmon. Harry Cohn had discovered her, just as he had discovered Joan Perry who was to become his second wife. Both women liked to paint landscapes, but their interests ended there. Joan Perry was the most important woman in 'King' Cohn's life and after some minor roles in feature films she became his wife, a celebrated Hollywood hostess and the mother of a young family.

Kim Novak, on the other hand, had been carefully groomed by Cohn to be a Columbia star. She was thirty when she arrived in Ireland and to the Irish journalists who asked why she hadn't married her reply seemed suitably pious:

'I'm a Catholic and my marriage will have to be a lasting one, not just a fling.'

On leaving the airport she was driven to the Old Conna, a

country house hotel sixteen miles from Dublin and close to the studios. She was provided with a black Mark Ten Jaguar to match Harvey's and a Cockney chauffeur. The manager of the hotel, Cyril Count McCormack, conducted her to her suite on the first floor, a large sitting-room, bedroom and bathroom, looking across the countryside to Bray Head. More newsmen were waiting in the lobby and although she wanted to be rid of the Press she went down and talked to them. The Count found her a quiet girl.

During the film's preparation and the early days of shooting most of the actors and executives came to dinner at the Old Conna: Bryan Forbes, James Woolf, Robert Morley, Ray Stark of Seven Arts, the production company, and the film's director Henry Hathaway. Harvey didn't endear himself to Count McCormack.

'He struck me as being conceited and arrogant. He was the sort of person who would get up from the table and go to the still-room for a drink instead of asking a waiter to bring it to him. My staff didn't like that, nor did I. Kim wouldn't have done it, nor would anyone else in the hotel, but how could I rebuke him? I just had to put up with it.'

Kim Novak preferred to have her meals in her suite. She rarely mixed with the other guests. But the staff liked her. If she wanted some special dish and the chef apologised in his Cork accent because it wasn't on the menu, she would say persuasively, 'Come on, cheffy, make it for me.'

WHEN HENRY HATHAWAY arrived in Ireland he was sixty-five years old, had made eighty films and owned forty-two asphalt plants in California. In business he was a tycoon; in films he preferred to think of himself as a hired hand. When he began directing films after a career as a child actor he was in his early twenties, like Harry Cohn, John Ford and Irving Thalberg at the time. 'We were just kids making movies.' In those days Hollywood was run by young men; the same men were still running Hollywood, but they were a lot older. Hathaway had continued making pictures 'to stay alive'. He had made *Trail of the*

Lonesome Pine in 1936 and he had just completed the most expensive Hollywood Western, *How the West was Won*. He had made thrillers and war films, had given Richard Widmark his break in *Kiss of Death* and directed Laurence Harvey in the smallest role in *The Black Robe*.

He had wanted to make *Of Human Bondage* in the 'fifties with Marilyn Monroe as Mildred, but the studios had said, 'You want to put Monroe in such a movie? In a comedy this girl can make us four million dollars.' Now he would have preferred Tuesday Weld, who was ten years younger than Novak. He saw Mildred as a teenager, but he was willing to accept Kim Novak because she was one of the few actresses who could win the sympathy of an audience in such a promiscuous part. He was less concerned about his leading man. So long as Harvey learned how to walk with a club foot he was satisfied. The prospect that Harvey, having directed his own film, might not be willing to accept the status of an actor obeying a veteran director didn't bother Hathaway. 'I think he'll be happy to sit this one out,' he predicted.

Bondage would be Hathaway's eighty-first film, or at least he thought so; they turned out movies so fast in the silent days he lost count. His was the craftsman's approach to film making, not the artist's. Olivier had vowed never to work for him because he was too tough on actors. Hathaway's retort was that if actors couldn't take tough direction they shouldn't be in the business.

He wasn't worried too much about his actors as he settled into his suite in the Old Conna; he was more concerned about a union squabble that was holding up filming. The Irish and British electrical unions were arguing about which of them should supply the greater number of technicians, while the anxious Seven Arts' executives considered switching the film to Paris, Madrid or Rome, perhaps even to Hollywood.

When the film finally began shooting in the first week in March, Hathaway strode onto the set smoking a cigar. He was a large, handsome man with silver-grey hair. He wore a loose-fitting tweed jacket over a dark woollen shirt and his voice carried around the set.

'Anybody not in this scene get the hell out of it!'

Robert Morley declared he was happy to be directed by such a sweet, kindly, old gentleman. No one knew if he meant it as a compliment.

ERNIE ANDERSON, THE first publicist on *Of Human Bondage* decided there was no better way to launch the production before the world's film Press than with a lavish party on St. Patrick's Night. He arranged dinner in a rambling hotel overlooking Dublin Bay, the Shangri-La, which was run by an Irish tenor, Michael Dwyer, and his wife, Patricia. The tables were decorated with bowls of shamrock and a menu devised which included *Prawns Henry Hathaway, Omelette Surprise Kim Novak, Sirloin Steak Laurence Harvey* and *Gaelic Coffee Siobhan McKenna*. The invited columnists included Earl Wilson, Roderick Mann and Charles Hamblett, who wrote a poem in praise of Novak. He had written poetry and was a friend of Anderson.

Peter Powrie joined Harvey in the Shelbourne for drinks before the party. Harvey opened bottles of champagne for Powrie, but confined himself to Pouilly Fumé. Around eight o'clock they drove to the Shangri-La, where they had more drinks before the dinner. The guests having taken their places, Anderson asked Powrie, 'Who are you?'

'Peter Powrie.'

'Oh, you're one of the Harvey party.' He showed him to a place at one of the side tables, far from Harvey.

'I'm not sitting here,' declared Powrie and started to walk away.

Anderson followed him. 'Mr. Powrie, where are you going?'

'I don't sit twenty yards from my friend when I'm his guest. I'm leaving.'

Harvey and Anderson coaxed him back to the table. A bagpiper, another of Anderson's folksy inspirations, had started the evening playing doleful Irish music. Powrie, now seated beside Harvey, looked across and saw Kim Novak.

'Hi, Kim!' he called.

The waiter placed a dish of *Prawns Henry Hathaway* before him, and Powrie, who wasn't feeling well, passed out. Harvey and Bryan Forbes lifted him from his chair and carried him from the restaurant. Michael Dwyer insisted they put him to bed in the hotel.

'He made such a marvellous entrance,' said Harvey. 'A pity we have to carry him out.'

Kim Novak popped a cork from a methuselah of champagne. By the time the *Gaelic Coffee Siobhan McKenna* was served the guests were dancing to *céilí* music. Anderson had brought along Brendan Behan's elderly father, a Joxer figure who drank pints of Guinness in preference to champagne. Despite his age the little man danced a jig with Novak.

Of Human Bondage and its problems could wait until next morning.

THE GATES OF Ardmore Studios were closed to everybody not involved in the film, especially when Kim Novak was on the set. Expected to play the teenage Mildred Henry Hathaway had envisaged, she was also struggling with a Cockney accent and taking lessons from a dialogue coach who had been flown from London. Hathaway was impatient with her, but at the start he vented his feelings on others.

'If you're not in this one, please clear off the goddam set. Kim can't emote with people watching. She's got to have peace of mind.' Even Bryan Forbes, who had written the screenplay and was playing Harvey's medical student friend, was ordered off. Hathaway made it obvious he didn't like the script.

Harvey, sensing the film was lost when it had only begun, sent up his own part and the parts of his fellow-actors. His frustration was due as much to Novak's problems with Mildred as to Hathaway's style of direction. They were filming the early scenes in a replica of a Victorian London tea-rooms to which Hathaway

had added a bar and a pool table. He didn't want audiences to
think his love story was, as he said, a piece of crap about long-
haired tea drinkers. Whenever Novak fluffed a line, Hathaway
would say, 'Cut', and Harvey would add, 'Christ, not again!'

Hathaway's method of drawing a good performance from his
actors was to growl, 'Come on, come on! React, can't you?' After
a few days Harvey wasn't quite sure what he was supposed to be
reacting to. The Maugham novel was reduced to a series of
novelettish situations in which the student with a complex about
his club foot had an affair with a waitress who tried to ruin him
before conveniently dying of syphilis.

When Harvey dined at the Soup Bowl he would tell friends it
made a change to watch another director making a fool of himself.
When not on the set he would cross to the studios' administrative
offices where film editor Ralph Kemplen was in a basement
cutting room editing *The Ceremony.* The fact that he could see his
own film in its final assembly eased the tensions created for him on
the set of *Of Human Bondage.*

He liked to discuss new projects in the Soup Bowl until the
small hours of the morning, sometimes until seven, when it was
time for Harry Barr to drive him to the studios.

'Come on, come on!' he would urge Barr, ordering him to push
the Jaguar over the ton on the south lanes of the dual carriageway.
They would take a side road to the studio complex and park
behind the construction block so that Harvey could slip into his
dressing room unnoticed.

Hathaway didn't like to be kept waiting. When Harvey strolled
onto the set in his student gown, the script in its leather holder
under his arm, Hathaway would look at his watch.

'Larry, we do have to work this morning.'

'Unavoidable, Henry. That damned chauffeur of mine delayed
me. I waited and waited outside the hotel. One can't trust these
Irish drivers.'

When the sound stage door was rolled up and the actors and
technicians strolled out for lunch, Harvey would greet Barr with
a wide grin.

'I told them I'm going to sack you, Harry.'

Soon after Kim Novak arrived in Dublin, Harvey asked her to dinner. She made the excuse of another engagement.

'Well, what about to-morrow evening?' he asked.

'I don't think so. Not to-morrow.'

'What about an evening later this week?'

'I guess I don't know what I'm doing later in the week.'

His pride was hurt because few other women would have refused an invitation to dinner with Laurence Harvey.

When Yousef Karsh arrived for a special photographic session with Novak at the Old Conna the Ardmore carpenters were ordered to transform a room in the hotel into a studio. A few days later a woman photographer arrived from the United States to take pictures of Harvey for a chain of Japanese papers.

'I'm as popular as *saki* over there,' Harvey said.

The tension on the set became intolerable. Harvey was rude to Novak. She, miserable over her efforts to come to grips with Mildred, was asking Seven Arts to find another director. Hathaway was getting angry with Harvey and losing patience with Novak. After a particularly poor 'take' Hathaway called, 'Cut', adding, 'I can't take any more of this goddam picture.'

And he walked off the set for good.

Seven Arts acted swiftly. Writer-director Bryan Forbes was named temporary director until another director could be found. The set at Ardmore was closed. Interviews were forbidden. No outsiders were allowed past the gates. But the security measures didn't stop thieves taking Kim Novak's wallet and passport.

The scenes Forbes directed were with Harvey and Siobhan McKenna, who was playing Nora, the other woman in Philip Carey's life. Kim Novak was unavailable. The Old Conna said she had left for a tour of Ireland. Three days later she was seen boarding the last 'plane out of Dublin for London. She was rumoured to be bound for Paris, Berlin, even Scotland. She was, in fact, visiting the Fleet Street columnist Roderick Mann and the London papers announced that the couple planned to marry.

The Vatican newspaper *Osservatore Romano,* usually critical of film people, decided to praise the actress. The paper reported that she had walked out of the film because the producer insisted she wore low-cut dresses.

> *Once again the stars appear better than the production, which for calculations of earnings seeks to impose the least decorous and dignified considerations, often harmful to the moral and artistic dignity of the person.*

A day later, just as Seven Arts were admitting they had no idea where she was, Novak came striding through the customs hall of Dublin Airport wearing a black suit, black stockings and a cossack hat. 'I've lost interest in this film,' she announced. 'I'd like someone else to take over my part. But if they can't find a replacement I'm prepared to go on with it because I feel I'm under an obligation.'

The production company told reporters, 'Kim is a good girl. We knew she wouldn't let us down.' Behind the scenes they had sought to persuade Elizabeth Taylor to accept the role of Mildred, and Novak knew this. Ken Hughes, who had been named as the director to take over from Forbes, left Dublin for dinner with Elizabeth Taylor at London's Dorchester Hotel.

HARVEY BELIEVED LIFE was to be lived and enjoyed, and because he lived for the present he was not nostalgic. He continued to dine at the Soup Bowl. Sometimes Joan Cohn was with him, sometimes James Woolf, but just now his dinner companion was Bryan Forbes. The evening would start pleasantly enough. He would order fillet of steak with cauliflower *au gratin,* sprinkled with grated Parmesan cheese, and Mornay sauce. He never ate the meat, preferring to chew it, swallow the juice and place the residue on his plate. The conversation might be about Hathaway, and Harvey would remark that he disliked discipline and people who shouted at him – it reminded him of South Africa and the

Army. He and Forbes would argue about how the film should be directed now that Hathaway was gone.

Harvey disliked taking direction from Forbes as much as he had from Hathaway. Forbes was a contemporary and a friend, which made it imperative that Harvey should have the last word. When the argument became noisy Kathy Powrie would ask him:

'If you want to have a board meeting, go upstairs.'

If they pretended not to hear, she would say to Harvey:

'It's all very well, Larry. You started us off in this restaurant, but we can't carry on if you continue to make scenes. Nobody will come in.'

Larry would look at her, take his glass of Pouilly Fumé and walk upstairs followed by Forbes.

The two men, Harvey tall and elegant, Forbes small and dapper, would continue the debate out of the other diners' earshot. Then Forbes would come downstairs, get into his white Rolls-Bentley and drive away. Harvey would follow in the Jaguar.

Half an hour later they would both be back.

'Oh!' Kathy would exclaim, 'so you've decided to stay?'

ON THE MONDAY after Kim Novak's return to Dublin, production resumed under the new director, Ken Hughes, a slight, prematurely grey forty-year-old, who had his own ideas about the film. Seven Arts thought highly of his talent. He had just made *The Small World of Sammy Lee* and his future was promising. 'A brilliant young man,' was how they described him. 'He's going to do the picture his way. Furthermore, he's a writer and he may decide to re-write entire scenes.'

This was news to Bryan Forbes, who considered himself, and was, an experienced writer and was already at work in a penthouse suisuite of the Gresham Hotel preparing a mammoth screenplay on the life of Winston Churchill. It was also news to Siobhan McKenna who had been directed in most of her scenes by Forbes. She was so upset she became ill.

When Harvey heard that Forbes was also to be replaced in the cast by another actor, Jack Hedley, and that Hughes was to re-shoot most of the film, he felt he could not continue. James Woolf and the Seven Arts producers Ray Stark and Kenneth Hyman were trying to keep *Bondage* on the rails, and the head of MGM, the distributors of the film, arrived in Dublin to see if there would be any film to distribute. Any hopes Harvey had of a new Mildred were dashed when Elizabeth Taylor, despite the persuasion of Ken Hughes, turned down the part of Mildred. After *Cleopatra* and *The V.I.P.s* she said she was tired.

Hughes spent the week before Easter shooting the love scene between Harvey and a nude Kim Novak. Harvey was less than passionate.

'He has been eating an onion,' said a disconsolate James Woolf.

JAMES WOOLF HAD flew into Dublin ahead of Laurence Harvey and Kim Novak, and was installed in an office at Ardmore studios. He had stayed long enough at the Shelbourne Hotel to enquire about a suitable suite for 'my friend Laurence Harvey.'

When the manager suggested Suite 226 he inspected it, but immediately rejected it.

'This will not do for Mr. Harvey,' he told the manager. 'I won't have it. Can't you make Suite 316 available?'

'I'm sorry, sir, it's occupied.'

Woolf was adamant. 'Then I shall have to go elsewhere.'

Suite 226 looked onto grey government offices, whereas 316 had a sylvan view of St. Stephen's Green. The management, anxious not to lose Harvey's custom, made Suite 316 available a few days after Harvey's arrival in Dublin. The saturnine and quietly-spoken Woolf moved into a penthouse suite at the Gresham Hotel. He was seldom seen around the Shelbourne once Joan Cohn had arrived to join Harvey there, although the actor and producer sometimes dined together at the Soup Bowl where Peter Powrie would uncork Woolf's favourite wine, Hospice de Beaune.

'Jimmy Woolf was sophisticated and civilised,' Powrie remembered, 'with a quiet sense of humour. There was a tremendous rapport between him and Harvey; they respected each other's talents and theirs was a unique friendship. Woolf was Harvey's closest friend.'

Powrie sensed that Woolf was a sick man. When Woolf argued with Harvey about the artistic side of film-making and what was best for him, it was plain that he was in command.

'I suspected he didn't believe Larry was serious about Joan Cohn, though he may have feared that Columbia Pictures would manipulate Harvey's career if he were to marry Joan.'

Woolf had a routine. His chauffeur called to his hotel in the mornings around nine to drive him to the studios. In the evening he returned directly to the Gresham where he rarely dined, preferring to cross the Liffey to the Russell Hotel. He smoked large cigars with Churchillian aplomb and felt vulnerable in those early Spring days without his heavy sheepskin coat. His chauffeur bought his cigars at a tobacconist's near the studios and collected his barbiturates from the local chemist's.

The ferment surrounding the production of *Bondage* affected Woolf, a highly sensitive man. He grew more reticent and Harvey found him edgy, even caustic.

One evening when Woolf was dropped as usual at the Gresham he told his chauffeur to collect him next morning. He seemed to be paler and more tense than usual. He had had angry words with Harvey and the actor had left him, peeved by the row.

Woolf went to his suite and called the Shelbourne. He asked for Harvey. Joan Cohn said he wasn't available. Woolf called again and was given the same reply. Harvey had told Joan that he wasn't taking calls from Woolf.

Later that night, after dinner at his hotel, Woolf was found by a housemaid, unconscious in his suite. The house doctor summoned an ambulance and Woolf was rushed through the back door of the hotel to the nearby hospital at Jervis Street, suffering from an overdose of barbiturates.

Harvey was entertaining friends at the Shelbourne when he was told that Woolf was seriously ill. He had given his chauffeur the night off and Barr had taken the Jaguar. He dashed down the stairs to the lobby where the doorman called him a taxi. He went first to the Gresham, then to Jervis Street. He paced the dreary, green-walled waiting room of the hospital until they told him that Woolf was out of danger.

Next morning he rebuked Barr.

'Never take the Jaguar again without telling me where I can contact you in an emergency.'

As they drove to the studios, he asked, 'What did you hear about Mr. Woolf?'

Barr said, 'I did hear something . . .'

'Don't you bloody believe it,' said Harvey. 'There's nothing wrong with Mr. Woolf. He's taking pills because he's in pain. He had a serious operation for haemorrhoids in America.'

'How is Mr. Woolf?' Barr asked.

'It was a near thing,' admitted Harvey.

The story of Woolf's overdose was kept from the newspapers and the hotel was discreet about the incident. At the studios it was agreed that he was lucky to be alive. Most people who had heard the news believed that Woolf had taken twice his usual dose of pills by mistake.

At the Soup Bowl that night Harvey talked emotionally to Powrie about his friend, who was still in hospital.

'I hope he'll be okay. Jimmy's my life and my love.'

When Woolf recovered he returned to his office at the film studios and resumed his place at Harvey's table in the Soup Bowl. He made light of what had happened. Powrie remembered, 'Although he looked ill he was the same man to me. He chatted and even laughed with Larry about the film business.

'I liked Jimmy very, very much.'

17 | 'Has my book created such problems?' asked Maugham.

ON THE THURSDAY BEFORE EASTER, FOUR DAYS AFTER KEN HUGHES had taken over as director, the unit of *Of Human Bondage* disbanded for the holiday week-end. Harvey flew from Dublin to Paris to make arrangements to meet the man who had created the character of Philip Carey, the novelist Somerset Maugham, now ninety years old. He then flew on to Nice, drove to St. Jean-Cap Ferrat and up to the Villa Mauresque with the Moorish sign against the Evil Eye on the garden wall. At the top of a steep driveway stood the great house, overlooking the Mediterranean and the curving coastline.

Harvey, who had not condescended to ask either John Braine or Richard Condon about their screen characters, was making a pilgrimage to seek the advice of The Master.

Maugham, a slight, frail, solitary figure, came out to greet him as he reached the terrace. When they sat down for drinks at a table beneath the cypresses Harvey began to talk about the book and the character of Philip Carey.

The old man listened, his wizened face turned to the young actor. Then he said, drily:

'I'm in complete agreement with you. But I must tell you I haven't read the book since it was published in 1915. It contains memories that for their pain I want above everything to forget.'

Harvey knew that Maugham's most popular novel was autobiographical; he knew of Maugham's all-consuming attachment to his mother and of his pronounced stammer, still perceptible, which had been transmuted into the club foot of Philip Carey.

When they adjourned for lunch in the dining-room downstairs Maugham surprised the actor with his questions about the film. Who had written the screenplay? Who was the director? How far did the locations in Dublin approximate to Victorian London? And who was playing Mildred?

Harvey outlined the production problems to Maugham and wondered if the old man understood.

'Has my book,' asked Maugham almost apologetically, 'created such ... difficulties for you?'

As they finished lunch the author mentioned Mildred.

'She did exist, you know. She had this ... terrible fascination for every man who ... met her, and we were all her victims. I admired her honesty in ... spite of her faults.'

He grew silent at the table; then he said, 'She ... died only a few years ago.'

When they parted on the terrace Maugham shook Harvey's hand. 'Thank you for coming, young man. Your youth and ... pep have quite cheered me up.'

Harvey hesitated, as if seeking the Master's *imprimatur* for his role in the film. As though he had read his mind, the author said, 'I'm glad you are playing the part ... of my hero.'

He hadn't told Maugham that during a break in the filming he had 'phoned a Seven Arts executive in New York half-intending to ask for his release from the production. The executive remarked, 'This picture has cost 750,000 dollars to set up.'

Harvey was silent. The voice asked, 'Are you still there?'

'Yes,' he answered. 'I was just wondering where I could raise 750,000 dollars.'

Back in Paris he remembered Kathy Powrie telling him how difficult it was to find her favourite perfume in Dublin. He bought her two eight-ounce bottles of Sortilège La Galliene, and Joan bought her an enamelled perfume spray and an umbrella with a black diamanté handle.

KEN HUGHES, PLEASED about his direction of *The Small World of Sammy Lee,* and undaunted when called on by Seven Arts to take over *Bondage,* pushed ahead with his plans to re-write Forbes' script and re-shoot Hathaway's scenes. He was surprised to discover the producers filming such a photogenic story in black and white. And when they checked him into a suite at the Old Conna next door to Kim Novak's, he could only assume they were in such a state of nervous tension they were not reacting normally.

'By the time I came to the production it was rather like a mutinous ship aboard which I was expected to keep the peace,' he recalled. 'They had given up the budget and the schedule. It was a job that demanded more tact than discretion. I could only describe it as horrendous.

'My relationship with Kim Novak went from instant love to instant hate. She was pretty tempestuous. She started out by thinking that I had come to save her life, but when she discovered that I was just another director I think she set out to 'tame' me.

'But my job was to bring the picture in, so I didn't care. They had told me about her dislike of Henry Hathaway; now I felt she hated me, which put me in good company. I used to think, "Well, Hathaway couldn't handle her and he has made more films than I have seen." '

WHEN A FINAL print of *The Ceremony* arrived from the film laboratories Harvey decided to screen it for his friends in a small art cinema on the Dublin quays. Beforehand there was a lavish party in the Soup Bowl. It would have been wiser to hold the party *after* the screening.

The tables were laden with cold meats, roast chicken, plovers' eggs, fresh salmon, Dublin Bay prawns and bottles of Pouilly Fumé. The small restaurant was so crowded that some people took their food and wine into the laneway. Just before midnight the high-spirited guests made their way from the Soup Bowl to the cinema. The numbers were greater than Harvey had anticipated.

Word of the late-night screening of a new Laurence Harvey film had spread and a crowd had gathered outside the cinema. When the auditorium was so crowded that even the aisles were filled with sprawling figures the street doors were closed.

Above the hubbub Harvey lifted the 'phone at the back of the stalls and ordered the operator to start the screening. There was a respectful silence as the curtains parted and the titles for *The Ceremony* came up. The print was poorly projected and, as much of the film had been shot at night and many of the scenes were in dark prison interiors, it wasn't easy even for the more sober guests to follow the story. The audience soon became restless. After the Pouilly Fumé many were taken short. The cinema had only a centre aisle, so those in the seats nearest the walls had difficulty in getting past other guests to reach the aisle. Then they had to step over people seated on the floor to reach the toilets. The toilet doors swung to and fro and from within could be heard the sound of cisterns flushing.

Outside the cinema those who had arrived late were hammering at the glass doors. Harvey rushed into the foyer. His own voice could be heard simultaneously with his dialogue on the screen. He shouted to the crowd outside:

'Go away! Piss off! We're trying to watch a serious work of art.'

Afterwards a subdued audience filed out, not quite sure what they had seen; some of them had slept through the film and could not be expected to give an opinion. Harvey was dejected, but he invited everybody back to the Soup Bowl.

Even if they had not been asked they would have gone.

The Ceremony was soon forgotten. A drunken writer edged his way up to Harvey to ask, 'D'you know who's throwing the party?'

'I'm not quite sure who the host is,' Harvey said, 'but I know I'm the star.'

Joan Cohn had returned to California. *Of Human Bondage* dragged on. Harvey planned other films of his own. Whatever the fate of *The Ceremony* at the box office, he intended to press on with Alistair MacLean's *The Golden Rendezvous,* which he felt contained humanity, terror and a dash of Ian Fleming. But this

time he would hire a co-producer. He had also bought the film
rights of *The Reason Why* from Herbert Wilcox, who had once
considered making it at a great cost and with a large cast headed
by his wife Anna Neagle. Harvey didn't want to make self-in-
dulgent films, but he believed a film-maker should say something
worthwhile, no matter what the *schmoeks* behind the executive
desks in Hollywood might think.

He was irritable and could not conceal his impatience. One
afternoon Harry Barr drove from the studios to the local town of
Bray to collect his secretary's shoes. When he got back Harvey was
waiting outside the administrative block. He got into the car with
his secretary. To Barr he said curtly:

'Where were you?'

'Collecting your secretary's shoes, Mr. Harvey.'

'I see. Let's get back to the hotel. I'm late.'

Barr knew he wasn't late. They drove into Dublin in silence.

At the Shelbourne, Harvey confronted the chauffeur.

'Remember this', he said. 'The Jaguar is mine. I use that car and
nobody else. If my secretary wishes to collect her shoes then she
can hire a car or take a taxi or have her shoes sent to her, but
under no circumstances must you or my car be used to fetch other
people's messages.'

'I understand, Mr. Harvey.'

In the mornings he would examine the Jaguar. The wheel rims
had to be shining, the tan leather upholstery spotless, the ashtrays
clean. Joan Cohn and James Woolf were among the few friends
allowed to ride in the car. He would drive past people he knew.
'Don't stop. Not on your life,' he would say to Barr.

He was drinking brandy again. One night he called the room
service waiter and complained that his drink had been watered.
The waiter sampled the brandy from the bottle. It was true, he
admitted. The brandy had been jipped by some person unknown.
Harvey strode towards him shouting, 'Do you want your head put
through the mirror?'

The waiter drew back, apologising and insisting that neither he
nor any of the hotel staff had tampered with the bottle.

'Don't lie to me!' screamed Harvey. 'I'll put you through that bloody window!'

When his anger subsided he talked to the waiter of his lousy day on the film set. 'I come from Lithuania. Did you know that? I'm Jewish and I've had a rough life. But whatever I've got for myself through hard work I intend to keep.'

Novak, he vowed, wouldn't stand in his way. On the day they filmed the hospital scene in which she was supposed to be dying he said to her, 'You bitch, I hope you never get off that bloody bed.'

Her chauffeur warned Barr, 'One of these days, mate, I'm going to take a poke at that Harvey. He gave Kim a hell of a time on the set to-day. She was in tears all the way home.'

Harvey 'phoned Joan Cohn in Hollywood. She listened sympathetically. He had called her every night since she returned to California and sometimes they talked for half an hour. His old sinus complaint was bothering him. Once it pained him so much he knocked his head in agony against his bedroom wall. He arranged for a doctor to come from London to treat him.

'I brought a man from Harley Street,' he said afterwards. 'I paid him his 'plane fare and hotel expenses and what happened? He charged me a hundred quid.'

ONE AFTERNOON towards the end of June they finished filming *Of Human Bondage*.

'Is that it?' asked Hughes.

The lighting cameraman nodded. 'That's it, Ken.'

'Then print the last take.'

Hughes walked off the set and got into his Ford Galaxie. He never wanted to hear about *Of Human Bondage* again. He didn't want to see it. He wanted no say in the editing. He was going to drive to Dublin Airport, put his car on the air ferry and drive to Italy for a holiday.

But there was one last chore. He had bought a toy machine-gun and, as he reversed his car outside the administrative block and turned towards the driveway, he saw Kim Novak.

He grabbed the gun from the seat, pointed it through the window at her, and shouted '*Rat-tat-tat-tat-tat!*'

HARVEY GAVE a farewell party in the Soup Bowl. He was relieved that the filming was over and pleased that he had been able to reach people in Dublin as he never could in London, Paris or New York. He would return to Hollywood next day. It was six thousand miles away, but he reckoned he would pass through Shannon now and then.

Siobhan McKenna said to him during the party, 'You know, Larry, you don't look at people any more.'

Her words jolted him.

'You should look actors in the eyes,' she continued, 'but you're not doing that.'

'I look at you, Siobhan.'

'Yes, but you used to look at your fellow-actors.' She meant that actors must respond to one another, but because of the trouble-ridden production Harvey had been playing it solo.

'I wasn't aware of it,' he told her.

'I'm sorry if I've hurt your feelings, Larry. But we've always been truthful to each other.'

He knew what she said was true.

Barr drove him to the airport in the Jaguar. The Rolls would be waiting for him at Los Angeles. He had asked the chauffeur to come to California with him to be his driver and Joan's.

'You're coming back with me, Harry,' he said.

But Barr, a family man, decided not to accept. Harvey put his arm around him and began to cry. The chauffeur, standing there in his navy blue uniform and cap and the gloves Harvey had bought for him, was touched, but embarrassed.

IT WAS ONLY when *Of Human Bondage* had been running in London's West End for two weeks that MGM decided to invite the critics. Their verdict was 'repetitious', 'melodramatic', 'clumsy', 'pretty awful' and 'a colossal bore'. Kim Novak's Cockney waitress was praised at the expense of Harvey. 'Laurence Harvey as the student,' wrote one critic, 'looks desperate. Well he might.'

The London *Times* didn't even mention his name.

18 | 'I'll always think of Cabrillo as Larry Harvey's house.'

BEVERLY HILLS, JUNE 1974.

The house at the top of Cabrillo Drive lay still in the afternoon sun; it wasn't empty, for much of Harvey's eclectic furnishings remained, but it was tenantless. One drove there from Sunset Boulevard, along Beverly Drive until it plunged into Coldwater Canyon, then took a sharp, almost hidden, left turn into Cabrillo. At the top of the hilly, winding Drive, among the orange and lemon trees, stood the extraordinary, one-level white house.

The anonymous double doors didn't prepare one for the interior. All the major spaces looked towards Los Angeles and the Pacific Ocean, the white brick and plasterwork, the terrazzo flooring and dark walnut fittings forming a background for Harvey's paintings, sculptures and antique furniture.

The main area, comprising a living-dining-entertaining room, had a fifteen-foot oak bar with settees, chairs and footstools in a knubbly fabric to match the off-white carpets from Edward Fields in New York. From above the bar a movie screen could be lowered for 35mm projection from a special room adjoining the kitchen. In the master bedroom a canopy bed had blue linen to match the wallpaper and a study adjoined the bedroom with a Louis XVI desk and black leather sofas and chairs.

Even the toilet had its special elegance. The washbasin and bath were set in marble surrounds and the faucets were gold-plated.

The mirror above the washbasin was ringed with light bulbs like a star's dressing-room.

All these rooms faced onto the swimming pool and terrace, beyond which the hillside dropped towards the valley, and the distant city and ocean.

On the east side of the house Harvey had built an extension for himself, comprising a den, a barbecue room and a sauna. Even without the extension the Cabrillo Drive was probably the most expensive one-bedroomed house ever built. But that had been the briefing to two Hollywood architects fifteen years earlier.

WHEN HARVEY FIRST WENT to Hollywood he stayed, as did James Woolf, in an apartment at the pink-washed Beverly Hills Hotel. Later he rented a bachelor house with a small swimming pool at 9208 Cordell Mews, a tree-lined lane off Doheny Drive. When he was making *Butterfield 8* Helen Rose, the film's couturière, had just had a house built by two architects who lectured at the University of Southern California, Conrad Buff and Donald Hensman. She told Harvey about them and showed him her house. He liked it, and from the moment he met the architects there was rapport. Buff and Hensman realised he was a frustrated architect and Harvey saw his opportunity to create a dream house in a setting which appealed to him.

He had found a hillside site on Cabrillo Drive and sketched a rough outline of what he wanted: a modern house in classic style, a house that was elegant, timeless and spacious and devoid of the Spanish-type arches and vaults all too frequent in Californian houses. Although it was to be a one-bedroom house it would have a wine cellar, a swimming pool and a sauna room. He accepted the inevitable compromises between client and architect because he saw that Buff and Hensman were, like himself, young, energetic and enthusiastic.

While the house on Cabrillo was building he bought an already-completed house on Swallow Drive which he remodelled and fitted with a swimming pool. That house became James Woolf's when Harvey moved into Joan Cohn's mansion on North Crescent Drive across from the Beverly Hills Hotel.

'Our first Christmas gift to him,' recalled Donald Hensman, 'was a miniature drawing board with a tee-square and pencils. He loved it. He was forever sketching.' The only snag, Hensman said afterwards, was that Harvey was always on the move.

When he arrived back in California after *Of Human Bondage* Buff and Hensman were completing the building of yet another house which Harvey planned as the biggest and most beautiful on Malibu Beach. When he first went to Hollywood he loved to drive in the evenings along the Pacific Coast Highway to Malibu. He would park his Thunderbird by the roadside and stride down to the water's edge, declaiming to the breakers as they crashed on the beach under the dying sun. His friend Wolf Mankowitz considered Malibu a gilded slum, but to Harvey the beach and its people were the essence of hedonism as he sought it.

The plot he bought was seventy-foot wide with piles for building on. He took the house next door for Hensman so that he could be on the site to hurry the workmen.

The living room of the new house was sunk two feet below beach level, mainly to prevent passers-by from staring in, and the twenty-foot-high window had 184 stained glass panes. A dining room, kitchen and steam room opened off the living room and above them were two master bedroom suites, one of which could be used as a study, with redwood balconies on which one could sleep on warm nights. This part of the house was separated by a patio from the servants' quarters and garages which faced the highway. Some of the fittings had come from the set of *Of Human Bondage,* notably the big chandelier which hung in the living room and the bar handles that adorned the front door.

Don Hensman thought the house a miniature San Simeon. Harvey didn't argue about the cost, although his money was controlled by attorneys and accountants and the architects had to keep within a budget; he was more concerned with how his jewel-box of a house should look. Each time he returned to

California from across the world he would have conjured up additions to the house, adding thousands of dollars to the original cost.

'I guess it was the frustrated architect in him,' said Hensman. 'After he had been away for a while he would come back here as if to get the ideas out of his system.'

Harvey thought of buying a second beach house and installing a swimming pool.

'You're out of your goddam mind,' said Hensman. 'You never go swimming.'

But Harvey was thinking of his friends and his chauffeur. 'It would be rather nice,' he said.

Hensman knew that this plan would also undergo a sea change. 'He kept travelling to and fro across the Atlantic, never resting, never settling down.'

When the big jets began their scheduled flights between Europe and the States, Harvey and John Ireland were both working on films in London. They would arrange to finish their week's filming early on Friday in time to catch the afternoon 'plane to New York.

Everything would be arranged for them. They would have a drink in the VIP lounge at Heathrow, knowing their bags were stowed safely under their seats on the aircraft and the Pouilly Fuissé was chilling in the fridge. At New York a limousine would rush them from the airport to the smart '21' club on West 52nd Street where a fleet-footed doorman would open the car door so they could dash to the standup bar before a late lunch or an early dinner that was served from five in the afternoon.

Their bags would have been checked into the Sherry Netherlands Hotel where they would spend the weekend. On Sunday night they would fly back to London, arriving at six in the morning in time to reach the studios by eight.

Hensman discovered the best place to contact Harvey was in the smallest room; only in the toilet did the star find the privacy he secretly craved. At the Malibu beach house the toilet was fitted with a telephone, intercom and stereo music system. After taking his habitual laxative pills he would retire there to read scripts.

He detested wasted moments.

IN THE HILLS, at 1196 Cabrillo Drive, Cody Wietzel, a bearded young man in purple shirt, blue jeans and stetson, from Harvey's accountants' office in Los Angeles, stood looking at the white house among the trees.

'I'll always think of this as Larry Harvey's house,' he said. 'He lives on in this house. He was a gentleman – a combination of chivalry and temperament, and you don't get that any more.

'But, of course, I'm from the mid-west and this is really not my style of house.'

CLAIRE BLOOM HAD co-starred with Harvey in *The Wonderful World of the Brothers Grimm,* 'a film of which neither of us was particularly proud.' The few times they had talked together on that production the topic had been the theatre; both of them had been members of the Old Vic. 'I thought he looked a bit of a wide boy,' Claire Bloom recalled. 'It was something to do with the way he wore his hair. I suppose it was a kind of disguise.'

Early in 1964 she played his wife in a Western, *The Outrage,* with Paul Newman. 'It was nearly a good film,' she said. On this occasion she observed him more closely, especially during the six weeks they spent on location in the Arizona desert near Tucson.

When an open horse-drawn carriage in which they were travelling started overturning, Harvey jumped clear and caught her as she fell. 'He was very masculine in that way, yet he gave the impression of being effete. I had heard certain unsavoury stories about him, but I decided to take him at his face value. I realised he was a self-made man and attracted to people with power and money. There was nothing he could get from me, yet he was very protective, very charming and extremely thoughtful.

'He didn't let you see very deeply. He covered up with a lot of rubbish.'

At Tucson they stayed at an unprepossessing hotel. Harvey had brought his stereo recorder and tapes with him. When they returned to Hollywood they continued to film on location outside the city. 'There was a lot of hanging around. It took three days to film a particular scene. We were beside a hill, almost a mountain, and I remember Larry saying, "Let's climb it."

'We started off and he was moving much faster than me. Oh, my God, I thought. I know he likes only older women, so I've got to keep up with him.

'But climbing that hill with Larry was beautiful. That was a magical day.'

WHEN HE GOT back to Beverly Hills Joan Cohn was in London, recovering from pneumonia. He wrote to her:

Darling,
I've been continually kept informed as to your progress and am thrilled all seems to be going well. The house seems so empty without you and we all miss you so much. It's awful not to have you screaming at us and barking at us and putting your two fingers up at us and being annoyed with us and loving us and barking at us and playing with us and getting drunk with us and keeping sober with us. OH HELL, get well!
                                        Miss you and love you, darling,
                                        Larry.

IN MAY OF 1964 he wrote to Nahum from the house on Cabrillo Drive telling him of *The Outrage* and also of a play, *The Time of the Barracudas,* which had closed in California 'with an enormous loss to myself and the company.' He thought he had reached the end of his financial resources. Now it was 'almost like starting all over again in every way,' but this was one of the hazards of his profession.

I have very little to say about my life at the moment except that I have finally decided to stop the endless succession of pictures which have done my career no good at all as they were handled extremely badly and we always have to suffer for others' mistakes.

I am now determined to be much more meticulous in choosing what type of film and play I will do in the future, even if it means a great financial sacrifice. The longing that I have to get back into the theatre has finally resulted in my doing Camelot in London for a six month season and we start rehearsals at the beginning of July, opening at the end of August at Drury Lane. It will be a new experience for me as I have never been in this type of show before and I am exploring a new field as far as the theatre is concerned. I am now busy taking singing lessons (ha! ha! ha!) and devoting most of my time to the study of the part that I am to do in the play and at the same time trying to organise my life for whatever the future may have in store for me.

He flew to London in July to start rehearsals for his role as King Arthur in the Lerner and Loewe musical. Four years previously this musical version of T. H. White's book *The Once and Future King* had opened with Richard Burton in the lead on Broadway to advance bookings worth three million dollars. The role was a challenge to Harvey; he was expected to sing convincingly and dance creditably. The London impresario Jack Hylton was sinking more money in *Camelot* than he had sunk in any previous show, but although Harvey loved his part he had a six months' 'get out' clause written into his contract. His £400 a week from *Camelot* was not enough to live on.

During the rehearsals Joan Cohn remained in California. It was three and a half years since their first meeting and Harvey marked the occasion before leaving for London by posting her a gift from Los Angeles International Airport of a gold rose encrusted with diamonds. The accompanying note read:

Just a small token of my love always, darling, for your 3½ birthday. How miserable I am to be separated AGAIN. But I promise I'll get pissed with you regardless.

> *Love, Love,*
> *L. of Lithuania,*
> *South Africa,*
> *Great Britain and*
> *Ireland,*
> *Palm Springs,*
> *Beverly Hills.*

Elizabeth Larner, who was to play Queen Guinevere, was daunted by her co-star's screen reputation. But when Harvey squeezed her arm at the auditions and said, 'Heavens above, she's just a baby!', she felt reassured. Soon after rehearsals began she found him uncertain about his singing voice and suggested he take lessons from her teacher, Harold Miller. Every day before the show Miller gave him a short lesson and, despite the demands of the role, Harvey's voice showed no strain during the run.

He occupied the large number one dressing room at Drury Lane, which had an even larger receiving room. His Rolls Royce stood outside the stage door, an obvious status symbol. On the first night Alan Jay Lerner and Frederick Loewe, the show's creators, were in the audience and came backstage afterwards. Lerner was excited. He said to Harvey:

'We didn't have an ovation like that for the opening of *My Fair Lady.*'

'Fritz' Loewe was happy, too, but he surprised Elizabeth Larner by telling her:

'How does it feel to be singing the last lines of music I shall ever write?'

'The last lines?'

'That number you sing – *Before I Gaze At You Again.* That was the last song I wrote for the show. And I don't plan to write again.'

The walls of Harvey's dressing room were papered with telegrams. The Burtons' telegram said that if they had been able to choose a new Arthur it would have been Larry. Harvey, had they but known it, had wanted to play King Arthur since Moss Hart, the stage producer, had given him a copy of T. II. White's book at the time of *Room at the Top.*

Night after night, having slipped off his heavily-encrusted medieval costume for a white towelling robe, he greeted his visitors, some with kisses, all with champagne: James Woolf, John Woolf, Richard Condon, Noël Coward, Kirk Douglas, Natalie Wood, Rosalind Russell. Condon and his wife had gone to the show in some trepidation.

'I'll be damned,' said Condon afterwards, 'but he pulled it off. It was sheer nerve. He got out there and he sang. And how he could project his voice! I remember Sol Hurok saying that Larry could hit the back row with his voice.

'He wore a cloak in *Camelot* which was so heavy even Paul Robeson couldn't have stood up in it. It probably felt like a feather to Larry.'

Towards his guests Harvey behaved royally, towards his subjects in the cast he was never overbearing.

'At first we held him in awe,' said Elizabeth Larner, 'because he was the big star. But soon he was Larry to us all. He made the show happy and marvellous.'

Between matinées and evening performances his chauffeur would bring him two newly-laid eggs and fresh rye bread for tea. Invariably Harvey would give two slices of bread to his leading lady. With the favourable notices for *Camelot* he had salvaged a good deal of his waning reputation as a stage actor. Sitting in an armchair in his dressing room and flourishing a cigarette holder he held court to the journalists. To Godfrey Winn, who found him eating an egg for his tea, he said, 'I shall always feel a little different for having spoken Arthur's speeches and thought deeply about his philosophy. Something has brushed off on me.'

DURING THE RUN of *Camelot* he filmed in *Darling* for John Schlesinger, playing a modest but significant role as Julie Christie's decadent friend. He made the film without a salary because he believed in the project; he was so convinced of its success he agreed to take ten per cent of the distribution profits. He saw little chance of any returns from *The Ceremony* which had been screened at the Cannes Film Festival and stamped by the critics into the dust of their disfavour.

'Harvey performed like a cut-price Kirk Douglas,' wrote one critic. His direction was 'galumphing and slapdash.' The best they could say of him was that he 'assembled his clichés with enthusiasm'. However, the film had taken a bitter look at human nature and Harvey, unlike most of the British directors among whom he was numbered, had shown he was not afraid of emotion.

He was surprised and hurt by the reviews, although not unprepared for them after the Dublin débâcle. He had screened *The Ceremony* in Hollywood for Frank Sinatra, Margot Fonteyn and Vincente Minnelli. They had been enthusiastic, and Minnelli had told him, 'You've had the bad taste to be a good director the first time round.'

He had spent his days on *Of Human Bondage* looking forward to the evenings when he could work on the editing of *The Ceremony*. All he could say now was that his film may not have pleased everybody, but at least it was his own work.

SOON AFTER HARVEY had bought a £6,000 Maserati to supplement his Rolls in London, Don Hensman arrived from Los Angeles. The two men lunched at Wheeler's in London's Soho, drank a couple of bottles of Pouilly Fuissé and set off at high speed in the Maserati, not stopping until they reached Ascot and a famous antique firm. Harvey walked through the rooms identifying the items he had collected, remembering where each one was.

He told Hensman, 'Sambo, I'm going to open my own antique shop in California.' He had called him Sam since the first days of their acquaintance when, writing down the names of players in a poker game one night, he forgot Hensman's first name and wrote 'Sam'. When he was in good humour he called him Sambo.

As soon as *Camelot* was over, he said, he would start an antique business on Robertson Boulevard. Hensman told him the shop was too small to operate successfully. Harvey didn't agree. He was soon planning a branch in Palm Springs, and then he found a motel he dreamed of converting into a bigger antique shop, above which he would build an apartment block with penthouse suites, bars and sauna baths. Hensman told him his schemes made no sense financially.

Harvey's answer was, 'Nonsense, dear heart.'

19 | 'I enjoyed Larry the way I enjoy a meringue.'

IN BRADFORD THEY EXPECTED GRIT ON THE RAIN, BUT THE SUN WAS shining at 'Th' Top,' the cloth cap term for the well-to-do suburbs stretching to the Yorkshire Moors. The stars of *Life at the Top* were filming in style on the croquet lawn of a great house. Honor Blackman, unknown in the days of *Room at the Top,* had forsaken the leatherwear of *The Avengers* television series that had made her famous and was striding about in an elegant tweed suit. Michael Craig drove a vintage M.G. into the grounds of the house for a scene in the film, but he had parked his own Facel Vega around the corner. James Woolf was sitting in a canvas chair on the lawn behind the cameras, trying to look anonymous, which for him wasn't difficult. Jean Simmons was there, coaxed out of retirement to play Laurence Harvey's wife. And Harvey? He was playing the fool between 'takes', hitching up his trousers and looking, as they said in Yorkshire, 'proper gormless.' It was an indication that he wasn't taking the film too seriously.

Still living in Bradford was John Braine. Since *Room at the Top* he had written three more novels, one of them *Life at the Top,* a sequel to his first novel. Harvey had made a dozen films after *Room at the Top,* but only his Sergeant Shaw in *The Manchurian Candidate* had matched his Joe Lampton.

As they waited for the cameras to turn Harvey and Honor Blackman, croquet mallets swinging loosely in their hands, closed their eyes and turned their faces to the sun.

'You know, my love, it has certainly changed around here,' Harvey mused. 'When we were making *Room at the Top* you had only to step outside and you were ready to appear in a minstrel show. Now we're getting suntanned.'

It was 1965. Bradford had changed, with new office blocks replacing the grey buildings that had housed the industrious wool merchants and their workers. The trains were electrified, the air smokeless. But Harvey, although a film star of international repute, hadn't changed in John Braine's eyes, except perhaps that his crew-cut, so conspicuous in *Room at the Top,* had been replaced by his natural quiff.

'It was weird, but I saw no change in Larry Harvey, no change at all. He was still talking of film projects, but they were pretty appalling projects because Larry had no taste in films. He was perfectly amiable, perfectly charming; he was never anything else. But he still wore the mask.

'I think there was a human being somewhere in there, but the thing about Larry was that he belonged really to the past. He was a 'thirties' star, much what you'd expect a traditional film star to be.

'He never gave me the impression that he was using people or offending people. He just didn't give a damn. Maybe this is one of the occupational diseases common to all actors. Who knows, perhaps artists in the end become devoured by their art, even possessed by it? They may exploit others, but in the deeper sense they don't mean to. To be fair, to get anywhere on the stage or in films or television you've got to be ruthless to some extent. You've got to consider your own advantage. I don't mean you must be a thorough-going swine, but as in politics nice guys don't win in acting.

'I liked Larry. I enjoyed him as a good actor. As a personality I enjoyed him in the same way that now and then one enjoys a meringue, but I wouldn't try to live on meringues.'

Braine was unhappy about the approach to *Life at the Top.* He worked closely with the Canadian director Ted Kotcheff before the film began shooting. He helped him choose the locations, introduced him to mill owners and local people, and made suggestions about the story-line and the dialogue, which he believed would be more recognisable in Toronto than Bradford. He was incredulous when they told him the film was to be made in black and white. Kotcheff agreed that times had changed and that audiences expected colour, but James Woolf was adamant.

'It's just stupid,' Braine told Woolf. 'You'll drive audiences away. What you must do is make it in colour, using very lush interiors. Don't you realise the audiences must *feel* that this table cost a thousand pounds, that this woman's dress is real silk?'

He objected, as did Kotcheff, to the casting of Honor Blackman as Joe Lampton's other woman. Kotcheff had wanted Vanessa Redgrave, but Woolf didn't agree she was box-office. Braine thought Jean Simmons should have been given the part, but instead they cast her as Joe's wife. They should have used Heather Sears again. 'The interest to the audience was seeing the same characters again. Instead, they used the old star formula, which by then didn't work at all.'

Harvey, who saw no reason to approach Braine about his portrayal of Joe Lampton in this new setting, had made up his mind that it wouldn't be Lampton Strikes Again. Joe had achieved the riches he sought by paying the price the god of success demands. He and Kotcheff were in agreement about the character of Joe, though Braine believed they had it wrong. 'They were trying to prove precisely what is *not* the point of the book, that Joe had been corrupted by riches and power. The whole point of *Life at the Top* was Joe's dissatisfaction because he hadn't got enough riches and power, which is quite a different thing.

'I tried to get this message home, but nobody received it. I know that Ted had some fearsome quarrels with Jimmy Woolf, but I think if I had put my arguments forcibly to Larry he would have listened.'

Kotcheff, who had made only one feature, *Tiara Tahiti,* and was somewhat inexperienced with stars, found Woolf's interference extremely upsetting. Kotcheff's wife Sylvia noticed that Woolf was bitching about her husband, stirring up trouble which

52. *Above:* Harvey as the hero of *I Am a Camera,* the film of Isherwood's pre-war Berlin, with co-star Julie Harris.

53. *Above:* On location in Berlin for *A Dandy in Aspic* in 1967 Harvey with Mia Farrow.

54. *Below:* The scene Harvey promised would be discreet – Sarah Miles' nude love scene in *The Ceremony.* But the pictures appeared in world newspapers. Harvey is directing the scene.

55. *Below:* Couple with a difference – Harvey and canine friend during the filming of *The Spy With A Cold Nose.*

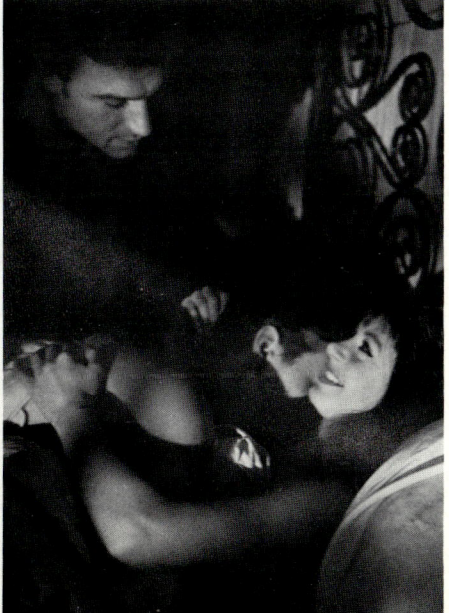

57. *Above:* The ceremony . . . and the kiss. Harvey and Joan
Cohn at their wedding in Nassau, October, 1968.

56. *Below:* Harvey and his second wife, the former Joan Cohn, at
a Hollywood party.

58. *Right:* Harvey's house and swimming pool on Cabrillo Drive. The windows and pool area overlook Los Angeles and the view stretches to the Pacific.

59. *Left:* Entrance hall to the house that Harvey built at the top of Cabrillo Drive in Beverly Hills.

60. *Right:* Living area of Harvey's house on Cabrillo Drive in Beverly Hills. Rear left is a 15-foot bar. From the ceiling a screen is lowered for 35 mm projection.

61. *Left:* Harvey in January 1973 with his new family: Paulene Stone, their daughter Domino (left) and Paulene's daughter Sophie.

62. *Above:* With Kim Novak in a scene from the crisis-ridden film *Of Human Bondage* in Ireland.

63. *Below: Left to right* Harvey, Elizabeth Taylor and Billie Whitelaw in a scene from the film *Night Watch.* Harvey had just returned to the film after a major operation.

producers should avoid. Obviously unwell, he treated those around him, with the exception of Harvey, like servants, ordering them to fetch his drink or his cigars, but more often his pills.

His already large intake of pills had increased. There was a story among the crew that he had given one of his pills to a young film director who was flying to New York and back for a meeting. 'Take one of these,' Woolf had suggested. 'It will relax you. You can have a little doze on the flight and you'll feel fresh when you reach New York.'

The director, it was said, took the pill, slept through the flight and was still sleeping two days later when they flew him back to London.

Kotcheff knew the Woolfs expected a successful film by using the ingredients of *Room at the Top*. Given a free hand, he would have cast the film differently. He would not have used Harvey, and this was no reflection on the actor's abilities.

If Harvey was the star, it was James Woolf who had the last word. When he and Harvey were together there was a curious look in the actor's grey eyes, as though he were under a form of hypnosis induced by Woolf. But there was also a detachment between the two men, not seen during *Room at the Top*. Woolf was now promoting other young actors, notably Terence Stamp, who visited Harvey on the set with the fashion model Jean Shrimpton when the unit returned to the studios.

A TABLE WAS reserved in the Caprice for Saturday lunch for Harvey and his friends, and James Woolf often joined them. No matter how splendid the lunch Harvey ate little. He toyed with his food, drank Pouilly Fuissé, chain-smoked Dunhills through a black-and-gold holder and talked about his projects. Occasionally he sampled an asparagus vinaigrette with a sauce he had created for the Caprice, *Sauce à la Harvey*. If he ordered Dover sole it was merely to nibble at the fish bones. And when he ordered baked potatoes the waiters knew what he wanted were the skins, bone-dry and grilled to a frazzle. If his guests hoped to impress him they pretended to a taste for potato skins.

Terence Stamp, who had made his debut as the innocent sailor in *Billy Budd* and followed this with the delinquent schoolboy in *Term of Trial,* was sharing a flat with a hard-up actor, Michael Caine, whose real name was Maurice Micklewhite. One Saturday Stamp asked him to come to lunch with Harvey.

'I can't afford the Caprice, mate, unless someone else is writing the cheque,' Caine said. 'It takes me all my time to buy Spaghetti Bolognese.' Stamp assured him that Romulus would pick up the cheque.

Caine found Harvey a flash character, but he was surprised when Harvey recalled he had seen him the year previously in a television play, *The Compartment,* a two-hander set in a railway carriage in which Caine had played a working class boy trying to communicate with an older man from the bowler hat class, Frank Finlay. Harvey had liked the play and Caine's performance; he even remembered that Johnny Speight was the author.

Caine was surprised at Harvey's memory for detail; obviously he wasn't the surface personality depicted by film publicists and newspaper columnists. Talking to him across the table at the Caprice, he saw him as creative, shrewd and witty.

When Lewis Gilbert acquired the film rights of Bill Naughton's play *Alfie* entrepreneur Leslie Grade agreed to become involved in the production. Then James Woolf bought his way in and suggested Harvey for the lead.

'Impossible, Jimmy', said Gilbert. 'Larry couldn't play this part. Does he even *want* to play it?'

Woolf argued so strongly that Gilbert eventually said 'Okay, then. If Larry plays it on Broadway and plays it well I'll take him.' But Harvey was in *Camelot* and committed to films as soon as he had worked out his contract, so Broadway was out of the question.

'I'm sorry, Jimmy,' said Gilbert, 'If Larry can't do the play he can't do the film.'

Woolf then decided that Terence Stamp would play Alfie on Broadway; he did, and the production was not a success. Stamp lost interest in the film, but suggested to Lewis Gilbert that his flat-mate Michael Caine might fit the part.

'To me,' said Caine afterwards, '*Alfie* was the only game in town. If I hadn't done *Alfie* I would have done nothing.'

When Harvey found that Caine had got the part, he showed no disappointment. He didn't want to be identified with a sleazy screen character who procured an abortion. It was an unsuitable role for a Hollywood leading man.

Caine said, 'Larry realised that the type of screen hero was changing, but he never did anything to alter his image as the archetypal leading man.'

JOHN WOOLF, SAID to be the business brain of Romulus Films, sat at a desk in a darkly-furnished room in the company's headquarters on London's Park Lane on a May morning in 1974. The room was less than a hundred yards from where Harvey and James Woolf had shared adjoining apartments in Grosvenor House.

By now John, the younger brother, had organised the Fred Zinnemann film of *The Day of the Jackal,* and had just returned from Berlin where his company was completing *The Odessa File.* He now owned, too, the only British film trade magazine which widely reported his film company's activities. Joe Lampton was a long time ago.

Woolf, small, shrewd and confident, agreed that *Life at the Top* had been less successful than its predecessor. 'As a book it rivalled *Room at the Top* in quality, but I don't think we made it as well. And, of course, the excitement had gone by then and the social climate had changed.' But had it? *Room at the Top* had, by general consent, broken through the 'sex scene' barrier.

'The highspot in Larry's career,' Woolf continued, 'was *Room at the Top,* but two or three years afterwards his career took rather a downward turn. Hollywood had been open to him because *Room at the Top* had been a highly successful film in America. My brother managed his career in California, but as the films became less successful at the box-office the parts he was offered became less attractive.

'In the last few years in the industry the big stars have been the McQueens and the Redfords, the he-men. Larry was never that. Larry was the dandy Englishman. I never thought his American accent convincing, and he certainly wasn't the type to play the parts that make big stars in America.

'Yet he had movie star style. He was a showman projecting a grandiose image and spending money as if he was printing it. He liked to be thought as living the life of a millionaire; that was something he wanted to project, rightly or wrongly. Inevitably, it made enemies for him; people are always jealous of another's success. In his flat in Grosvenor House there were dozens and dozens of suits, and dozens of pairs of shoes and hundreds of shirts. He spent a fortune on clothes.

'He was tremendously arrogant; that, perhaps, was part of his make-up. He wanted outsiders to know he believed in himself. I saw him play Henry V in New York and he was absolutely magnificent. If he had been content to stay with the Old Vic Company I think he could have had a great career in Shakespeare. But the critics never appreciated him. He had built up a reputation for being tough and unpleasant, particularly to the newspapers, and they never really gave him a fair chance. I don't think they ever visualised him as a Shakespearean actor.

'Still, I think it was wise of Larry to go to Hollywood. He did very well and my brother looked after his career and was responsible for it. But the type of film changed and he wasn't offered the big star parts. The part he wanted most, and which wasn't offered to him, was Arthur in *Camelot*. That hurt him badly.

'He gave the impression that he was able to get any screen role he wanted, and he would never admit his disappointment; that was a part of himself he wouldn't show the world. He was the supreme optimist.

'I'm convinced he would have been a successful film director, though he never asked me to let him direct. He would come to me

with books he wanted to buy, stories he wanted to film, scripts
that had been offered to him. He disliked turning anything down.
If he could have made half a dozen films at the same time he
would have been delighted.

'Whenever he came to see me in this office he might sit still for
a while; then he'd walk around the room smoking, talking and
drinking a glass or two of white wine. Larry must have been hell
to live with because he thought of himself first all day long. For
a successful actress, marriage to a man like that spelt doom.

'He never tried to break his contract with us. We released him
when he established himself in America. At the height of his
career he had a large fan mail which we looked after. I am still a
director of Laurence Harvey Productions which was formed back
in the 'sixties. Larry and I were the only directors of the company.
It's being wound up now. I only wish his career in America had
been more successful.'

JOHN BRAINE AND Laurence Harvey didn't keep in contact
after *Life at the Top*. 'I never 'phoned him,' Braine said. 'And he
didn't 'phone me, for the simple reason that he knew I had
nothing for him.'

Life at the Top didn't match *Room at the Top* at the box-office,
but Braine got double the money for the rights of his novel.

Wolf Mankowitz had refused to script the film, although
Harvey had wanted him to. He believed the low-key, downbeat
ending wrong for Harvey. Making Joe Lampton a loser, he felt,
would destroy the value of the character and at the same time
destroy Harvey's box-office image.

He was proved right.

20 | 'Can't someone knock on Mr. Woolf's door?'

LEWIS GILBERT AND 'CUBBY' BROCCOLI WERE SITTING IN THE dimly-lit Polo Lounge of the Beverly Hills Hotel on the evening of May 29, 1966, waiting for James Woolf to join them for drinks before dinner. They had arrived in Hollywood from Japan where they had been preparing to film *You Only Live Twice,* which Gilbert was to direct with Broccoli and his plump partner Harry Saltzman producing. In Los Angeles they hoped to find a Japanese actress for the film who would speak good English. Gilbert also wanted to discuss the film version of *Oliver!* which James Woolf was setting up and which he was to direct with Julie Andrews as Nancy and perhaps Harvey as Fagin.

Woolf had never agreed with Gilbert that Harvey was too prissy for romantic leads; he would admit only that he hadn't been getting the right parts. But Gilbert thought that behind a red beard Harvey could play Fagin splendidly.

He looked at his watch. It was after 7.30.

A table had been reserved for dinner, and if Woolf didn't hurry there would be no time for drinks. He chatted on with Broccoli until eight o'clock, then decided to call Woolf's suite from the telephone at their table in the lounge. There was no reply. He tried again. The operator checked and reported a 'Please Don't Disturb' sign on the producer's door.

'Can't someone go up and knock on Mr. Woolf's door?' Gilbert asked.

'I'm sorry, sir,' said the operator. 'When there's a "Don't
Disturb" notice on the door we can't interrupt.'

'That's nonsense', said Gilbert, though he knew that Hollywood
hotel staffs must be discreet.

At 8.30 he left Broccoli and went up to the second floor and
knocked on the door of Woolf's suite. There was no answer. He
saw a chambermaid in the corridor. 'Mr. Woolf hasn't been out all
day,' she said.

Gilbert knew that Woolf had not been well, but at least he
should answer the door. He went down to the lobby and found a
manager, who was apologetic, but repeated the 'phone operator's
explanation that when a 'Don't Disturb' notice was on a door he
could not interfere.

The film director was insistent. 'You've got to open up that
suite.'

Reluctantly the manager collected a pass key and they went up
to the suite together. When they opened the door the sitting-room
was empty. They crossed to the bedroom. The drapes were drawn
and the light from a bedside lamp lit the figure of James Woolf
sitting up in bed, propped comfortably against the pillows, his
thick-rimmed glasses on the end of his nose, reading *Valley of the
Dolls.* He was dead.

He appeared to have died from a heart attack. Not one of his
friends was there. His chauffeur, who usually travelled with him,
had stayed behind in London; Terence Stamp, who had been at the
hotel earlier in the week, had returned to England; and his first
protégé and closest friend, Laurence Harvey, was in the South of
France.

The police arrived and took away some phials they found in a
wastepaper basket.

JOHN IRELAND drove from Santa Barbara next morning on
Highway 101, crossing onto the San Diego freeway to reach
Sunset Boulevard and the Beverly Hills Hotel. He listened to the

music programmes on his car radio and didn't bother with the
news bulletins. At the hotel a doorman took his Cadillac and
drove it to the car park. Ireland looked at his watch. He was in
good time for his luncheon appointment with James Woolf.

'Mr. Woolf?' The desk clerk looked at Ireland. 'I'm sorry, sir,
Mr. Woolf has left us.'

'Checked out? My gosh, and I'm supposed to have lunch with
him.'

The clerk was embarrassed.

'When I said Mr. Woolf had left us, sir, I meant he – he has
passed away.'

HARVEY WAS AT the Hotel Colombe D'Or at St. Paul de Vence
when his secretary 'phoned him with the news. He had known
Woolf wasn't well; he had 'phoned him in Hollywood that day,
but he hadn't expected his death. He sat in his suite, stunned.

He called Joan who was at the beach house in Malibu. When
John Ireland 'phoned him he said:

'Yes, John, I know. But do something for me, please. They're
going to bury Jimmy in London. Please fly back with the body.
Will you do that?'

Ireland agreed. But other arrangements had been made. Woolf's
body was in a funeral parlour on Maple Drive in Beverly Hills and
was flown to London the next morning.

The funeral was held in the Jewish Cemetery at Golders Green,
North London. According to Orthodox tradition, when the plain
coffin was lowered into the grave a shovel was passed among the
chief mourners who each in turn heaped earth onto the coffin
below. Harvey didn't take the shovel. He stood impassively, his
grey eyes expressionless, his arms hanging limply by his sides. As
the grave was filled in and the mourners slipped away to their
cars, plucking tufts of grass and throwing them over their
shoulders according to custom, he remained alone at the graveside.

He stood there for a long time. Then he began to back away,

staring at the grave until it was out of sight among the headstones. Then he turned and walked quickly out of the cemetery.

His friendship with James Woolf had endured for more than fifteen years. 'My very personal friend, Mr. Woolf,' he had called him. Though they had seen less of each other in the last few years, though Woolf had made him empty promises, and though they had quarrelled, he still felt desolate.

In the months that followed he found himself trying to adjust not merely to a world without his closest friend and adviser, but to a world which no longer held film stars in awe. He slotted Beatles tapes in the new cassette player in his Rolls. He began to wear more casual clothes, spending less time with Carr, Son and Woor than with Dougie Hayward, the tailor to whom the fashionable young entertainers and pop stars were hurrying. He grew his hair longer, still maintaining his quiff. He went to discotheques instead of night clubs. He dined less at the Caprice and more often at restaurants like the Terrazza in Romilly Street, Soho.

It was at the Terrazza that he met a red-haired model, Paulene Stone, thirteen years his junior. His friends were more than surprised when the pair were seen dining and dancing together, for already news had reached London that he and Joan Cohn were talking of marriage. As though to assuage the pain of Woolf's death and forestall his own approaching middle-age, Harvey behaved like a man half his years, dating his new girl and calling her Redbird. The betrayal of the woman who had been his companion for eight years did not appear to concern him.

WITHIN A FEW WEEKS of Woolf's death he began rehearsals for *The Winter's Tale* which a scratch company (his own term), under the direction of Frank Dunlop, was to present at the Edinburgh Festival. He was playing Leontes, a challenging role which would enable him to prove himself to the critics and return to the stage where he had first shown promise before Woolf had led him into a different career. He was also filming *The Spy with a Cold Nose* at Shepperton Studios, where he renewed his friendship with Eric Portman, a reminder of the days of *Cairo Road* and Cornwall; but this time Portman was playing a supporting role and Harvey was the lead.

In spite of the reassuring love of Joan, the demands of his new girl and the pressure of work he felt terribly alone. An element in his life was missing. He talked compulsively about Woolf.

'I miss Jimmy,' he said. 'I feel utterly vulnerable without him.'

Conditions at Manchester twenty years earlier had been better than at Edinburgh in 1966. He rented a house outside the city for £100 a week. But his dressing room had neither a bath nor a shower. He was given a small tub in which to scrub off Leontes' body paint which he decided was adequate for a baby's ablutions. He sent the caretaker out with a fiver and he returned with a Victorian zinc tub which he had bought for thirty-five shillings. It was a monstrosity, but at least Harvey was able to lower his tall frame into it every night after the performance.

'Gentlemen,' he told the Festival organisers, 'I'm not a delicate orchid, but this is like something out of Dickens. One would imagine that civilisation had reached Edinburgh, but apparently it has not.'

For the first time he answered a critic publicly. After Ronald Bryden's notice in the London *Observer*, he wrote to the paper:

> *In a career that has spanned twenty years of the theatre and films, I have been the butt and centre of journalistic praise and emasculation. I had tried to remain impartial and unprejudiced, as I have always felt that the critics too must eat, even though they feed and profit in the barreness and fruits of our labour.*
>
> *Mr. Ronald Bryden with his last Sunday's notice of the Edinburgh Festival production of* The Winter's Tale, *has finally destroyed what compassion and understanding I may have had, and made me do what I have never done before – reply.*
>
> *His obsession with Mr. Richard Burton is justifiably his own business and, much as I admire Mr. Burton, I have never been privileged to see him either in* Camelot *or in* The Winter's Tale. *In fact, I have never seen*

The Winter's Tale. *I cannot understand Mr. Bryden's comparisons and references. Whatever contribution I have made as an actor, I have prided myself on originality of performance and concept. . .*

I think what Mr. Dunlop has managed to achieve out of what is Shakespeare's most difficult play is remarkable. He has made it a coherent and highly stimulating evening. All the subtleties, nuances and meanings in the play, which have heretofore been unexplored by Shakespearean critics and scholars alike, are brought out for the first time in this production. Mr. Bryden failed to notice them, or simply chose to ignore them, with what I assume can only be total ignorance.

What, in fact, Mr. Dunlop is trying to do is to bridge the gap between the National and Stratford's closed shop and the commercial theatre, and to have a company where actors can work, be encouraged and given an opportunity to play in an atmosphere that isn't strangled by bureaucratic rule and self-indulgence.

As a scratch company we dug deeper than the surface and superficiality of your criticism. What greater satisfaction is there than for the actor to play to capacity audiences and leave the theatre with cheers ringing in his ears?

> *Laurence Harvey,*
> *Edinburgh.*

THE NEWSPAPERS REPORTED that James Woolf, aged 46, had left £31,241 nett (£53,268 gross) before estate duty of £11,972. The rest of his estate was to be split between Harvey and John Woolf. A bequest of £20,000 was made to his chauffeur.

His brother John Woolf immediately contested the will, claiming that two witnesses were not simultaneously present when it was signed. He vowed to fight the case to the bitter end.

Towards the end of 1967 the action was settled out of court on what the British legal system describes as 'Agreed Terms'.

21 | 'Mother clung to Larry every moment of his visit.'

HARVEY HAD PROMISED HIS PARENTS REPEATEDLY THAT HE WOULD visit them in their new home in Israel where they had moved from South Africa in 1955. When he failed to keep his word they were deeply disappointed. Eventually his brother Nahum wrote to him, 'Please, Larry, we are all most anxious to see you, but if you are not one hundred per cent certain of your visit don't announce it beforehand. Don't tell us months ahead you're coming and then not come.'

Harvey's mother longed to see him. When her son disappointed her she would say, 'I'm going to America to get hold of that Larry and give him a good telling-off.'

What his parents did not realise was that Harvey did not want them with him in England or America. There must be no family intrusion into his private life. Even his letters to Nahum and Henya maintained a certain discretion.

Nahum was aware of the psychological problems in his brother's attitude towards his mother. He had rebelled against her possessiveness, yet never rejected her; he was willing to help her provided she remained at a distance. It was one of the paradoxes of the man whose letters to his brother and sister-in-law gave little hint of his extravagant way of life. When Harvey finally decided to make a weekend visit to his parents in the spring of 1967, Nahum knew it would be an immense strain on all of them.

Tel-Aviv's Lod Airport was crowded with sightseers on the Friday afternoon of Harvey's arrival. When he stepped off the 'plane he was dressed casually in a jacket and polo-neck sweater. A Columbia car took him to the Tel-Aviv Hilton.

Nahum and Henya, who lived in Beersheba, came to Tel-Aviv for his visit and stayed at the apartment of Ber and Ella Skikne. They knew that Harvey would have put them up at the Hilton, but they didn't want to arouse Mrs. Skikne's jealousy.

On the Sabbath Harvey was driven to the parents' apartment. Nahum remembered, 'Mother had prepared his favourite dishes of gefillte fish and roast meat, but Larry could hardly enjoy them. He told me, "My guts are buggered. I can't eat". He smoked a lot and drank white table wine.

'Mother called him Larry because for years he had signed himself Larry in his letters. She could not take her eyes and arms off him. She clung to him every moment.'

At last Nahum understood why his brother had put off his visits in the past.

On the Sunday Nahum arranged a cocktail party at the Desert Inn on the outskirts of Beersheba where he was a city councillor.

'I could have invited the whole town and still be told I had forgotten somebody.'

In the afternoon before the party Harvey and the Snehs' son Nachshon, now twenty-one, climbed Masada, the site of the fortress on the Dead Sea where in the second century Jewish soldiers had killed themselves rather than fall into the hands of the enemy. Harvey was tired, but tanned by the sun, when he arrived for the party at the Desert Inn. He met friends of Nahum's from South Africa and sat at their table, feeling at home.

He had decided at the last moment to come to Beersheba and it would be the only time that he and Nahum would be alone together. After midnight, when most of the guests had gone and only a handful of close friends remained, the two brothers withdrew to a quiet corner and talked for twenty minutes.

'Larry asked me about my health. There were some questions concerning our parents. Then he said, "You are so undemanding,

Nahum. I know the parents are a burden to you and I appreciate
what you are doing. The money I'm sending sometimes seems so
insignificant in comparison to the problems involved. How can I
help you financially?''

'I wanted to go back to university for a refresher course, to
renew my store of knowledge. I told him if he could help me to
do this I would appreciate it. But he was prepared to do much
more.'

Next morning Harvey visited the flat where Nahum and his
wife and their son lived.

It was a modest apartment, constructed during the first years of
Beersheba's development, and similar to a post-war English
council flat. Beersheba had been a village of one street, a few shops
and a mosque when captured by the Israeli army in 1948. It was
in the middle of the desert, but the Israelis had built houses,
gardens, workshops, factories, hospitals and schools. Nahum and
Henya wanted Harvey to see their flat, not to arouse his sympathy,
but to imply that their view of life was not materialistic.

'I can see,' he said to them, 'that it's my brother's house. It's full
of books.'

He played with their cocker spaniel, Kusuka, and remarked that
he kept dogs in Beverly Hills.

'Nahum', he asked suddenly, 'how would you like me to buy
you a house?'

'No, thank you, Larry.'

'Henya, what do you think?'

Henya shook her head.

Two years later Nahum and Henya were able to buy a small
house through their own efforts. Friends who had heard of Harvey's offer told them they had been damned fools to refuse it.

That afternoon Harvey drove back to Tel-Aviv and met relatives
who had come to his parents' apartment. At the Hilton he gave
interviews to journalists and talked with producers who wanted to
make films with him. In the evening Lotte Matalon, the Columbia
representative, gave a reception at her villa. Though tired, Harvey
was propelled by his nervous energy. His mother had been carried

along by the excitement of his visit, but even she couldn't keep
pace with her son. She and Ber were extremely tired after the
reception and were about to leave for home when Harvey invited
Nahum and Henya to join him at a night club. Mrs Skikne said
to Nahum, 'So you're going to have a nice time with Larry and
send us off to bed?'

Nahum couldn't explain to her that he and his brother simply
wanted to spend a little more time together. 'So like good children
Henya and I went back to our parents' apartment.'

During that weekend in Israel Nachshon and some friends
stayed in the Hilton at Harvey's invitation. Nachshon got on well
with 'Uncle Larry', who had never forgotten him in his letters to
Nahum. Harvey was proud that his eldest brother had been a
pioneer, a kibbutznik who had cultivated the desert. And he
envied him.

'With all my fame, Nahum, I lack one basic and important asset
which you possess. I have no son.'

He got little sleep the night before he left Tel-Aviv. He stayed
at a night club until almost dawn and delayed his arrival at the
airport until the last moment. Nahum and Henya and the parents
had been driven to Lod earlier that morning and the car returned
to collect Harvey at the Hilton. He had said to Nahum the night
before:

'Tell Mother if she makes a scene, I won't see her again.'

When he reached the airport it was crowded with well-wishers.
The El Al captain had been asked to hold his aircraft for a Very
Important Passenger. Harvey rushed from the car into the departure lounge. He hugged and kissed his mother and father, his
brother and sister-in-law and their son, and was gone.

Afterwards, when the parents had returned to their apartment
in Tel-Aviv, Mrs. Skikne became hysterical.

BRIAN GIBBS, the new chauffeur, looked after a dozen cars for
Harvey, as well as making frequent trips down London's Park

Lane to buy Harvey's laxative pills from a chemist's in Curzon Street. Gibbs was a sturdy, fair-haired young man of twenty-five when hired by Harvey and his first job was to drive him to Edinburgh for *The Winter's Tale* in a new Pontiac Bonneville.

He kept tabs on three Rolls: a black convertible and a bronze hardtop with a black leather roof which were shipped to and fro between England and the United States, and a dark blue hard-top Rolls, usually kept at Joan's house in Beverly Hills, and on two Austin Cooper Minis coachbuilt at Park Royal at a cost of more than £4,000 each and kept in London. There were two Maseratis: the first, a Mistrale, was shipped to the States and Gibbs flew to Italy to pick up a second model, the Gibley, which was later sold to Bernard Cornfield. And there was the Moke, a tiny, Shelby-converted Fiat which was kept at Palm Springs.

Harvey also had an arrangement with Columbia by which he collected new cars every year from Pontiac and used them in his films. There were two station wagons, the Bonneville, a GTO and a Firebird, which Gibbs drove to Berlin for *Dandy in Aspic*.

'He expected his cars to be immaculate,' said Gibbs. 'He noticed every mark, the slightest dent. If he got into a car and there were fag ends in the ashtray he'd be furious.

'But I saw places with Larry Harvey I thought I'd never see. Some bosses say they'll take you here, there and everywhere, and you go nowhere. But Larry took me everywhere.

'We had arguments. I walked out on him twice, once in California, another time in Italy. But when I came back it was as though we had never quarrelled.'

He would take Gibbs to the Caprice or the Terrazza, even to the Bunch of Grapes in Shepherd Market, Mayfair, where he would point to a window across the laneway from the pub, and say:

'That's where I lived when I first came to London.'

HE WAS FRIENDLIER TO MIA FARROW during *Dandy in Aspic* than he had been to any actress since Elizabeth Taylor on *Butterfield 8*. The film went smoothly until the director Anthony

64. *Left:* Michael Caine – one of Harvey's circle of close friends.

65. *Right:* John Ireland . . . a twenty year friendship with Harvey.

66. *Left:* Film producer James Woolf, close friend of Laurence Harvey, who formed Romulus Films with his brother John in 1949. Together they produced many films including *Pandora and The Flying Dutchman, Room at the Top* and *The L-Shaped Room.*

67. *Above:* Siobhan McKenna announces her one woman show,
Here Are Ladies, at a reception in London in 1970. Harvey and
Wolf Mankowitz (centre) were her producers.

68. *Below:* Hollywood dinner party 1973. Harvey and wife Paulene
with Rex Harrison and wife Elizabeth (left).

69. *Above:* Harvey and Fabergé executive Stan Krell beside the Fabergé private jet.

70. *Above:* Harvey and George Barrie at Las Vegas in 1973. On the right, Harvey's wife, Paulene.

71. *Below:* Elizabeth Taylor links Harvey in Rome. The actor had stopped off in the city during a round-the-world flight in the Fabergé jet in the summer of 1973.

72. *Below:* Harvey at a Las Vegas golf tournament in 1973. Included in the picture: Cary Grant, Billie Jean King, George Barrie.

73. *Left:* Harvey's widow
Paulene weeps at his
funeral at London's Golders
Green crematorium in
November, 1973.

74. *Right:* The floral
tribute from Elizabeth
Taylor and Peter Lawford.
The message read 'We love
you. Elizabeth and Peter.'

75. *Left:* Memorial service
at St. Paul's Church ('The
Actors' Church') in Covent
Garden, London. Harvey's
widow, Paulene, arrives
with her two children,
Sophie (left) and Domino.

Mann collapsed and died two weeks before the end of shooting. Harvey, who was playing a brain-washed espionage agent, had been working closely with Mann and took over the direction. When filming was finished he persuaded Columbia to let him take charge of the post-production work, which, he argued, could be handled only by someone who understood all aspects of the film. *Dandy* was completed in London and Harvey, elated at directing again, was full of new ideas. He flew to the South of France to talk to author Graham Greene: he wanted to produce and direct *The Living Room* in which he would co-star with Mia Farrow. He would produce a repertory season of classical plays with Frank Dunlop in Los Angeles. He would open a Shakespeare theatre in New York.

Richard Condon said of these days: 'He had a lot going against him, but he was very forthright about that. He lived like a man who expected to die young. He was reckless with his money, his whole verve was reckless. He was extravagant emotionally. My view of Larry was that he was afraid of nothing. If he didn't like people he wouldn't be rude, but he'd be glad to see the back of them. If they persisted in staying, then he got rude, sure. If people behaved badly he bawled them out in the open.'

There were no parts in Hollywood for Harvey at this time, as Jack Cushingham knew. 'Larry was a very proud guy. He'd never go up to a producer and ask for a part. He felt he should have got certain parts and couldn't understand why he didn't get them. He was never really accepted by Americans. I think it was because of his behaviour, his I-don't-give-a-damn attitude. So far as I was concerned he handled himself ridiculously. He would say things he shouldn't say, or didn't mean to say. For he really did care deeply and had a lot of pride.

'What he didn't want to do was to hang around Hollywood without work, so he would go anywhere to make a picture. When they offered him a picture abroad off he'd go, re-write the script, work on the director and the actors and end up by putting his own money into the venture. I kept saying to him, "These pictures aren't doing you a damned bit of good." '

Richard Condon believed Harvey had arrived in Hollywood at the right time. 'Larry made some twelve pictures for which his average fee must have been around three hundred thousand dollars. He travelled the world and lived in the best hotels. I think he had no interest other than spending his money and projecting himself. Naturally it was only human to think that such a life was never going to end.

'Nor would it have ended if the film industry hadn't collapsed.'

Rebus was one of a series of films Harvey made abroad at this time. It was made on location in the Lebanon, and Harvey's spirits sank when he arrived at Beirut Airport to find a battered Cadillac waiting to take him to the Phoenicia Intercontinental Hotel. This was to be his car for the film, and he shared it with the director, the production manager and an Arab driver.

He carried a new passport because the Lebanese authorities would have refused him entry if they had seen the Israeli stamp on his old passport. Soon after filming began a Beirut newspaper carried a front-page photograph of Harvey and his family during his visit to Israel. It was just after the Six-Day War and Frank Sinatra's and Elizabeth Taylor's films had been banned because the stars supported Israel. Harvey was taken aback. He kept the door of his hotel room locked and asked his production manager for a gun. When his good humour returned he began to joke on the set, 'What d'jew know? What d'jew say?' But as the crew were Italian they didn't understand him.

He made a film for Orson Welles in Yugoslavia in two and a half weeks. When he got back to Hollywood Welles called him and asked him to return for an extra scene.

'Just buy the ticket and come over,' Welles said. 'We'll refund you the fare when you get here.'

Harvey bought the ticket, took John Ireland with him and collected Paulene Stone in London. The flew to Geneva and on to Zagreb. At the hotel there were no reservations for them. Harvey tried to 'phone Orson Welles at the location, but Welles wasn't taking any calls. Not even from Laurence Harvey.

The hotel was full, so the three of them climbed into a car with the crew from the Yugoslav airline and drove around the town until they found a small boarding house which put them up for the night. Harvey didn't meet Welles and never filmed the scene.

Paulene Stone would say later that she became pregnant on the trip.

Harvey was not long back in California before he packed his grips again to make a film on an Italian island, *She and He,* the story of a relationship between a man and a woman which was almost metaphysical. The 'He' of the title was a romantic poet who falls in love with a beautiful independent woman demanding physical love without sentiment. The woman regards the man as a stud and a source of money. She humiliates him by swimming naked before an audience of mechanics and waiters and allowing garage hands to make love to her while he is forced to watch. The poet realises that his only way to freedom is through death, so he allows her to run him down with her car.

Friends advised Harvey not to become involved with the film which seemed too anti-feminist to succeed. He claimed it was a truthful study of woman in modern society, draining man with her demands for love and possessions.

When the original backers pulled out he decided to invest 400,000 dollars of his own money in the picture, fifty per cent of the production cost. He would produce the film, write the script, direct it himself. But a group of Italian backers who became involved insisted on an Italian director and when the film was finished cut it themselves. Harvey brought a print of *She and He* back to Hollywood, but could find nobody to distribute it. When it was screened privately some viewers remarked to him that 'She' had won at the end of the story.

'Oh, no,' he protested. 'He wins, because he's free of her at last. And if you had lived a full life, with all that you wanted from it, I can't think of a better way to go.'

He had been offered a role in *Ice Station Zebra* that might have saved his Hollywood career. His name would have gone beneath Rock Hudson's on the titles, but he would have earned 250,000 dollars for ten weeks' work.

He had sold the house at Malibu to pay for *She and He* and was building another beach house next door. Don Hensman said over drinks one evening, 'What the hell is wrong with you, Larry? Why don't you take the part? You're not doing anything else right now. It means ten weeks in California and the money will pay for the new house. And you'll be able to keep an eye on the work. What could be better?'

Harvey thought for a moment. 'Sam, how can I explain it? If someone asked you to design a two-million dollar residence in French provincial style, would you do it?'

'You've got me there, L.H. The answer's no, I couldn't'.

'Well, that's how I feel about this picture.'

Ernest Borgnine got the part.

IN LONDON HE reclined on the saffron velvet sofa heaped with cerise pillows in the apartment at Grosvenor House which he had shared with James Woolf, and which now was his, airing his views to the columnists on acting and women. He still prepared his quotes carefully and polished his aphorisms until they seemed original, but occasionally he contradicted himself and just as often was repetitive.

The columnists, enchanted by the apricot silk-covered walls, the white sculptured marbles, the 18th-century gilded chairs and the Moorish mosaics, drank the proffered glass of Pouilly Fuissé and accepted a Dunhill from a silver box on the coffee table of Russian malachite, and betrayed no surprise.

All of them knew of his eight-year friendship with Joan Cohn and a few of them knew of his friendship with Paulene Stone, the model girl who lived in a flat in Aberdare Gardens in London's Hampstead. They could be excused for surmising that marriage didn't enter into his relationship with either woman. But could they be sure? They had not predicted his marriage to Margaret

Leighton on the Rock of Gibraltar. And who could predict if he would marry Joan Cohn? But they recognised that marriage to the widow of Harry Cohn would help his career in Hollywood.

22 | 'Larry, who are you really?' Joan asked.

'YOU'LL BE MARRIED ON OCTOBER 17, 1968.'

The prediction of Maurice Woodruff, whom Joan Cohn described as 'my friend more than my clairvoyant,' was accurate. Woodruff must have forseen that Harvey's flight from New York to the Bahamas on October 16 would be cancelled.

Joan was waiting for him at Nassau, but Harvey was forced to take a later 'plane which arrived there at 9.05 p.m., unaware that marriages were not permitted on the island after nine p.m. It was a law that was vigorously enforced because drunken late evening marriages among the islanders usually ended in divorce.

Harvey, tense and impatient, wanted the wedding to go ahead as he and Joan had planned, not as Woodruff had predicted, on October 16. He asked his lawyer Frank Wells to try to arrange the ceremony on board the 'plane when it landed. But even 9.05 p.m. was too late.

Next day, October 17, the ceremony took place at the exclusive Lyford Cay Club and was conducted by the island's magistrate John Bailey. Jean Louis, the fashion designer and Harvey's Malibu neighbour, was Joan's witness. One of the guests in the small wedding party was Joan's twenty-three-year-old son by her marriage to Harry Cohn.

The couple exchanged rings. Harvey gave his bride a gold ring, half an inch wide, designed by a London silversmith. The following day he removed his own ring and hung it on his key-chain; he hated jewellery on his fingers.

Time Magazine printed the item in their 'Milestones' column:

> *'Married. Laurence Harvey, 40, the movie's handsomest heel* (Room at the Top, Darling) *to Joan Cohn, ex-wife of shoe manufacturer Harry Karl, and his constant companion for the past eight years. He for the second time (he was divorced by British actress Margaret Leighton in 1961) and she for the third, in Nassau.'*

The honeymoon began in a private cottage in the secluded grounds of Lyford Cay Club and continued at the Malibu beach house.

Few people had expected the marriage. Three years previously Joan Cohn had said:

'How can you improve on something that is perfect? Perfect is the only word for our relationship.'

Yet they had talked together about marriage for nine years after their first meeting on St. Valentine's Night, 1960.

Hermione Baddeley, who was rightly or wrongly convinced that marriage to Harvey had changed Margaret Leighton into 'a jibbering mass of nerves', was asked by Joan, 'What do you think of Larry? I've fallen for him hook, line and sinker. He adores me and I'm so much in love with him.'

'Don't marry Larry', Hermione told her.

Could Joan be sure she knew him? One night at her Beverly Hills home she had asked him:

'Larry, who are you *really?*'

His reply was, 'Larushka Mischa Skikne.'

She was anxious to know more about his background. They had been together in many places, enjoying life to the full at Harvey's hectic pace. She counted a dozen visits to Paris with him, staying at the George V or the Raphael. He was a friend of Rudolf, the head barman at the George V; they had been buddies in the South African army. They dined at New Jimmy'z, Éléphant Blanc, Maxim's and other fashionable restaurants. He taught her about antiques and accompanied her to the couturiers when she ordered her clothes.

But his early life was something he didn't talk about.

Within a few months of their marriage he had put Malibu on the market to raise money for *She and He*. He claimed he took nothing from Joan professionally or privately. She was the largest single stockholder in Columbia Pictures and her wealth was estimated at two million pounds. If he had married her for her money, he said, that would mean he was a ponce.

He turned his attention to building a house in Palm Springs. He had been hooked on Palm Springs ever since he and Joan had leased Kirk Douglas's home there. They bought a house and remodelled it and then Joan bought the house next door. They called the houses Palm Springs One and Palm Springs Two. Now Buff and Hensman were planning Palm Springs Three for them. This was to be Harvey's ultimate home, his most ambitious venture, costing over 300,000 dollars. He sketched the original plans which the architects drew professionally and refined. They would sit by the pool at Crescent Drive at weekends and Don Hensman would busy himself with a sketch pad. Joan would view the sketches and say, 'That's nice' or 'That's great'. Or they might sit outdoors at Palm Springs late at night with a bottle of champagne. Joan would spread her sable coat on the sand and they would huddle around the sketch pad discussing where the pool or the sauna room should go.

Palm Springs Three was to be a single-storey mansion, a miniature country club, with a large dining room and bar area, a master bedroom and study, two master bathrooms, two guest suites, servants' quarters, a large sauna room, a giant swimming pool, jacuzzies, fountains, loggias, garages, a tennis court and a putting green.

When the house was being built, Hensman would fly to Palm Springs at weekends in the twin-engined Air Commander Harvey had acquired, or by helicopter. When Harvey was in New York or on location in Europe he would invite Hensman to join him to discuss the progress of the house. He planned the colour schemes, designed the carpets, decided what he wanted in furnishings and chandeliers. Hensman realised he was more interested in creating and building the house than living in it.

Yet he had a passion for Palm Springs, its spas and groves of date palms and its perfect weather. His routine at the Springs was to rise before noon and mix himself a bullshot of vodka, consommé, lemon juice and Worcester sauce. Lunch at two o'clock consisted of salad and cheese with white wine and was followed by a couple of hours in a sauna until late afternoon and party time. In the evening he would organise a barbecue, cooking the steaks himself and dispensing the wine.

Hensman, like Harvey's other close friends, observed his need to retreat to a sauna or a super toilet. At Joan's mansion on North Crescent Drive Harvey remodelled a cabana some distance from the house as a combination of living room and bedroom with a jacuzzi and sauna. He would sit and talk there with his friends, or read and listen to music, until it was time for dinner; and although twenty guests might be waiting he would invariably be late.

JACK CUSHINGHAM said, 'When you went to Joan's house Larry would be out taking the sun and forgetting about dinner. That was his big hangup. He'd arrive at nine-thirty for eight. He never had any idea what time it was. Yet when he came in he had everyone eating out of his hand.'

Cushingham never knew where Harvey got the money to finance his projects. 'But he always came up with it,' he remembered. 'He spent money like a drunken sailor. Twice a month he'd send the Rolls in for repairs because of some minor annoyance. When I first knew him he had two Rolls and a Maserati and he didn't even use them, but they were all special to him. He'd go to a firm in Ascot, near London, choose 50,000 dollars' worth of antiques, pay 20,000 dollars to have them transported to California and within a few weeks he'd send them back again.

'It cost thousands just shipping that stuff all over the place. He , started his own antique business against everybody's advice, and he'd go off on a film and come back after six months to find his firm in the red.

'When I first met him he used to tell me about his struggling days, but when I knew him he wasn't struggling, but living it up pretty good. He fitted into Hollywood in the early 'sixties. Joan had just become a widow and Larry zoomed in on her. They got on great together. They had a ball.'

WHEN HARVEY WAS filming *She and He* in Italy in 1968 Joan decided to visit his family in Israel. She was curious to know if her husband was really Larushka Mischa Skikne. She had seen Nahum Sneh's name on air letters to Larry and arranged through him to meet the family. She had never bothered Harvey during his film-making with social and personal demands and he didn't question her departure from Rome on the two-hour flight to Tel-Aviv.

The family were at Lod Airport to meet her. Mrs. Skikne, who was waiting in a car outside the terminal building, embraced Joan and kissed her. Joan invited them all to dinner in the Hilton.

When Harvey had married Margaret Leighton his mother's reaction had been violent. She could not accept that her son had married a *shiksa,* and when she heard of the divorce her comment was: 'Good riddance.' For some reason she assumed that Joan was Jewish. During dinner Joan was asked by Nahum about the bracelet she wore on her wrist. When she told him it was part of a pearl Rosary, she suddenly saw Mrs. Skikne, who was seated beside her, stiffen.

'Yes, Mother,' Joan said, 'I'm a *goy.'*

Mrs. Skikne put down her knife and fork. For a moment she wasn't prepared to believe her ears.

'I'm a *goy,'* Joan repeated, 'but I happen to like Jewish men.'

The moment passed and Mrs. Skikne never referred to the matter again. Her husband Ber had impressed upon her years before, 'If you want your son to be an actor, Ella, then you must accept his way of life.'

She accepted Joan Cohn Harvey.

JOAN'S BOY PRINCE sat on the throne of 'King' Cohn in the mansion on North Crescent Drive. He may have wondered if Columbia Pictures would one day be his, if a plaque would hang over the studio entrance in Gower Street beside his predecessor's:

> Harry Cohn 1891-1958, co-founder of Columbia Pictures.
> 'In him the strength of the leader, the flame of the creator.'

What had happened made lyric writer Sammy Cahn rub his eyes. Harry Cohn had cherished Cahn like a son in the Hollywood of the 'forties. 'I think all the old guard of the motion picture business did one smart thing in their lives: they went into the motion picture business and to this day they've not been able to ruin it. Harry Cohn was just one of those fools who believed his own publicity. He developed the reputation of being a hard, coarse, crude man and he worked at it. Our relationship came to a brutal and inelegant end when he ordered me from his house, yelling, "Get out!"

'I left that house assuming I'd never return. But when I did go back, there in the chair in which Harry Cohn had sat was a totally different man. Laurence Harvey.

'If I had to give you one word to sum up life as I understand it, it would be *paradox*. It was a paradox to find Larry Harvey sitting in Harry Cohn's chair. Every time I think about it I chuckle to myself. Larry liked me and I liked him. I loved his flair for life. I'm not sure where he learned it or how he came by it, but he certainly lived to the manner born and turned that house of Harry Cohn's into a showplace. He had elegance in all his conduct, and Joan has elegance.'

At the parties in the Crescent Drive mansion Harvey would tell

anecdotes by the hour. Guests demanded imitations of Otto
Preminger on board a 'plane with landing gear trouble or Carol
Channing singing 'Hello, Dolly!'

Joan preferred home living. As in Harry Cohn's day, there was
a staff to look after her needs from the first moment in the
morning when she pressed a switch by her bedside for the drapes
to swish open and a servant brought her orange juice and the *Los
Angeles Times*. But even in a thirty-room house her new husband
was restless. He ate at home because he enjoyed the screenings of
his films for the guests who descended from the dining-room to
the 35mm theatre which Harry Cohn had built at pool level.
When they dined out his favourite restaurants were Chasens,
Perino's, Trader Vic's and the Bistro, which he partly owned and
where he liked to sit facing the mirror-clad walls so that he could
watch the other diners and himself.

Not everyone believed him when he claimed he hadn't married
Joan for her wealth.

'She has her money and I have mine. I ask for nothing and she
gives me nothing.'

So far as Columbia Pictures were concerned he said his pride
would not allow him to approach them with a project.

Joan was not unaware of his relationships outside marriage,
although he was discreet. She was loyal when asked about him.

'My husband is a wonderful man', was her reply.

During the interval of a performance by the Royal Shakespeare
Company in Los Angeles in January, 1969, she remained calm
when two English girls approached Harvey. He stood aside to talk
to them. Joan overheard one girl say:

'Paulene's pregnant. She's asking for you.'

Harvey kept his composure. He looked quickly at Joan, then
said to the girls, 'This is my wife.'

The other girl smiled and said to Harvey, 'We just thought
we'd give you the message.'

WITH PALM SPRINGS THREE almost ready he began to dream of another house in London, a house for Paulene Stone and his child she would soon bear. There was an air of desperation about his life. He was not feeling well and the stomach trouble that had bothered him since his youth had put him into hospital in Geneva with pancreatitis, a nasty inflammation of the gland that aids digestion. And even his best friends were unprepared for the guest role he took in the film *The Magic Christian*. He decided to play a striptease Hamlet. It was his own idea. The man who had been Stratford's Romeo and Orlando in the 'fifties walked onto a mock-up of the Memorial Theatre stage in the studios before a make-believe first night audience that supposedly included members of the Royal family.

He stripped as he recited the soliloquy *To be or not to be*. He wore a long wig tied behind his head with a velvet bow. He camped through the speech and at the crucial moment tugged at the bow so that the false hair fell and covered him. It was going to shock the hell out of people, he thought.

To his brother Robert Sinai it was a negation of all that Harvey had projected early in his career.

'Is that what it had all come to?' he asked.

23 | 'I don't want to involve you in the horrendous problems.'

HARVEY WENT TO CHICHESTER IN THE SUMMER OF 1970 TO APPEAR in two festival plays, *Arms and the Man* and *The Alchemist*. 'If I have roots anywhere then they are in England', he said. 'England has given me what little art and reputation I have.'

He was a regular commuter between Hollywood and London, but was spending more time in England now. Joan was with him in Chichester where they had rented a house for the season. Because of the proximity of Paulene Stone marriage had become difficult, their relationship strained. When Joan brought up the affair, he shrugged it off.

'It's nothing. Paulene's just a good kid.'

Joan had first heard about the affair after Paulene Stone had been interviewed by a London magazine. Although hurt, she didn't take the relationship seriously.

'I never really believed in it. I just thought it was someone else for him to kick around.'

She remembers she was in no way distressed about his betrayal. 'I couldn't watch him every minute, after all, and I would rather he went out with a girl than a boy. Anyway, I went out with men in Hollywood; they were friends of mine.' A patient woman, she had no intention of plunging into public debate about her husband's affair with a London model.

One evening as she and Harvey and his secretary played cards in their rented Chichester house the telephone rang. A woman's voice announced herself as Paulene Stone. She asked to speak with Mrs. Cohn Harvey.

'Joan, I want you to know that I have been Larry's lover for five years.'

Joan listened in silence, then said, 'Yes, I know. I was in a similar situation for eight years – and I loved every minute of it.'

Paulene hung up. Harvey had heard the conversation but when Joan returned to the card table he made no mention of it. Neither did she.

If her husband was indifferent to the gossip about his affair she had no intention of allowing the situation to become humiliating for her. She could not accept that the child born the previous Autumn was Harvey's, but the 'phone call had convinced her that the affair was not over.

Harvey attributed his neglect of Joan to the constant demands made on him as an actor. Joan hadn't returned to Beverly Hills, when, during rehearsals for *The Alchemist,* he fell on the stage and broke a bone in his leg. He turned his room at the London Clinic into a suite stocked with flowers and greeted his visitors with champagne, which the nurses poured obligingly.

In the following year, 1971, when he decided to appear in *Child's Play* in the West End, he asked Joan to join him in London. She didn't want to come. 'I didn't like living in London, and it was a real effort for me to go. But I knew Larry wasn't well and my secretary, Marge, persuaded me to make the trip. Love will take you to many places, but if you haven't love you'll stay at home. My enthusiasm had waned, and I was tired of travelling.'

The marriage seemed to be over. Through her attorney she filed divorce proceedings against her husband on the grounds of 'irreconcilable differences.' The papers were handed to Harvey when he stepped off a plane at Los Angeles International Airport.

It was St. Valentine's Day, February 14, 1971.

WOLF MANKOWITZ, with whom he had presented Siobhan
McKenna in a one-woman show, *Here Are Ladies,* begged Harvey
not to do *Child's Play.* But he had signed a contract almost
furtively, a habit he had acquired during James Woolf's last years.
The play was to be presented by Doris Cole Abrahams, a part-time
entrepreneur who was married to a clothing manufacturer, and
directed by Joseph Hardy, who had already directed the play with
success on Broadway. The theme was the relationship between
teachers and pupils in a boy's school, the premise being that evil
in an ideologically confined setting breeds evil. Those concerned
with the production decided to transfer the American setting to an
English Catholic public school. To the author, Robert Marasco, it
seemed an acceptable change.

Harvey said to Marasco before the opening night. 'The critics
will be gunning for me. They resent my success in America.' After
the first night party at the Café Royal Harvey and his friends went
on to Doris Abrahams' chic apartment in Lowndes Square to wait
for the reviews.

'It was a terribly painful experience,' recalled Joe Hardy. 'Larry
sensed what was going to happen. He had got blind drunk at the
Café Royal and could hardly stand up. The notices were rude and
the critics treated him abysmally.'

Hardy was angry because the critics refused to see Harvey as
anybody but Joe Lampton. 'Quite frankly, that's the image I had
of him, too, until I got to know him as an overly generous
person.'

'He was silly, he was irresponsible, but so is everybody else. He
had the image of a rotten fellow who used people to get where he
was, but I don't think he used people any more than the rest of
us do in the ordinary course of human events.

'I loved the way he lived. I loved the way he spent his wealth
on other people, too much of it, I gather. He adored the accou-
trements of fame, the houses and the chauffeurs and the Rolls –
and the Mini painted the same colour as the Rolls. When we had
dinner together he would demand that they bring up a vintage
port from the cellar and it was sheer ambrosia.

'I don't think he was ever happy or content because he was driven as a person and an artist. Marriage doesn't exist for such a man. Larry was married to his art and his own image, yet he never wanted to be alone with his daemon. By nature he wasn't an extrovert, not at all. He was shy, timid and easily hurt.'

Harvey was determined to save the play. Doris Abrahams worked hard on the publicity and Harvey gave interviews to the columnists. *Child's Play* jogged along for a few months; Harvey's name still attracted audiences. But he was depressed and his mood was reflected in the letter he wrote to Nahum in Israel in November:

My dear Nahum,

I have just received your last letter on a fleeting visit to London, before returning to America where, as you are no doubt aware, I am heavily involved in a Court action which could leave me destitute.

I am extremely distressed to hear of the ever worsening situation over there with our parents and I can assure you that my neglect in sending them funds has been due to no reason except that there have not been any.

My sojourn into the theatre has not even covered the rent and my dearest, about to be ex-wife, is making life extremely difficult and has threatened to put me on a rack that makes Chinese torture seem like a busman's holiday.

It is amazing how wrathful vengeance can be and, of course, the richer the party the greater the scorn.

I, personally, have been living on borrowed money, but have just called New York and asked them to send the parents 2,500 dollars immediately.

I don't know what you mean in your letter by them asking for an 8,000 Israeli pound deposit plus an 800 pound monthly charge when father has said that, if he doesn't like the home, he may want to move back into the flat. In the event we pay and he moves out, do we get our deposit back or do you have to forfeit it? I wish you would clarify this point to me as I am not in a position to throw money around like confetti.

Naturally, I will do everything in my power to look after them, but I am being torn financially, emotionally, physically and mentally in so many different directions that, quite honestly, I don't know whether I am coming or going. The film industry, as you have no doubt read, is in a very serious state of collapse, and for any work an actor does he is paid a minimal amount of money and given percentages of profits that he never sees.

I am writing this in great haste as I don't want to involve you in all the horrendous problems that one is being faced with, as even thinking about it merely adds another cancerous wound.

Please discuss this with the parents as soon as possible, find out the situation with the home and the flat and everything, and we will see what we are going to do about it.

In the meantime, by the time you receive this letter, they will have received their cheque, which will more than pay for the deposit for the home, but, before they do it, please make sure that, in the event they move out of it, they can get their money back as I can't go on putting down deposits and keeping the world's institutions open.

My love to everybody as ever,
Larry.

HARVEY HAD HOPED for a 'quiet and dignified divorce without publicity'. He was asking the impossible. Divorce involving the heiress of multi-millionaire film boss Harry Cohn was certain to attract world attention, and the presence of Paulene Stone and the child didn't help.

He said of Joan, as though to justify himself:

'Why should she want to break me? The older I get the less I seem to understand the incredible patterns of feminine behaviour. I opened up the world for her, but she wanted a more settled kind of existence. There were too many separations. She's not at the stage of her life where she wants to go around as I do.'

Joan obtained a court order in Santa Monica, California, preventing Harvey from molesting her. She also obtained an order barring him from removing any furniture, paintings or art pieces from their homes in Beverly Hills and Palm Springs.

Harvey claimed that on Joan's initiation they had signed a premarital agreement giving him no claim on her fortune. There was a second clause that, in the event of a divorce, she would leave him alone. He alleged that she was breaking that clause.

'Larry wanted to have his cake and eat it,' Joan said afterwards. 'He acted disgracefully. He told people I wouldn't divorce him, but he underestimated me.'

Yet nothing he said embittered her, though the rancour of his words shocked her friends. 'He received everything that was his when I divorced him. His recriminations didn't hurt me, as I had by then closed the door. Besides, everyone knew that he dramatized and exaggerated whatever story he wished to tell.'

Harvey admitted that life with Mrs. Cohn had begun promisingly enough.

'I adored her. In many ways she was good for me. But eventually it became an asphyxiating life.'

24 | 'He gave me more in terms of money than I gave him.'

IT WAS SATURDAY AFTERNOON IN THE SUMMER OF 1974 AT JOAN Cohn Harvey's hacienda near Santa Barbara in California. Callers parked beneath the trees at the end of the drive, in time for bullshots and a lunch of paella omelette, which everybody had helped to make, eaten at the big kitchen table.

Life at the hacienda at weekends was in extreme contrast to life at Joan Cohn Harvey's mansion on North Crescent Drive during week days. At the hacienda she lived without servants, looked after the horses and walked through the countryside with her dogs Jola and Jenny, the retrievers from Harvey's time. The name Jola was an amalgam of Joan and Larry, Jenny was called after Guinevere in *Camelot*. There had been other dogs with Arthurian names: Wart, a Great Dane, and Cammy (short for Camelot), a golden retriever. Wart, a birthday gift for Harvey from Brian Gibbs, was killed by a truck on the Pacific Coast Highway. Cammy had been killed in an accident at Joan's house.

The hacienda had a one-level ranch house, with views of the Ynez Mountains, and a 19th-century barn which Don Hensman was converting into a studio for Joan. The house itself had been restored and a swimming pool built into the courtyard formed by its three sides.

After lunch Joan Cohn sat by the pool under a wide sunshade.

Her blonde hair was carefully arranged, but in her print dress and apron she hardly seemed the hostess of North Crescent Drive. She remarked that her great-grandmother had been born out of wedlock – her mother had been one of three of the Emperor Maximilian's mistresses to produce a male heir, the Empress Carlota being barren.

Joan's father had married her mother against the wishes of his wealthy Southern parents. He found a job on the railroads to earn a living and support his wife and children. It wasn't until Joan, the fourth child, was born that the grandfather took the baby in his arms and the family was reconciled.

Joan was a New York model when she met Harry Cohn, Columbia's founder and business head. She married him, raised a family and kept house, studying art and psychology in her spare time. She was hostess to Cohn's Hollywood friends and associates, but somehow managed to live a sheltered life. Harvey changed all that after Cohn died. 'He took me out of myself. He showed me another world. Moss Hart said Larry was really a prince.

'I remember I had a sable coat and hat. Larry loved me to wear that hat. He'd say, "Now you remind me of my mother". When I met his parents for the first time in 1968 I found his mother was a big-boned woman, very Jewish-looking. She was white-haired, but she had been blonde. His father wasn't Jewish-looking in the accepted sense. I remember his grey eyes, like Larry's. Nahum has grey eyes, too. Toward the end Larry used to look in the mirror and say to me, "The older I get the more Jewish I look."

'He was interested in my Catholicism. When we went to Gary Cooper's funeral at the Church of the Good Shepherd in 1961 he was impressed by the ceremonial. It was like a film première, of course, with limousines drawing up and people saying, "There's Joan Cohn!" He stood and knelt in church just as I did. Harry used to say when he came to church with me:

' "I don't want to be conspicuous, so I'll do what everybody else does."

'When Larry disguised himself as a priest for a scene in *The Ceremony* I showed him how to make the Sign of the Cross, but he never got it right. He had been in so many fights his right hand was disfigured.

'He never did what the doctors told him. He wouldn't eat meat or drink milk. He had what I call Fats' Disease. He was terrified of getting fat. And when he did eat he'd bring it up afterwards. That's why I liked to go to Maxim's with him; at least he couldn't do it there.

'He began by taking one laxative tablet at each meal, but by the time we were divorced he was taking three or four at a time, like aspirin.'

She supposed he had ideas of becoming the head of Columbia Pictures.

'He was avid for money, fame and possessions. Everything had to be the very best: the best clothes, the best cars, the best homes. We put everything into Palm Springs Three: barbecue, sauna, swimming pool, a fifteen-feet bar. Larry always had to have a fifteen-foot bar – that was his stage.'

When she had given him a Rolls as a Christmas present he had sent her a pavéd diamond double-heart brooch with a note:

> *I can't compete BUT – it may remind*
> *you of my gratitude and affection and*
> *love for all your kindness.*
> *XXXX Larushka.*

'He was saying in effect that he couldn't compete with the other suitors who had given me presents. But over the years he gave me much more in terms of money than I gave him.'

As Margaret Leighton had done, Joan Cohn Harvey had kept her wedding photographs from Lyford Cay, and photographs of Harvey and herself in many places they had been together: arriving for film premières in London and Hollywood, cutting Harvey's birthday cake at the Malibu beach house and aboard Sam Spiegel's yacht in the Mediterranean. She had kept the letters he had written to her, even the cards he had sent with his gifts of

jewellery, reading simply, *All my Love – Larry.* She had also kept
a small, yellowing piece of paper with the words *Room at the Top.*

'Long before I met Larry someone had recommended the film.
I scribbled the title on this slip of paper to remind myself to run
it. Spooky, wasn't it?'

She remembered an Easter Eve party at Palm Springs. 'About
twenty of us had gone out to dinner and we all came back to our
house. I was wearing a yellow silk Givenchy dress and pearls and
diamond earrings – in those days you wore the real thing. Larry
and Richard Harris were standing talking by the deep end of the
pool. I went over to them and they suddenly caught me and threw
me in.'

'On the way down I told myself, "I mustn't come up angry".
When I surfaced I called to Larry, "Darling, is my mascara
running?" '

'Larry and Richard jumped in fully clothed and as the three of
us swam around. Larry kissed me and said he had fallen in love
with me all over again.'

Harvey and Harris were not so friendly after Harris got the part
of Arthur in the film of *Camelot.* Harvey had considered the part
his own since Moss Hart had given him T. H. White's book.

Joan and Harvey and Moss Hart saw a great deal of one another
at Palm Springs before Hart's death in 1961. At a tribute to Hart
at the University of Southern California nine years later Harvey,
wearing a medallion Joan had given him, recited the last
soliloquy, *Run, Boy, Run,* from the musical.

'Everyone said he spoke it more beautifully than they had ever
heard it spoken. I thought so, too. It was such an emotional
experience that immediately after the performance a woman was
carried out dead – she had suffered a fatal heart attack'.

When Harvey heard that Joshua Logan had cast Harris for
Camelot with Vanessa Redgrave as Guinevere he dismissed them
as 'dirty Richard Harris and that female impersonator'.

There had been many parts he wanted to play, Joan recalled,
and many parts he had been promised. 'Jimmy Woolf promised
Larry the role of Fagin in *Oliver!,* as he promised many, many

other things to him without fulfilment. But Larry's name had never ever been mentioned to Columbia in connection with the film by Jimmy or by any of his staff.'

During a Columbia management meeting at the Racquet Club at Palm Springs the studio heads came to Joan's for tea. James Woolf was a house guest at the time. When Woolf had gone to bed in the afternoon, Joan asked the Columbia chiefs if Harvey had been considered for Fagin. They didn't think so. Mike Frankovitch telephoned Lionel Bart, the composer of the show, in London and asked him what actors had been mentioned for Fagin. Bart gave him four names, one of them Ron Moody's.

'Has Larry Harvey been mentioned?' asked Frankovitch.

'Never,' said Bart.

When Woolf came into the living room later Joan offered him tea. The producer was talking about Harvey's potential as a screen Fagin.

'My stomach turned over', said Joan. 'I said to him:

' "Why don't you stop it! You know perfectly well that Larry has never been mentioned for the part."

'He disliked me after that. He thought I was good for Larry and had promoted our relationship until I caught him out in that lie. Larry was drifting away from him in the last years. Larry had such a strong sense of loyalty it was rough on him to realise that he couldn't believe Jimmy any more.'

The Laurence Harvey she loved was both very affectionate and very vague with extreme moods of gaiety and melancholy. 'He had no real schooling, but he was intuitive. When the Bolshoi dancers came to Los Angeles he talked to them in Russian. It probably wasn't good Russian, but he was able to carry it off. It came from somewhere in his head. He was at ease in any country and in any language.

'But he never had any stability. He would build a house and before it was finished he wanted to get rid of it. Let's see, he had one, two, three, four, five, six, *seven* houses. And he was always juggling cars about.'

When the break-up came Joan didn't face it until she had to.

'They say the wife is always the last to know. That's perhaps because she doesn't want to know. But when I found out about the house at Hampstead – that was the last straw.

'I'm only sorry we didn't marry earlier. That was our mistake. I felt loved by Larry. But how can one measure the depth of love?'

BEFORE THE DIVORCE was final Father Bernard Lohmann drove Joan from her house on North Crescent Drive to the beach house at Malibu belonging to Jean Louis and Maggie for a meeting with Harvey, who was living four houses away.

Father Lohmann was a Paulist priest who had instructed Joan in Catholicism before her reception into the Church in 1953. He knew Jean Louis and his wife as hard-working Catholics and they and Jack Cushingham had arranged a small get-together in a final attempt to reconcile Harvey and Joan.

Joan had agreed to come along provided Father Lohmann was present.

'There had been a number of attempts at reconciliation', Father Lohmann recalled, 'but one of the big stumbling blocks was the lady Larry had in London. That was a big, big stumbling block, and Joan was pretty fed up at this stage of the game.'

When Harvey arrived at the beach house he had been drinking heavily. Probably to get his courage up, thought Father Lohmann. 'Both of them were a little fearful of getting hurt. They sat at a high table between the kitchen and the dining room.

'Jack had urged Larry to try to make it up, but Larry's emotionalism turned Joan off. He told her how much he needed her, but she wasn't buying it.'

The attempt had failed, and Harvey ran back along the beach to his house, crying.

25 | 'I've had to pay dearly for my mistakes.'

EARLY ON A JUNE MORNING IN 1972 HARVEY WALKED INTO A SMALL make-up room at Elstree Studios near London clutching his stomach. Pale and drawn, he sat before the mirrors without speaking a word. The actress making up beside him didn't feel snubbed by his silence. She was accustomed by now to Harvey's bad mornings.

Billie Whitelaw was one of the three stars of *Night Watch*, a thriller being made in the studios and on location in London. Elizabeth Taylor was playing Harvey's wife. That morning in the make-up room Billie Whitelaw knew that Harvey wasn't well. After a long silence, he remarked with a forced casualness, 'Ugh, this nervous tummy of mine.'

'You ought to see a doctor, Larry,' she told him. 'I'm sure you can take something for the pain.'

'Not to worry, love. I've had it all my life.'

She assumed it was an ulcer. Watching the tired man sitting in the make-up chair she thought how different he looked to the Laurence Harvey she had met a few weeks earlier in the Grand Hotel in Rome. 'It was about eleven o'clock at night and I had gone to the producer's suite for an appointment with the film's hairdresser. They had suddenly decided that my mane of hair would have to come off, and like a bloody fool I said okay.

'We used the producer's bathroom. The hairdresser lopped off six inches of my hair and then put my head under the taps. When Larry walked in I must have looked a terrible mess and he probably imagined I was a script girl.

'I had seen him around the hotel, but we had never met. He came bounding into the suite, projecting what he assumed was everyone's idea of a Hollywood actor. I just sat there quietly without saying a word and for about an hour and a half watched his extraordinary performance. It wasn't until he realised I was his co-star that he came down a few notches and stopped leaping around.'

When they began to work together in London on the film she thought at first that the real Laurence Harvey didn't exist, that the actor was a figment of his own imagination. Gradually her impression of the man changed.

They were filming on location in a London house at Bayswater where they began by shooting the conclusion of the film, which included stabbings and knifings. They had a limited time in which to complete the scenes because the owners of the house wanted them out. 'They were getting fed up with us. The police were fed up with us. Everyone in Bayswater had had enough of us.'

In the small hours of the morning, when the human spirit is most vulnerable, Billie Whitelaw began to study Harvey more closely. 'Then I saw the man rather than the image, a man far more nervous than he liked people to think. I suddenly realised that his projection of a devil-may-care Hollywood actor living up to his printed image really had nothing to do with the man.'

When they had coffee in the make-up room in the mornings he would start to talk: 'I don't know why people think that actors just learn their lines and step in front of the cameras. Christ, if they only knew the agonies we go through to sweat this stuff out.'

All actors are nervous and Billie Whitelaw's nervousness made her feel inadequate before the cameras.

'My heart pounds so much I'm convinced the microphone is going to pick up the noise.'

Her husband, writer Robert Muller, held the theory that people project what they do not feel. 'It seemed to me that Larry was so frightened of revealing his nervousness that he behaved in an extraordinary way. He became over-excited, emotionally high and obviously covering up. He never seemed relaxed in front of the cameras. He was extremely professional and worked very hard, but he would know when a scene wasn't right and this would make him more tense and agitated.'

After two weeks' location in Bayswater the director, New Yorker Brian Hutton, became ill with bronchial pneumonia and the production was halted. It was the first of a series of misfortunes. When filming resumed two weeks later Billie Whitelaw's son Matthew was rushed to hospital with meningitis on his fifth birthday. She remembered, 'I wanted to pull out of the film, but they begged me to hang on. It was touch and go for Matthew. He was in University College Hospital in the most appalling pain and I lived there during the crisis. They kept a studio car standing by and after I had done my night scenes on location they would rush me back to the hospital. Then I'd return to do another scene and dash back to the hospital again.

'As soon as the location filming was finished I told them I was out of the film until my son was over the worst of his illness. After a couple of weeks he was out of pain and the wise professor at the hospital told me to go back to work. I went to Elstree, waiting for a 'phone call to tell me whether Matthew had responded to the treatment, or whether they would have to begin it all over again.

'Both Larry and Elizabeth were marvellously tactful. Larry said nothing, just gave my hand a squeeze. I realised he knew what I was feeling.

'We were rehearsing a scene, the first in which Larry, Elizabeth and I appeared together, when someone came up to me and said:

' "Billie, your son is on his way home."

'Larry smiled at me and said, "Good. It's okay."

' "Yes", I said. "Now let's get on with the film."

IT WAS AT this time that Harvey's mother underwent a serious
operation in Tel-Aviv. When Harvey heard the news he wrote to
his brother:

My Dearest Nahum,

*I am desperately sorry to hear about mother. The sad thing about it all
is that one's life seems to have been plagued by a succession of tragedies,
and somehow I wonder, on reflection, if there have ever been any true
moments of happiness. Maybe these moments have never been recorded or
talked about, and the only time there seems to be any need for corres-
pondence is through despondence.*

*I am afraid it appears that, after the age of awareness and respon-
sibility, life keeps heaping it on with a mechanical shovel. I am fully
aware of what the problems are and will, of course, make every effort to
meet whatever financial aid is required of me.*

*I hate to have to write this, but as you well know and understand I,
too, have to maintain whatever standards and day to day needs are
required of me and, because of my foolishness, stupidity, and irrationality,
I have had to pay dearly for my mistakes, not only emotionally, but
financially as well.*

*Regrettably, one feels oneself in a position today in this industry where
one's rewards in the past have been numerous, but agents, lawyers,
accountants, government, housekeepers, secretaries, children, and
everything have taken a heavy toll, and, not being one who has ever
thought of the future, we are now all forced to gamble along with the
companies and somehow none of us manage to see a penny for the fruits
of our labours.*

*The only reason I am going on about this is that I don't want you to
feel that I have a licence to print my own money, but rest assured that I
will, as I have said, do everything in my power to meet whatever demands
the parents make of me.*

*I would be most grateful if you would keep me informed of mother's
operation and progress, and let me know if and when they intend to move.
I have given instructions for a cheque to be sent to them immediately for
the moment and it should, hopefully, get there in the next couple of weeks.*

*Please give the parents my love and tell them that I am thinking of
them.*

Also hope that all is well with Nachshon and Henya.

Love as ever,

Larry.

IN MID-AUGUST, a few weeks after Billie Whitelaw had returned to the film, Martin Poll, the producer, 'phoned her to say that Harvey was ill. He had been rushed to hospital in the middle of the night with acute appendicitis and filming had come to a standstill again.

The executives of Brut Fabergé, the film backers and cosmetics firm of which George Barrie was head, went into conference with the insurance companies. According to the hospital, it would be two or three weeks before the star would be able to work again. Crew and artists were laid off.

'No one got paid,' Billie Whitelaw recalled. 'We should at this time have been finished, but the film seemed to be going on for ever. If someone had pulled the plug on the production there would have been a great sigh of relief.'

After five weeks Harvey returned, having recuperated in the South of France. He was tanned and buoyant, displaying his operation scar which extended from his navel to his crotch. He accepted the sympathy of people on the set who told him, 'Larry, we're surprised you're here at all!'

'We realised that his operation was not for appendicitis,' said Billie Whitelaw, 'but outwardly he seemed to be enjoying the story of how they had taken away yards of his intestines.'

Production stopped twice again because of Elizabeth Taylor. In July she was knocked unconscious on the set during a scene in which she had to run backwards. She tripped and fell against a wall and they thought she had broken her neck. But all that was broken was the second finger of her left hand. Soon after Harvey had returned, Billie Whitelaw answered another late night 'phone call to learn that Elizabeth had fallen again and injured her right arm. 'By this time everyone was getting a bit fed up because our small fees were spread rather thinly. What had seemed okay for five or six weeks' work was now spread over months and none of us could take on other work.

'When Elizabeth resumed she was wearing a great strapping bandage from her elbow to her wrist for which all her dresses had to be altered. But she and Larry exploded a myth for me about superstars. The both kept on working. And by this time I hadn't slept for six or seven weeks because I had been nursing Matthew. So the three of us, Larry, Elizabeth and I, were in a mess.

'Elizabeth had a scene in which she sees a body in a window across the garden. She faints, and Larry and I had to lift her from the floor. We had to be very careful not to touch her broken finger or her injured arm. Larry was kneeling, trying not to bend after his operation. They were lighting the scene and as we held our positions I could see he was making an effort not to show how much pain he was in.'

'Are you all right, Larry?' she asked him.

'If they don't shoot this bloody scene quickly I don't think I can hang on.'

His dressing room was next to hers and occasionally she saw him resting on his couch when he thought nobody was around. He admitted the surgeons had removed part of his colon. It gave him an excuse to say, 'Now I suppose I'm a semi-colon'.

A few weeks before the film ended Billie Whitelaw began to have shooting stomach pains. She thought the worry about her son had brought them on, and she and Harvey joked about how they shared a nervous tummy. Then her doctor told her she would have to have her appendix out.

'If I had gone back to Martin Poll and told him this I think the man would have had a heart attack. I decided to finish the damn film before the operation. Sometimes I could hardly walk. I started taking pain-killers and Larry was taking them too.'

Over lunch on the last day in the studios, in the special dining room with the off-white carpet and mirrored walls where the stars ate, Harvey told her he was planning to make another film, *Welcome to Arrow Beach,* probably in Vancouver, and asked her to star in it. Would she care to read the script which he had with him?

She said, 'Larry, I won't even look at it. I can't go abroad and leave Matthew at this time.' But she was surprised at her disappointment at having to refuse his offer.

'When I first met Larry Harvey, I thought I wasn't going to

enjoy working with him,' she remembered. 'But having gone through those awful five months on what was quite the most bizarre film I ever made I wanted to work with him again.

'In those last weeks he had deteriorated physically and looked exhausted. I felt he shouldn't go on to do another film. I remember saying to my husband, "Larry isn't well." And that turned out to be the understatement of the year.'

On the day *Night Watch* finished shooting Billie Whitelaw went into the London Clinic and next morning had her appendix removed.

DURING THE MAKING of *Night Watch,* Laurence Harvey threw a party to celebrate his quarter of a century in films. Simultaneously he announced his engagement to Paulene Stone, the mother of his child Domino, now three years old. He wore dark glasses to the party to hide a black eye, the result, he admitted, of an accidental meeting with his fiancée's right hand. He felt reborn, he told his friends, totally free, newly independent. His divorce from Joan had come through and he had thrown off the 'solid gold shackles'. So far as Domino was concerned he said he hadn't revealed her existence until now so as not to embarrass Paulene.

He believed his new fiancée would be able to keep pace with his energy and vitality, but he wondered if she would understand the importance of his work, his obsession with cleanliness and order and his need for moments of solitude.

The couple had moved into a large house on Kidderpore Avenue in Hampstead, which Harvey had altered structurally, changing floor levels, tearing out ceilings, introducing tall, smoked-glass windows. The stolid, well-to-do neighbours looked askance at the white house with the swimming pool which seemed more suited to California.

During the filming of *Of Human Bondage* in Ireland Harvey had talked to Vincent Donohue, a young designer at the studios, about the idea of an organic room. By the time Harvey had moved to Hampstead, Donohue was a freelance designer in London. They met in Shaftesbury Avenue one afternoon and over drinks in a pub Harvey asked Donohue to create the organic room in his new house.

Donohue remembered, 'The corners were to be curved, as though you had chiselled your way into a solid block of concrete. Floors, walls and ceilings were to be sprayed with black velvet flocking. He wanted dream screens, not hanging on the walls, but appearing to support the room. He wanted his stereo music, but no telephone; no contact, in fact, with the outside world. He hadn't expressed or executed anything like this in his previous houses and to me it didn't conform to his past.

'I think he had come to need a room where he could be a recluse. This was to be his escape pit.'

Donohue found that Harvey changed his mind quite often.

'He was altering his house cosmetically when he would have preferred to demolish it and start again. There were plans and plans. He would visualise an idea and then decide he wanted something else.'

The escape pit never became a reality. Harvey telephoned Donohue in the autumn of 1972 to say he was going to California, but to sit tight.

'Later I had a letter from him regretting that it might be six months before he was back in London, but he would take up the plans again when he returned.

'I went to work in France and after that we lost contact.'

HOLLYWOOD HADN'T forgotten Harvey's nasty swipes at Joan Cohn after their split. He had hurt one of Hollywood's most esteemed women and opinion in influential quarters, notably at Columbia Pictures, had turned against him. He was no longer looked upon as the dandy English actor with the smooth quiff and the deadly charm. Jack Cushingham said:

'He estranged himself from the studio heads. He was crazy.'

But he was a sick man. When he and Paulene agreed to marry on New Year's Eve, 1972, they both knew that he was seriously ill, but they hoped he would survive. Courage was never lacking in his make-up. After the ceremony at the home of writer Harold Robbins in Beverly Hills, Harvey and his third wife gathered a group of Hollywood friends together and returned in the evening to the Robbins' house.

Grace and Harold Robbins were due to hold their annual New Year's Eve party within a few hours. They were spending 25,000 dollars on the party, which spread itself through the house into a giant tent, and the entertainment included what was described as an 'orgy room' filled with water beds with music performed by the Mystic Knights of the Oinga Boinga.

When the Harveys arrived back they were accompanied by so many people there was no room for them. They left before Robbins remembered to give Harvey his marriage licence.

Less than a week later Paulene had returned to London to arrange for her elder daughter's return to boarding school. Harvey began work on *Welcome to Arrow Beach,* with which he hoped to retrieve his reputation. The excuse he gave to columnists for his succession of mediocre films was that he had been offered nothing better except blue movies.

'I won't lower my trousers, however ecstatic such a revelation might be.'

WUSA, the film he had made with Paul Newman and Joanne Woodward, was released just as he was beginning work on *Arrow Beach.* The critics found it improbable, with Harvey as a whisky preacher speaking what was described as left-over dialogue from a dozen 'B' movies. *The Manchurian Candidate,* it seemed, had said it all ten years before ten times better.

When *Night Watch* was released one critic, obviously unaware of the problems during the filming, found it surprising that the backers should have put money into such a production.

'What's amazing about the film is that it's so bad. In fact, it almost defies description.'

AT THE TIME of the Academy Awards in April Michael Caine and his wife were among a group dining with Harvey at a Hollywood restaurant. Caine, who hadn't seen him for some time, noticed how much weight he had lost and realised he was very ill. After the party had broken up he and his wife, Shakira, went on with Harvey to Cabrillo Drive.

'Larry didn't want to go to bed. He never wanted to go to bed. We stayed at Cabrillo until two in the morning talking about our plans. I was going back to Europe to make *The Black Windmill*, and he was still immersed in *Arrow Beach*, but he showed me his designs for altering the house and enlarging the swimming pool.'

Harvey brought Caine down to the wine cellar, which he had not shown him before. Although the racks were lined with the Pinot Chardonnay he once claimed, tongue-in-cheek, came from grapes handpicked and trodden underfoot by virgins from a French convent, he selected a bottle of Mouton Rothschild '59.

'That's a hellishly expensive bottle,' Caine said to him. He suddenly realised it was to mark their last night together.

'I think he already knew he was doomed.'

In the vast living-room, with the fifteen-foot bar and the knubbly off-white furniture, Harvey played Cole Porter. 'It was nostalgia. He was looking backwards. His taste in music never went beyond the 'sixties, the last peak of an exciting period for us British mob. Larry was definitely stuck in the 'sixties.

'Of course, he never looked too far back. He never mentioned his early years. He expected people to overcome their past and didn't consider it good taste to raise the subject.

'We talked a lot that night. Larry always talked a lot. But he did get on with his work. It takes a lot of work to put a film together, and he had done that with *Arrow Beach*. He was so full of energy and so enthusiastic about what he was going to do next he almost convinced me that nothing was wrong with him.'

At two in the morning Caine and his wife called a taxi to take them back to the Beverly Wilshire Hotel. Harvey was standing at the picture-window of the living-room, his back towards them, looking down on the lights of Los Angeles when the taxi arrived.

Caine said to him, 'We'll let ourselves out, Larry.'
He recalled, 'Larry said good night. But he never turned round.'

AFTER *WELCOME TO ARROW BEACH* was finished and
Harvey had undergone further surgery both he and Paulene knew
for certain that he had cancer. In London the previous August the
surgeons thought the malignancy had been removed and had told
Harvey they had taken away part of his colon, but the cancer had
spread so fast there was no further surgery they could do. Harvey's
only chance lay in chemotherapy treatment. Towards the end of
May, 1973, less than a month after his operation at the UCLA
Medical Centre in Los Angeles, he wrote to his brother to say that
'fate has dealt us a bitter blow in striking this poor, battered body
yet again, and laying it low.'

*I don't know whether there have been any reports in the newspapers about
my condition. Needless to say, the journalists do tend to dramatize these
incidents, although I must confess that this time what I have gone through
has shattered even me.*

*I have been forbidden to work for at least six months, which for me can
only cause economic disaster.*

*Despite all this, please reassure the parents that every effort will be
made to continue their allowance. I don't want to enumerate my problems,
as I suppose my concern should be for the parents, which it is, and I hope
that they are making satisfactory progress with their own problematical
conditions.*

*I had intended to come to see you all at the end of May, at the
invitation of the Israeli government and the Prime Minister, but regrettably have been forced to cancel because of this unexpected problem.*

*I trust that you and your family are well, and please read this to the
parents so that they are aware that I am still thinking about them.*

PAULENE, WHO HAD returned to California during the
making of *Welcome to Arrow Beach,* stayed on at the house at
Cabrillo Drive until July. It was a difficult, testing time for both
of them, with Harvey struggling to come to terms with his illness.

She found, as his previous wives had found, that his close relationships were strong until demands were made to which he could not respond. From such demands he ran away.

Friends believed that Paulene loved Harvey and had learned the lessons early. She knew she would lose him if she tightened her grip beyond a certain point, so she kept him on a long tether.

With age Harvey found he needed privacy; marriage and friends drained him. In company he was an extrovert, but the fatique of playing to an audience, even in his own house, required that he spend more time alone. One afternoon he stormed onto the lawn at Cabrillo where Domino and Sophie were playing with their young friends.

'What are all these children doing here?' Harvey asked.

'They must have other children to play with,' Paulene protested.

'Keep them out of my house,' he said. 'I don't want them touching my things.' And he added, 'When the new wing is built they won't be allowed into it. Nor will you.'

Though he had the house at Cabrillo and houses at Malibu and Hampstead, he continued to maintain the apartment in Grosvenor House at a rent of a hundred pounds a week. He always believed that one day he might need it. It was a place to run to, a luxurious cell in which to hide.

A week after Paulene had returned to London she telephoned her husband in Beverly Hills to learn he had set off on a world trip in the Fabergé jet. She was astonished that he had even contemplated such a journey. But his Los Angeles doctor, Harold Karpman, who travelled with the small party as far as Sydney, said afterwards it was much better for him to travel than to lie in bed. 'He was aboard a luxurious 'plane, and he didn't do any hiking or sightseeing, and he was among friends.

'He was creatively happy those last years I knew him. I think George Barrie gave him a free hand with projects, and in terms of his development he felt more gratified creatively those last two years than he had for a long time.

'Larry was restless, but being restless doesn't imply instability. It was just that his creativity carried him from one place to' another. Larry had tremendous drive which he tried to maintain at the same level in many places.

'When George suggested that last trip he knew how ill Larry had been and wanted to give him a feeling of accomplishment, a continued sense of being needed.

'When I left them in Sydney Larry was talking to a group of reporters. He didn't even notice I was leaving.'

SAMMY CAHN SAW Harvey in a Hollywood restaurant soon after his return from the world trip. 'All the brave talk and the brave attitude of the people around him couldn't disguise the fact that Larry was dying.'

Cahn had observed the same courage some years previously when his neighbour Humphrey Bogart had cancer. When Bogart invited Cahn to his house across the street he found him sitting in his beautifully-furnished den, dressed casually, but immaculately.

'I could see he was ravaged, but he brought it off, like Larry, with a touch of elegance.'

At one period, when Bogart first returned home from hospital, Cahn thought he might recover. Bogart telephoned him to complain that Cahn had signed a release for a neighbour who wanted to sell off part of his estate.

'He was screaming and yelling, and I was happy. I thought, "My God, I think he has it beaten!"'

'Larry showed the same bravura as Bogie, but I never thought Larry had his cancer beaten. Well, maybe I did, but only for a few moments.'

STAN KRELL, George Barrie's display director at Fabergé, was astonished at Harvey's thinness when he saw him in a sauna. He said, 'Larry, you know the old school story, "You're so skinny if you turned sideways the teacher would mark you absent." '

'He was stoic', Krell recalled. 'He never griped. He was a beautiful guy.'

26 | 'One's own life hardly serves as a model . . .'

Laurence Harvey,
1196 Cabrillo Drive,
Beverly Hills,
California 90210.
August 1, 1973.

My dearest Nahum,

I have just returned from a quick fourteen-day around-the-world trip to promote the two films which I have made over the past twelve months. Unfortunately, the extra burden of my physical condition denied me the full measure of enjoyment that I would normally have had, but therapeutically it came at a time when I needed to get away.

Apart from the physical pain that one has to endure from day to day, the biggest problem is overcoming psychological pressures. The weekly treatments and depletion of one's strength continually serve as a reminder, plus the fact that the doctors have forbidden me to do any work. Having been so active all my life, I find it extremely difficult to be suddenly so inoperative and helpless. I am trying to prepare various scripts for the future, and to keep as busy as I possibly can under the circumstances.

I am enclosing a letter to Nachshon and his wife which I would appreciate your forwarding. I am aware of your feelings regarding the match and am in total agreement with your current attitude. He is, after all, at an age where he thinks he knows his own mind and has to fulfil his youthful needs. It would be ludicrous for any of us to offer our advice, as, on reflection, one's own life hardly serves as a model for the younger generation.

How fabulous that Aunt Rachel should have visited you and the parents after so many years. I was always very fond of her, and it would have been nice to have seen her again. It seems unfortunate that she should have come at a time when the parents are in such a poor state of health.

It is regrettable that we all have to grow old and suffer the humiliation and indignities that seem to plague the human body.

I do hope that all your problems with regard to the parents and Canada will resolve themselves soon. It seems when fate decides to deal its ugly blows, it does so with a vengeance. It is difficult enough trying to survive the daily problems with which we are confronted continually, without having these added burdens to contend with.

Keep me informed as to what is happening and give my love to the parents. Tell them I think of them constantly.

> *Love to you all,*
> *Larry.*

27 | 'I just want to go home', he said.

TWENTY-SEVEN YEARS AFTER HE HAD ARRIVED IN LONDON AS A gangling, unknown youth in a worn South African Army uniform, hoping to be an actor, Laurence Harvey, the Hollywood star of more than fifty films, flew into Heathrow Airport in a TWA Boeing 747. It was the morning of September 3, 1973, and his close friends knew he was desperately ill and unlikely to see again his house on Cabrillo Drive.

Paulene, his wife, refused to accept that there was little hope for her husband. In their home in Hampstead Harvey tried to settle down as a parent for the first time. He did not intend to slow the pace. 'I want to go on living as though everything were normal,' he said, not prepared to give in to the pain that racked his body. He dined out with friends and towards the end of September gave a private screening of *Welcome to Arrow Beach*, followed by dinner at Les Ambassadeurs. He looked frail, his jumpsuit scarcely making contact with his body. He was having blood transfusions, and his terrible pain remained with him in spite of daily injections. His weight was down to almost ninety pounds. His first tailor Edward Woor would not have recognised his old customer who had once measured 42 inches across the chest and had the best figure of anybody on the books of Carr, Son and Woor.

The star whose reckless life style had become legendary was now living with a simplicity that mocked his earlier frenetic involvement in films and plays and party-going. He was cast in a role he had not rehearsed, a role not of his choosing, and the other players in the drama were his friends.

He treasured life so dearly he was prepared to part with all his possessions for his health. He regretted his neglect of his body, once so perfect, and his indifference to doctors who might have diagnosed his sickness in time to save him.

On his forty-fifth birthday on October 1 he drew on his failing reserves of energy to play host to friends who had flown halfway across the world to see him. It was a glittering celebration, with Elizabeth Taylor, John Ireland, Kirk Douglas and Peter Lawford among the guests, but Harvey was just a shadow of the man who had delighted them in Hollywood. At dinner the guests spoke softly, knowing their host lay ill in the four-poster bed upstairs. Meeting people exhausted him, but when they came to his room he drank draught Guinness and talked of future plans.

Watching Domino playing in the garden at Hampstead he was surprised at his tolerance. Children had once irked him, but now he felt close to Domino and his step-daughter and he wanted them to grow up to face the world without fear.

When dining at the Guinea restaurant in the mews off Berkeley Square where they had once lived, he met his first wife, Margaret Leighton, and her husband Michael Wilding. He forgot the long silence between them and crossed the floor to talk to her. Margaret said afterwards, 'The air had been cleared and Mrs. Cohn wasn't in the picture any longer. To my surprise he greeted me like it was the old days. It was as though nothing had happened between us. I hadn't known he was so ill. I told him I would send him some books.'

Jack Clayton was planning a screening of his latest film, *The Great Gatsby,* and wanted to have Harvey along. 'I had heard he was ill, but I didn't have any idea how ill. When I called him he sounded cheerful and said, "Jack, I'd love to come."

'A few days later I asked Paulene if it would be good or bad to have Larry at the screening.

'Paulene said, "Neither good nor bad, Jack. Larry is confined to his room most of the time. I think it's best to forget about it." '

Instead, Clayton went to see him.

'Lying there in bed, he looked like a stick. Although he was drugged he was full of memories. He talked about our days together on *Room at the Top*. He joked and I knew he didn't want to give in. It was a shattering encounter.'

In spite of blood transfusions and injections the strain of trying to behave normally was proving intolerable for Harvey. He accepted an invitation to dine with John Woolf at Les Ambassadeurs rather than admit how ill he was.

For Woolf, who had known Harvey in his most scintillating days, the reality was startling.

'He tried to turn on the old verve,' Woolf remembered, 'but he had shrunk and faded to nothing. He was bent almost double with pain. I could see that people who hadn't met him for a long time and who came up to our table to talk to him were shocked at the change. But Larry put on a brave front.

'During the meal he never mentioned his illness by name, although he did say he was in absolute agony and never without the terrible pain. He turned to me and said, "I don't know, John, how I'm going to get rid of this thing inside me."

'It was clear to me that he never would.'

When Bryan Forbes came over to talk to him at Les Ambassadeurs Harvey said, 'For Christ's sake, old love, don't ask me how I am.'

Even at this stage he was planning films and plays. He was promoting a novel of Wolf Mankowitz's which he wanted to direct as a film; he had called in a Hollywood writer to work on a screenplay. He was also planning to star in a play by Alun Owen on Broadway.

Owen went to see him at Hampstead and Harvey received him in the sunken living room. Before they began discussing the play, Harvey poured him a glass of Pouilly Fuissé.

'I drink only whisky,' said Owen.

Harvey changed the drink.

When Owen saw the star's physical condition he knew there was no possibility of him appearing in his play.

Even his voice was fading.

WHENEVER JOHN IRELAND telephoned him from Santa Barbara he listened carefully to Harvey's voice. Sometimes it was strong, but more often weak, and this Ireland attributed to the drugged condition of his friend who was having shots of morphine to ease his pain.

Ireland called Harold Karpman in Los Angeles and they discussed Harvey's condition.

'I guess it looks pretty bad,' Dr Karpman said.

'How bad?', asked Ireland.

'It could be any time now, John.'

'Do you think I should go over to London to see him?'

'I suppose you could.'

Ireland called Harvey to say, 'I'm coming over, Larry.'

'I'm happy, John,' Harvey said. 'That makes me feel good.'

Ireland stayed for two weeks at the house at Hampstead. The night nurse would call him in the small hours of the morning. 'Mr. Harvey's awake now,' she would say. Although it might be four in the morning he would go into his friend's bedroom and have tea and toast with him until the nurse gave Harvey a shot of morphine.

When he slept Ireland would return to his own room. 'Larry would wake up again two or three times later and have more tea and toast, or maybe a cup of coffee.'

When Ireland prepared to leave for lunch in town, Harvey would say, 'Don't go without me, John.' So they would go together.

'Before leaving for the restaurant he'd get a shot and although he'd be a little drowsy over the meal he didn't seem to be in pain.'

In Wheeler's in Soho, Ireland would order sole. Harvey would say, 'Don't order fillet. I'll eat the bones.'

When the meal was served he would nibble at the bones and Ireland would eat the fish. Then he would say, 'Now, let's have some cheese.' And he would sip a little white wine.

HARVEY WAS PLAYING his final role among a cast that excluded his parents, Ber and Ella Skikne, and his brothers Robert and Nahum. Day nurses and night nurses moved across the stage. Most of the other players had spoken their lines and departed.

Robert Sinai saw it as the tragedy of a man's collapse. 'My brother's cancer,' he believed, 'was a product of his own self-destructiveness, of his suicidal impulses. I don't think Larry could bear the burden of acting all those parts and behaving as he did to others.

'He was destroyed by his desire for material comfort. And he was mean. It is true he kept our parents afloat during this time, but sometimes he wouldn't send them money for months and they were very insecure. They depended on him.

'He had no relationship with them in the last years. He wrote to them, but he wrote about his income tax and his financial problems. I'm sure he spent more on his flunkeys than he did on them.'

A colleague of Harvey's who had known the actor since he came to London in 1946 noted that his Svengali, James Woolf, was missing from the tragedy being played out at the house in Hampstead. 'After Woolf's death,' he said, 'Larry managed on his own, but the sheet anchor of his career had gone. He changed radically after Woolf's death. His life became a shambles, a frenetic life without any visible results.

'I remember Larry as a frightened young man of nineteen with a chip on his shoulder, possibly because of his origins and his background. He had very little schooling and his language was foul. His attitude was, "Who is trying to get at me?"

'He had tremendous ambition, yet he doubted himself. He was an irrational person who calculated issues on simple terms that barely reached a conscious level. He reasoned, "If I marry Margaret Leighton I'll get into the theatre." Or, "If I marry Joan Cohn I'll get Columbia." Later he would try to disguise these motives. If he married Paulene Stone, he reasoned, there was nothing for him to lose. He could make the gesture without expense.

'Deep down there was a maternal fixation of an incestuous nature.

'Larry is a peculiar study in failed ambition. He wanted to be at the top of the ladder. He lived as though he *were* at the top, but he wasn't.

'Only one thing was anathema to him – to be ignored. He was sensitive, but he didn't take other people's sensitivity into account.

'He wanted to be great. But to be great you must have compassion and humility, and these qualities were in short supply.'

FRIENDS OF HARVEY'S, knowing his affection for California, tried in the early days of November to bring him back to America. Joan Cohn Harvey heard he had said to Peter Lawford, who visited Hampstead, 'I just want to go home.'

John Ireland recalled his friend's wish to be buried in California. When they had visited Ronald Colman's grave overlooking the Pacific, Harvey had said, knowing that Ireland and his wife Daphne were buying a plot there:

'I'd like to buy one, too, John. Then we could all be together.'

Joan said to Ireland, 'If Larry wants to come back here and you can figure a way of getting him back, I'll pay the expenses.' She knew he was dying and she believed that people who were living with death should have a choice of where they wanted to die. She saw her gesture as 'a token of farewell'. Harold Karpman told her he was visiting Europe and would call on Harvey and, if possible, bring him back to California.

A few weeks earlier Harvey had told a reporter from the *Los Angeles Times* that a new treatment was shrinking his tumour and he expected to be in Hollywood a week later to discuss a film deal. 'I'm feeling fine,' he said.

But when Karpman arrived in London he found Harvey a lot sicker than he expected.

'I knew he missed Los Angeles, for he loved his home there. He liked England, but not in the same way. I thought when I got to London I would find him well enough to return to Cabrillo Drive with me, but he wasn't.

'On the Saturday before I left for home I had lunch with him in his bedroom: caviar, eggs and onions. Larry sat there with a small jar of caviar. Although he was very ill he was determined to live a life-style that was uniquely Harvey.

'Nothing more could be done for him realistically. I knew his chances of recovery were very slight.'

When Dr. Karpman returned to Los Angeles he told Joan that Harvey would not have lived through the eight thousand-mile trip.

EARLY IN NOVEMBER Nahum received a message from Los Angeles that his brother was gravely ill and hadn't the courage to tell him.

'Larry had never mentioned family affairs. It took us a day and a half to find the Hampstead 'phone number through the international exchange.

'Henya and I wanted to go to London, but we didn't have the means and, anyway, we could not leave the parents. Larry didn't say come, neither did Paulene.

'When I called the number Paulene was very correct in her attitude. I thought how different it was from the old days when Joan would 'phone in the middle of the night and say, "Joan speaking".

'I said to Paulene, "I'm Nahum, Larry's brother from Israel."

'She replied, "Mr. Sneh? Do you want to speak to Larry?"

'I said to her, "I'd like to thank you for taking good care of him."

'During our short conversation with him, I said, "Larry, how are you?"

' "Trying, fighting, Nahum."

' "Never give up," I told him. "*Chazak veematz!* – Be strong and of good courage!"

'I think he was surprised to hear from us. His voice was the voice of a dying man. But I didn't realise it as much as Henya.'

Henya recalled, 'It was more terrible for me. For six months I had lived in fear of his death.'

THE LAST ACT of the tragedy in the house on Hampstead Heath was enacted. Harvey sent for the restaurateur Mario Cassandro from the Terrazza and asked him to cook a spaghetti served with a vintage red wine. It was a gesture in the old expansive Harvey style.

George Barrie believed that Harvey might still return to Cabrillo Drive. He would telephone him from the Brut Fabergé office at Burbank in California or from the New York office on the Avenue of the Americas.

'I had a special time call to Larry's home in Hampstead. I knew there was a 'phone beside his bed and another 'phone across the room with a different number and no extension to the bedside. Many times I called him on this second 'phone to see if he could make it from the bed.'

On the night of Thursday, November 22, Barrie and Cary Grant telephoned the Hampstead house and talked to him, but the conversation was brief. Harvey was obviously exhausted.

He had lost fifty pounds in weight in six months. But he was calm and resigned now that his audience had dwindled.

On Sunday, November 25, he slept for long spells. When the doctor called to see him he told Paulene that her husband had suffered a stroke and was dangerously ill.

The stage was almost empty. Harvey died that evening, peacefully. The curtain had come down with no one to applaud the star who loved an audience.

WHEN HARVEY'S MOTHER heard of his death she begged Nahum:

'Bring him to Israel and bury him here as a Jew.'

Nahum pointed out that Harvey had a family in London. 'We have no right to interfere', he said.

Harvey's remains were cremated at Golders Green crematorium and his ashes taken to a vault in St. Paul's, the actors' church, in Covent Garden. At the Memorial Service the recorded voice of Harvey was heard singing the title song from *Camelot,* in which he had starred a few streets away in Drury Lane, and *The Alamo* was recalled with *The Green Leaves of Summer.*

Elizabeth Taylor was a patient at the UCLA Medical Centre when a Memorial Service was held at St. Alban's Church in Westwood, Los Angeles. She was allowed to leave the hospital to attend the church.

John Ireland delivered the eulogy, beginning:

'We who have been pricked by the sharpness of his wit, comforted by his abundant generosity, warmed by his humour, feel the void left by this dear person. Thank you, Larry, for caressing us with your friendship and your love. . .'

He stumbled over his words and could not go on. Elizabeth Taylor began to weep.

'I still can't believe I'll never see him again', she said. 'He was a part of the sun.'

After the Service her friend Henry Wynberg and Peter Lawford accompanied her back to the hospital, after a stop at Gatsby's. She had promised to return by eight-thirty; she was just fifteen minutes late.

When Rabbi Max Nussbaum of Hollywood's Temple Israel heard that the Memorial Service had been held in an Episcopalian church he called it 'an utter scandal'. But Lawford, who had arranged the Service with Elizabeth Taylor, retorted:

'I never thought about it. I held a Service at St. Alban's for my mother. Larry was hardly a practising Jew. Come to think of it, he would have preferred the room at the Bistro. Only it was taken.'

AT THE FUNERAL Wolf Mankowitz had given close friends copies of the Elegy he had written for his friend of twenty-five years:

> *So for the last time*
> *your laughing sardonic face*
> *looked into the pit*
> *and creased with pain,*
> *then*
> *grinned finally*
> *as with a shrug*
> *you carefully lifted*
> *your elegant bones into the wings.*
>
> *O demon lover, white wine poet,*
> *Litvak lunatic, little monster,*
> *your positively last appearance*
> *as a man*
> *was so true that*
> *only death could upstage you.*
>
> *Rest now, lonely friend,*
> *as you never did before,*
> *In utter peace.*

LAURENCE HARVEY LEFT no will. This presented difficulties for Paulene and those who had expected to be remembered by her husband. John Ireland recalled that his friend of twenty years had promised him some of his wines. But when he drove to the house on Cabrillo Drive to examine the contents of the cellar the staff refused him entry.

'There is no question of John Ireland having been left any wine', said Paulene.

Joan Cohn Harvey had sent no flowers to the Memorial Service. 'I would have been a hypocrite to do so', she said. But she telephoned Nahum in Beersheba to try to help him find his brother's will. She remembered that all Harvey's property, his cars, houses and antiques, was held by the Magla company (an amalgam of Margaret and Laurence) for tax reasons. She had once asked Harvey, 'Do you really know what you have, Larry?'

'I know where everything is,' he said.

'I don't think he did', said Joan. And lawyers had told her that his affairs would never be unravelled.

28 | The caller at the house on Cabrillo Drive.

GEORGE MCLEAN, AN ARCHITECT AND DESIGNER WHO HAD BEEN A neighbour of Harvey's and Joan's for many years at Palm Springs, called to the house on Cabrillo Drive a month before Harvey made his last journey to London. McLean wanted to give Christian witness to his friend.

McLean had become an enthusiastic Christian when his son, 'lost to drugs and rock music', had recovered his health after his mother prayed for his recovery. McLean regarded his son's healing as a miracle and began to explore the Scriptures.

Early one August afternoon he drove up to the house on Cabrillo Drive and knocked at Harvey's door. He remarked, 'As I knocked I thought how absurd my gesture was in calling on Larry, as unspiritual and irreverent a man as you could wish to meet. He wasn't expecting me, but when I told him I wanted to talk to him about eternity and would prefer if we could be alone, he said:

' "Okay, George. Let's find a quiet spot." '

The two men talked sitting on the terrace by the pool, and later in the living room. Harvey's secretary came into the room a few times, but he waved her away.

'No 'phone calls. Not now.'

McLean said afterwards, 'He was excited about the Biblical evidence and I saw he was deeply moved. After we had talked for about an hour and a half I gave him a brotherly hug and left.

'When he closed the door behind me, I thanked God. I felt he had been touched.'

McLean told Elizabeth Taylor about the meeting; he was the godfather of her son Christopher. Other people in California also knew about the attempt to bring Christianity to Harvey before his death. Among them were Jean Louis, the couture designer, and his wife Maggie, who had been Malibu Beach neighbours for years.

Just as McLean was convinced that Harvey 'had accepted Jesus as his Messiah', the designer and his wife believed that he had become a Christian before his death. 'He was willing to be baptised,' said Jean Louis. 'He told us so.'

The couple had been in London en route to Paris when Harvey was dying. For more than a week they visited him every day at Hampstead. Maggie remembered he hated taking medication and fought off the injections, fearful of losing his faculties. 'When the dope wore off he would be in real agony, but his mind was fabulous, and we would talk for an hour with him until the nurse came in.

'I talked to him about becoming a Christian and he respected what Christianity stood for. He intended to be buried in Christian ground, not caring what anybody in his family thought, for this was something between him and God. The last time I saw him I gave him a medal of the Blessed Mother and the Sacred Heart, which he kissed and pinned to his pyjamas.

'On the day he died we had left for Paris to take care of some business.'

Hymie Siegel, a driver with a Hollywood studio, stated he had given witness to Harvey in 1972 by the pool of the Sheraton Universal Hotel.

'I told him that I, too, was Jewish and believed the Lord Jesus Christ to be the Messiah of Israel, the Saviour of the world. I told him how I was saved at a street corner in Brooklyn twenty-five years before. He seemed very interested and I gave him a Prophecy Edition of the New Testament, which he said he would read. He asked me to leave it on the front seat of his car in the parking lot.'

Siegel, who described himself as a Hebrew Christian, claimed that the same New Testament was beside Harvey's bed when he died. The Prophecy Edition was a special Bible published by the Bethany Fellowship, a group witnessing specifically to the Jews.

IN THE AUTUMN of 1974 Patricia Duschak, who called herself a Christian counsellor, claimed that Laurence Harvey had accepted Jesus through her. A friend of hers had foolishly given Harvey a copy of a booklet, *Death Made Easy,* on the day he had been told of his terminal cancer in the hospital at UCLA. Realising her mistake she 'phoned Patricia Duschak long distance to Vancouver in the State of Washington to ask her advice. Harvey had suffered a trauma when told the nature of his cancer, she said, and now the gift of the booklet had made him distraught.

'All you can do,' advised Patricia Duschak, 'is stay out of it. Don't apologise. Do nothing.'

Poor man, she thought. Such an unfortunate, offensive gesture. She recalled, 'My heart was heavy for him. I wanted to cry. Six years previously doctors had given me six weeks to live. They were proved wrong, but at the time it was frightening. I thought I must offer this man encouragement and prayed that I could reach him.'

A few days later another Los Angeles friend asked her to get in touch with Harvey who wanted to talk to somebody who had been close to death. Poor thing, Patricia Duschak thought. 'He was almost under guard at the hospital, so I doubted if I could get through. But when I dialled the number I had been given he answered. I told him I knew of his ordeal and wanted to encourage him. I didn't mention Christianity.

'He asked me to call him again and after that first call we talked on many occasions. I told him how to find value and meaning in life, of how important it was not to be fearful. He questioned the existence of God and argued about death. For him there was nothing beyond the grave.'

'God is gracious and merciful,' she told him. 'Maybe in His kindness He'll let you have that nothingness. But I know there is more – if you want it.'

When Harvey returned to Cabrillo Drive for the last time Patricia Duschak prayed for a chance to meet him. She knew he had overcome his fear of death, but, to her, that wasn't enough.

George McLean had 'witnessed to him and laid the groundwork.' She had arrived in Los Angeles to work as a visiting counsellor when a friend arranged for Harvey to meet her before he left for England.

'This friend drove me to the house on Cabrillo and left me there, saying they would return in an hour. My only way out was to call a taxi. It was a nasty trick to play on the man, but I was convinced that God was in it and was smiling.

'When I was shown into the house Laurence Harvey was obviously very ill. He apologised because he couldn't stand up to greet me. He hadn't noticed that I was blind. In our telephone conversations I had alluded to my blindness, but he hadn't accepted it as a physical fact.

'I left my white cane at the door and walked into the room without stumbling and was able, with my built-in radar, to find my way to a small footstool.'

As they talked Harvey mentioned an object across the room. Patricia Duschak said, 'I can't see.'

'What?'

'I'm totally blind.'

Harvey sat up suddenly. 'You really are, aren't you? Goodness, how do you manage?'

'God helps me,' she said, 'and He has brought me to you.'

She knelt in front of him and took his thin hands in hers. 'This is a very precious moment for both of us,' she told him. 'Do you believe that?'

He said he did.

'Then ask God to take away everything that is not right in your life. Don't go into details. He has the list. Just tell Him you are contrite about what has happened, whether it was a small anger against a loved one or some horrendous sin. Then you can be sure of eternity.'

According to Patricia Duschak's account they both began to cry. She prayed and he responded:

'Heavenly Father, I know there have been episodes in my life that You haven't been happy about. But I'm giving You my life, past, present and future, to take for all eternity for Your dear Son's sake . . . '

'I knew he was taking Jesus into his heart,' she said afterwards. 'We clung to each other at the end, and then he leaned back in his chair. He dozed a little. I stayed on my knees and held his hand. When he awoke he said, "You're still here", but he kept holding my hand.

'I asked him if he felt all right. "I've never felt so all right in my life," he answered.

' "Then I'll be seeing you," I told him.

' "We'll both be seeing each other in a little while," he said. "We'll have all eternity to talk." '

THREE DAYS AFTER Nahum and Henya had broken the news to Ella Skikne about her youngest son's death she began to live in a world of the past. Harvey had promised to visit his mother earlier that year. He had sent his parents photographs taken in Beverly Hills, one of Paulene and the two children at the wedding in Harold Robbins' house, the other of himself and Domino – 'Larry *mit de madel* – with the little girl', Mrs. Skikne remarked. Neither she nor her husband could quite accept the fact that their youngest son was a father.

'You have three grandchildren, not two', Nahum would say to his father.

'Yes, yes, of course', Ber Skikne would nod.

For Mrs. Skikne each advance in the personal life of her youngest son represented a further estrangement. 'Why did he have to have a child at his age?' she asked.

Nahum was angry. 'How can you speak like that, Mother? Larry's not an old man, and he always wanted a child.'

The photograph of Harvey and Domino, which had been placed on a cabinet containing the silverware and cutlery given to the parents by Harvey, could not be found after his death. Nahum knew his father had a habit of storing letters and receipts on top of cupboards in the kitchen. During the week's *shiva,* or mourning, according to custom, he climbed on a chair after his parents had gone to bed one evening and took down the bundles from the cupboards and sifted through them. He found the two photographs.

On March 3, 1974, Ber Skikne died, aged 78. He had nursed his wife until a month before his death when she entered a private nursing home for the chronic sick. Her mind was a muddle of past and present, and she seldom mentioned his name until the day before he died when she said to a neighbour who had come to visit her, 'Naomi, I think I have a husband no more.'

She talked to herself in Yiddish, and would remark, 'See what has become of the elegant Mrs. Skikne!'

She was 76 when she died on April 5 that same year.

When they were clearing out the parents' old apartment Nahum and Henya found the sable hat which Ella Skikne had often worn, the hat that Harvey remembered when he first saw Joan Cohn wearing sable.

IN THE SUMMER of 1974 Nahum and Henya arrived in London, bringing most of their personal belongings with them for a two-year stay in England during which Nahum would work for Mapam, the Israeli United Workers' Party. While they searched for a flat they took lodgings in a house in West Hampstead, a Jewish area with a synagogue and delicatessen stores with matzos on the shelves. Their room at the top of the house was as small as the room Harvey had rented when he first arrived in London and far from the luxury of the house on Kidderpore Avenue, on the other side of Hampstead, with its sauna and barbecue rooms and garaging for seven cars.

In their luggage were the letters Harvey had written to Nahum and Henya since they left for Israel in 1941. Nahum took them out of a bulky folder and fingered the yellowing pages lovingly. It was curious, he observed, that his brother had written to him usually in times of crisis and stress. Even the letter he had written to Nachshon for his barmitzvah in May, 1959, was mainly to assure the boy that he was remembered and that his Confirmation would not be the unhappy event that Harvey had known in Johannesburg when he looked in vain among the faces of the guests for his brother and Henya.

'I regret so much that I shall not be with you,' he had written, 'but I will be thinking of you. I know you will be a great credit to your parents and I look forward to the day when we shall all be together . . . '

Nahum returned the letters to the folder which he bound with a rubber band and locked in the cramped bedroom cupboard.

Remembering Mrs. Skikne's wish to have her son's body brought back for burial to Israel, Nahum and Henya set out to look for Harvey's grave at Golders Green, and found there was none.

He had been cremated, they were told, and his ashes were in a church in Covent Garden.

The chasm had widened between Ella Skikne and her son Hirsch Moses Skikne, otherwise Laurence Harvey.

Index